AAT

ASSESSMENT KIT

Intermediate Unit 6

Cost Information

August 2000 second edition

- Practice activities
- Four Practice Devolved Assessments
- Two Trial Run Devolved Assessments
- The AAT's Sample Simulation for this Unit
- Four Practice Central Assessments
- Three Trial Run Central Assessments for this Unit

All Simulations and Assessments have full answers included in this Kit

FOR 2000 AND 2001 ASSESSMENTS

BPP Publishing
August 2000

First edition August 1999
Second edition August 2000

ISBN 0 7517 6238 5 (Previous edition 0 7517 6172 9)

British Library Cataloguing-in-Publication Data
A catalogue record for this book
is available from the British Library

Published by

BPP Publishing Limited
Aldine House, Aldine Place
London W12 8AW

www.bpp.com

Printed in Great Britain by Ashford Colour Press

We are grateful to the Lead Body for Accounting for permission to reproduce extracts from the Standards of Competence for Accounting.

Page

INTRODUCTION

How to use this Assessment Kit - Assessment Strategy - Unit 6 Standards of Competence

(v)

ORDER FORM

REVIEW FORM AND FREE PRIZE DRAW

BPP PUBLISHING

HOW TO USE THIS ASSESSMENT KIT

Aims of this Assessment Kit

To provide the knowledge and practice to help you succeed in the devolved and central assessments for Intermediate Unit 6 *Recording Cost Information*.

To pass the devolved and central assessments you need a thorough understanding in all areas covered by the standards of competence.

To tie in with the other components of the BPP Effective Study Package to ensure you have the best possible chance of success.

Interactive Text

This covers all you need to know for the devolved and central assessments for Unit 6 *Recording Cost Information*. Icons clearly mark key areas of the text. Numerous activities throughout the text help you practise what you have just learnt.

Assessment Kit

When you have understood and practised the material in the Interactive Text, you will have the knowledge and experience to tackle this Assessment Kit for Unit 6. In addition to practice activities, this Kit contains four practice devolved assessments, two trial run devolved assessments and the AAT's Sample Simulation. It also contains three of the AAT's Central Assessments for Unit 6 plus relevant questions from the AAT's Sample Central Assessment and central assessments set under the previous version of the Standards.

Recommended approach to this Assessment Kit

(a) To achieve competence in all units, you need to be able to do **everything** specified by the standards. Study the text very carefully and do not skip any of it.

(b) Learning is an **active** process. Do **all** the activities as you work through the text so you can be sure you really understand what you have read.

(c) After you have covered the material in the Interactive Text, work through this **Assessment Kit**.

The Kit is divided into three sections.

(i) **Section A** contains a number of practice activities. These are short activities which are designed to reinforce your learning and consolidate the practice that you have had doing the activities in the Interactive Text. Try all the practice activities. Answers to practice activities are to be found at the end of this Section.

(ii) **Section B** contains a number of practice devolved assessments, trial run devolved assessments and the AAT's Sample Simulation. The practice devolved assessments are designed to test your competence in certain key areas of the Standards of Competence, but are not as comprehensive as the ones set by the AAT. They are a 'warm up' exercise, to develop your studies towards the level of full devolved assessment. Once you have tried the practice devolved assessments, try the trial run devolved assessments and then try the AAT's Sample Simulation, which gives you the clearest idea of what a full assessment will be like.

(iii) **Section C** contains full central assessment standard questions which give you plenty of practice in the type of question that comes up in the central assessment. Many are taken from central assessments set by the AAT under the previous versions of the Standards. All have full answers with tutorial notes. Finally, we also include three of the AAT's Central Assessments for the Unit with full answers provided by BPP - it is probably best to leave these until last and then attempt them as 'mocks' under 'exam conditions'. This will help you develop some key techniques in selecting questions and allocating time correctly. For guidance on this, please see Central Assessment Technique on page (vii).

(d) This approach is only a suggestion. You or your college may well adapt it to suit your needs.

Remember this is a **practical** course.

• Try to relate the material to your experience in the workplace or any other work experience you may have had.

• Try to make as many links as you can to your study of the other units at this level.

ASSESSMENT STRATEGY

This unit is assessed by both **central assessment** and by **devolved assessment**.

Central assessment

A central assessment is a means of collecting evidence that you have the **essential knowledge and understanding** which underpins competence. It is also a means of collecting evidence across the **range of contexts** for the standards, and of your ability to **transfer skills**, knowledge and understanding to different situations. Thus, although central assessments contain practical tests linked to the performance criteria, they also focus on the underpinning knowledge and understanding. You should in addition expect each central assessment to contain tasks taken from across a broad range of the standards.

Central assessment technique

Passing central assessments at this level is half about having the knowledge, and half about doing yourself full justice on the day. You must have the right **technique**.

The day of the central assessment

1   Set at least one **alarm** (or get an alarm call) for a morning central assessment

2   Have **something to eat** but beware of eating too much; you may feel sleepy if your system is digesting a large meal

3   Allow plenty of **time to get to where you are sitting the central assessment**; have your route worked out in advance and listen to news bulletins to check for potential travel problems

4   **Don't forget** pens, pencils, rulers, erasers

5   Put **new batteries** into your calculator and take a spare set (or a spare calculator)

6   **Avoid discussion** about the central assessment with other candidates outside the venue

Technique in the central assessment

1   *Read the instructions (the 'rubric') on the front of the paper carefully*

   Check that the format of the paper hasn't changed. It is surprising how often assessors' reports remark on the number of students who attempt too few questions. Make sure that you are planning to answer the **right number of questions**.

2   *Select questions carefully*

   Read through the paper once - don't forget that you are given 15 minutes' reading time - then quickly jot down key points against each question in a second read through. Select those questions where you could latch on to 'what the question is about' - but remember to check carefully that you have got the right end of the stick before putting pen to paper. Use your 15 minutes' reading time wisely.

3   *Plan your attack carefully*

Consider the **order** in which you are going to tackle questions. It is a good idea to start with your best question to boost your morale and get some easy marks 'in the bag'.

4   *Check the time allocation for each section of the paper*

Time allocations are given for each section of the paper. When the time for a section is up, you must go on to the next section. Going even one minute over the time allowed brings you a lot closer to failure.

5   *Read the question carefully and plan your answer*

Read through the question again very carefully when you come to answer it. Plan your answer to ensure that you **keep to the point**. Two minutes of planning plus eight minutes of writing is virtually certain to earn you more marks than ten minutes of writing.

6   *Produce relevant answers*

Particularly with written answers, make sure you **answer the question set**, and not the question you would have preferred to have been set.

7   *Gain the easy marks*

Include the obvious if it answers the question, and don't try to produce the perfect answer.

Don't get bogged down in small parts of questions. If you find a part of a question difficult, get on with the rest of the question. If you are having problems with something, the chances are that everyone else is too.

8   *Produce an answer in the correct format*

The assessor will state **in the requirements** the format in which the question should be answered, for example in a report or memorandum.

9   *Follow the assessor's instructions*

You will annoy the assessor if you ignore him or her. The **assessor will state** whether he or she wishes you to 'discuss', 'comment', 'evaluate' or 'recommend'.

10   *Lay out your numerical computations and use workings correctly*

Make sure the layout fits the **type of question** and is in a style the assessor likes.

Show all your **workings** clearly and explain what they mean. Cross reference them to your answer. This will help the assessor to follow your method (this is of particular importance where there may be several possible answers).

11   *Present a tidy paper*

You are a professional, and it should show in the **presentation of your work**. Students are penalised for poor presentation and so you should make sure that you write legibly, label diagrams clearly and lay out your work neatly. Markers of scripts each have hundreds of papers to mark; a badly written scrawl is unlikely to receive the same attention as a neat and well laid out paper.

12   *Stay until the end of the central assessment*

Use any spare time **checking and rechecking** your script.

13 ***Don't worry if you feel you have performed badly in the central assessment***

It is more than likely that the other candidates will have found the assessment difficult too. Don't forget that there is a competitive element in these assessments. As soon as you get up to leave the venue, **forget** that central assessment and think about the next - or, if it is the last one, celebrate!

14 ***Don't discuss a central assessment with other candidates***

This is particularly the case if you **still have other central assessments to sit**. Even if you have finished, you should put it out of your mind until the day of the results. Forget about assessments and relax!

Devolved assessment

Devolved assessment is a means of collecting evidence of your ability to carry out **practical activities** and to **operate effectively in the conditions of the workplace** to the standards required. Evidence may be collected at your place of work or at an Approved Assessment Centre by means of simulations of workplace activity, or by a combination of these methods.

If the Approved Assessment Centre is a **workplace,** you may be observed carrying out accounting activities as part of your normal work routine. You should collect documentary evidence of the work you have done, or contributed to, in an **accounting portfolio**. Evidence collected in a portfolio can be assessed in addition to observed performance or where it is not possible to assess by observation.

Where the Approved Assessment Centre is a **college or training organisation,** devolved assessment will be by means of a combination of the following.

- Documentary evidence of activities carried out at the workplace, collected by you in an **accounting portfolio**.

- Realistic **simulations** of workplace activities. These simulations may take the form of case studies and in-tray exercises and involve the use of primary documents and reference sources.

- **Projects and assignments** designed to assess the Standards of Competence.

If you are unable to provide workplace evidence you will be able to complete the assessment requirements by the alternative methods listed above.

Possible assessment methods

Where possible, evidence should be collected in the workplace, but this may not be a practical prospect for you. Equally, where workplace evidence can be gathered it may not cover all elements. The AAT regards performance evidence from simulations, case studies, projects and assignments as an acceptable substitute for performance at work, provided that they are based on the Standards and, as far as possible, on workplace practice.

There are a number of methods of assessing accounting competence. The list below is not exhaustive, nor is it prescriptive. Some methods have limited applicability, but others are capable of being expanded to provide challenging tests of competence.

Assessment method	Suitable for assessing
Performance of an accounting task either in the workplace or by simulation: eg preparing and processing documents, posting entries, making adjustments, balancing, calculating, analysing information etc by manual or computerised processes	**Basic task competence.** Adding supplementary oral questioning may help to draw out underpinning knowledge and understanding and highlight your ability to deal with contingencies and unexpected occurrences

BPP PUBLISHING

Assessment method	Suitable for assessing
General case studies. These are broader than simulations. They include more background information about the system and business environment	Ability to **analyse a system** and suggest ways of modifying it. It could take the form of a written report, with or without the addition of oral or written questions
Accounting problems/cases: eg a list of balances that require adjustments and the preparation of final accounts	Understanding of the **general principles of accounting** as applied to a particular case or topic
Preparation of flowcharts/diagrams. To illustrate an actual (or simulated) accounting procedure	**Understanding of the logic** behind a procedure, of controls, and of relationships between departments and procedures. Questions on the flow chart or diagram can provide evidence of underpinning knowledge and understanding
Interpretation of accounting information from an actual or simulated situation. The assessment could include non-financial information and written or oral questioning	**Interpretative competence**
Preparation of written reports on an actual or simulated situation	**Written communication skills**
Analysis of critical incidents, problems encountered, achievements	Your ability to handle **contingencies**
Listing of likely errors eg preparing a list of the main types of errors likely to occur in an actual or simulated procedure	Appreciation of the range of **contingencies** likely to be encountered. Oral or written questioning would be a useful supplement to the list
Outlining the organisation's policies, guidelines and regulations	Performance criteria relating to these aspects of competence. It also provides evidence of competence in **researching information**
Objective tests and short-answer questions	**Specific knowledge**
In-tray exercises	Your **task-management ability** as well as technical competence
Supervisors' reports	**General job competence**, personal effectiveness, reliability, accuracy, and time management. Reports need to be related specifically to the Standards of Competence
Analysis of work logbooks/diaries	**Personal effectiveness**, time management etc. It may usefully be supplemented with oral questioning
Formal written answers to questions	Knowledge and understanding of the **general accounting environment** and its impact on particular units of competence.
Oral questioning	**Knowledge and understanding** across the range of competence including organisational procedures, methods of dealing with unusual cases, contingencies and so on. It is often used in conjunction with other methods.

BPP PUBLISHING

UNIT 6 STANDARDS OF COMPETENCE

The structure of the Standards for Unit 6

The unit commences with a statement of the **knowledge and understanding** which underpin competence in the Unit's elements.

The unit is then divided into **elements of competence** describing activities which the individual should be able to perform.

Each element includes:

(a) **A** set of **performance criteria** which define what constitutes competent performance

(b) A **range statement** which defines the situations, contexts, methods etc in which competence should be displayed

(c) **Evidence requirements**, which state that competence must be demonstrated consistently, over an appropriate time scale with evidence of performance being provided from the appropriate sources

(d) **Sources of evidence**, being suggestions of ways in which you can find evidence to demonstrate that competence

The elements of competence for Unit 6 *Recording Cost Information* are set out below. Knowledge and understanding required for the unit as a whole are listed first, followed by the performance criteria, and range statements for each element. Performance criteria are cross-referenced below to chapters in this Unit 6 *Cost Information* Interactive Text.

Unit 6   Recording Cost Information

What is the unit about?

This unit is concerned with recording, analysing and reporting information relating to both direct and indirect costs. It involves the identification, coding and analysis of all costs, the apportionment and absorption of indirect costs and the presentation of all the information in standard cost reports. The candidate is required to carry out variance analyses, different methods of allocation, apportionment and absorption and adjustments for under/over recovered indirect costs. There is also a requirement for information to be systematically checked and any unusual or unexpected results to be communicated to management.

Knowledge and understanding

The business environment

- Main types of materials: raw materials; part finished goods; materials issued from stores within the organisation; deliveries (Elements 6.1 & 6.2)

- Methods of payment for labour: salaried labour; performance related pay; profit related pay (Elements 6.1 & 6.2)

- Main types of expenses: expenses directly charged to cost units; indirect expenses; depreciation charges (Elements 6.1 & 6.2)

Accounting techniques

- Basic analysis of variances: usage; price; rate; efficiency; expenditure; volume; capacity (Elements 6.1, 6.2 & 6.3)

- Procedures for establishing standard materials costs, use of technical and purchasing information (Element 6.1)

- Methods of analysing materials usage: reasons for wastage (Element 6.1)

- Procedures for establishing standard labour costs: use of information about labour rates (Element 6.1)

- Analysis of labour rate and efficiency: idle time; overtime levels; absenteeism; sickness rates (Element 6.1)

- Methods of stock control (Element 6.1)

- Methods of setting standards for expenses (Elements 6.1 & 6.2)

- Procedures and documentation relating to expenses (Elements 6.1 & 6.2)

- Allocation of expenses to cost centres (Elements 6.1 & 6.2)

- Analysis of the effect of changing activity levels on unit costs (Elements 6.1 & 6.2)

- Procedures for establishing standard absorption rates (Element 6.2)

- Bases of allocating and apportioning indirect costs to responsibility centres: direct; reciprocal allocation; step down method (Element 6.2)

- Activity based systems of allocating costs: cost drivers; cost pools (Element 6.2)

- Bases of absorption (Element 6.2)

- Methods of presenting information orally and in written reports (Element 6.3)

- Control ratios of efficiency, capacity and activity (Element 6.3)

Accounting principles and theory

- Relationship between technical systems and costing systems - job, batch, unit, systems (Elements 6.1 & 6.2)

- Principles and objectives of standard costing systems: variance reports (Elements 6.1, 6.2 & 6.3)

- Relationships between the materials costing system and the stock control system (Element 6.1)

- Relationships between the labour costing system and the payroll accounting system (Element 6.1)

- Relationships between the expenses costing system and the accounting system (Elements 6.1 & 6.2)

- Objectives of depreciation accounting (Elements 6.1 & 6.2)

- The distinction between fixed, semi-fixed and variable costs (Elements 6.1 & 6.2)

- Effect of changes in capacity levels (Element 6.2)

- Arbitrary nature of overhead apportionments (Element 6.2)

- The significance of and possible reasons for variances (Elements 6.1, 6.2 & 6.3)

The organisation

- Understanding of the ways the accounting systems of an organisation are affected by its organisational structure, its administrative systems and procedures and the nature of its business transactions (Elements 6.1, 6.2 & 6.3)

- The reporting cycle of the organisation (Element 6.3)

BPP PUBLISHING

Element 6.1 Record and analyse information relating to direct costs

Performance criteria	Chapters in this Text
1 Direct costs are identified in accordance with the organisation's costing procedures	2-4,9
2 Information relating to direct costs is clearly and correctly coded, analysed and recorded	2-4, 7-9
3 Direct costs are calculated in accordance with the organisation's policies and procedures	2-4, 9
4 Standard costs are compared against actual costs and any variances are analysed	10, 11
5 Information is systematically checked against the overall usage and stock control practices	10, 11
6 Queries are either resolved or referred to the appropriate person	2-4, 7

Range statement

1   Direct costs: standard and actual material costs; standard and actual labour costs; standard and actual expenses

- Materials: raw materials; part finished goods; materials issued from stores within the organisation; deliveries

- Labour: employees of the organisation on the payroll; sub-contractors; agency staff

- Expenses: direct revenue expenditure

2   Variance analysis: Materials variances: usage, price; Labour variances: rate, efficiency

Element 6.2 Record and analyse information relating to the allocation, apportionment and absorption of overhead costs

Performance criteria	Chapters in this Text
1 Data are correctly coded, analysed and recorded	2-4, 7
2 Overhead costs are established in accordance with the organisation's procedures	2-4, 9
3 Information relating to overhead costs is accurately and clearly recorded	2-4, 7-9
4 Overhead costs are correctly attributed to producing and service cost centres in accordance with agreed methods of allocation, apportionment and absorption	5
5 Adjustments for under or over recovered overhead costs are made in accordance with established procedures	5
6 Standard costs are compared against actual costs and any variances are analysed	10
7 Methods of allocation, apportionment and absorption are reviewed at regular intervals in discussions with senior staff, and agreed changes to methods are implemented	5
8 Staff working in operational departments are consulted to resolve any queries in the data	2-4, 7

Range statement

1   Overhead costs: standard and actual indirect material costs; standard and actual indirect labour costs; indirect expenses; depreciation charges

2   Methods of allocation and apportionment: direct; reciprocal allocation; step down method

3   Variance analysis: Overhead variances: expenditure, efficiency, volume, capacity; Fixed overhead variances: expenditure, volume, capacity, efficiency

Element 6.3 Prepare and present standard cost reports

Performance criteria	Chapters in this Text
1 Standard cost reports with variances clearly identified are presented in an intelligible form	11
2 Unusual or unexpected results are identified and reported to managers	11
3 Any reasons for significant variances from standard are identified and the explanations presented to management	11
4 The results of the analysis and explanations of specific variances are produced for management	11
5 Staff working in operational departments are consulted to resolve any queries in the data	11

Range statement

1   Methods of presentation: written report containing analysis and explanation of specific variances; further explanations to managers

2   Types of variances: Overhead variances: expenditure, efficiency, volume, capacity; Materials variances: usage, price; Labour variances: rate, efficiency

PART A

PRACTICE ACTIVITIES

CHAPTER 1: COST INFORMATION

Practice activity 1

For a mixed farm, growing crops and raising cattle, suggest *one* cost unit and *two* cost centres.

Practice activity 2

Indirect materials costs can also be called indirect expenses. True or false?

Practice activity 3

Prime cost is
A   all costs incurred in manufacturing a product
B   the total of direct costs
C   the material cost of a product
D   the cost of operating a department

Practice activity 4

What is the advantage of charging as many costs as possible to cost units rather than treating them as overheads?

Practice activity 5

Suggest the cost units which would be appropriate for management information systems in the following industries.
(a)   A building contractor
(b)   An airline

Practice activity 6
(a)   Suggest two suitable cost centres for a hospital.
(b)   Suggest two suitable cost units for a hospital.

CHAPTER 2: MATERIALS

Practice activity 7

A company has established reorder levels for each of the major materials it holds. Give *two* factors which influence a reorder level.

Practice activity 8

Explain briefly the purpose of establishing stock levels for each type of material in a stock control system.

Practice activity 9

What is the purpose of:
(a) a stores requisition?
(b) a purchase requisition?

Practice activity 10

In a period of rising prices which of the following methods of pricing issues would place the lowest value on the closing stocks?
(a) Weighted average
(b) FIFO
(c) LIFO

Practice activity 11

Annual demand for a material is 200,000 units. It costs £3.20 to hold one unit in stock for one year. Ordering costs are £18 per order. What should the reorder quantity be in order to minimise stock administration costs?

Practice activity 12

At a time of rapidly rising prices a manufacturing company decides to change from a FIFO to a LIFO system of pricing material issues. What would be the effect on the following?
(a) Stock valuation
(b) Cost of materials charged to production

Practice activity 13

Give four factors which should be considered in deciding the optimum level of stocks of component parts to be held in a stores which serves a mass production assembly line.

Practice activity 14

Explain how the term 'reorder level' differs from 'minimum level' and 'maximum level'.

Practice activity 15

On what factors does a maximum stock level depend?

Practice activity 16

What are the main advantages of using a system of numbers to identify stock held?

CHAPTER 3: LABOUR

Practice activity 17

What is differential piecework?

Practice activity 18

List two advantages of paying employees by the results achieved.

Practice activity 19

Give two reasons why the majority of employees are paid on the basis of time, eg hourly rates of pay.

Practice activity 20

How would additional payments to production workers for weekend working be treated in the cost accounts?

CHAPTER 4: EXPENSES

Practice activity 21

A personal computer costing £3,000 was expected to last for four years and to have a resale value of £200. The company policy is to depreciate assets using the straight-line method of depreciation.

(a) What is the annual depreciation charge to the administration cost centre?

(b) The computer was replaced after three years with no resale value. Calculate the obsolescence charge and state where this charge should be shown in the cost accounts.

CHAPTER 5: OVERHEADS AND ABSORPTION COSTING

Practice activity 22

Give *two* significant overhead costs likely to be incurred by an international firm of management consultants.

Practice activity 23

The overheads of a cost centre were substantially over absorbed last period.

(a) What is the costing treatment for this?

(b) Will it increase or decrease the costing profit for the period?

Practice activity 24

The actual overheads for a department were £6,500 last period and the actual output was 540 machine hours. The budgeted overheads were £5,995 and the budgeted output was 550 machine hours. Calculate the under- or over-absorbed overhead and state whether it would increase or reduce the profit for the period.

Practice activity 25

With activity-based costing, 'cost drivers' are used.

(a) Are cost drivers a means of:

    (i)   establishing the overhead cost of activities; or

    (ii)   calculating the value of the direct materials used; or

      (iii)   determining the most suitable cost centres.

(b)   Suggest a suitable cost driver for the purchasing department of a large manufacturing company.

Practice activity 26

Suggest suitable cost drivers for the following cost pools.

Production scheduling costs
Despatch costs

Practice activity 27

The overhead absorption rate for the machining department at Jefferson Ltd is £5 per direct labour hour. During the year to 31 December 1,753 direct labour hours were worked and overheads incurred were £9,322. During the twelve-month period overheads were therefore over absorbed. True or false?

Practice activity 28

Suggest an appropriate basis for apportioning each of the following overhead costs to production cost centres in a manufacturing company.
(a)   Canteen costs
(b)   Heating and lighting
(c)   Building maintenance

Practice activity 29

Explain briefly the machine hour rate method of absorbing overhead costs into cost units in a manufacturing organisation.

Practice activity 30

Explain briefly the function of cost drivers in an activity based costing system, giving an example.

Practice activity 31

When using absorption costing, explain why the use of an overhead absorption rate based on direct labour hours is generally favoured over a direct wages percentage rate for a labour intensive operation.

CHAPTER 6: COST BEHAVIOUR

Practice activity 32

Draw graphs to illustrate the following cost behaviour patterns.
(a)   Variable cost
(b)   Fixed costs
(c)   Step costs

Practice activity 33

The cost of operating the stores department of Lake Garda Ltd for the last four years have been as follows.

Year	Output volume units	Total cost £
1	70,000	1,100,000
2	80,000	1,150,000
3	77,000	1,110,000
4	60,000	970,000

Task

What costs should be expected in year 5 when output is expected to be 75,000 units?

CHAPTER 7: BOOKKEEPING ENTRIES FOR COST INFORMATION

Practice activity 34

Fraternity Ltd manufactures a range of products which are sold through a network of wholesalers and dealers. A set of integrated accounts is kept, and for the year 20X0 the following information is relevant.

(a) Production overhead is absorbed into the cost of products on the basis of a budgeted rate of 80% of direct labour cost.

(b) Finished stocks are valued at factory cost.

(c) The selling price to wholesalers and dealers includes a profit margin of 25% on actual production cost.

(d)

	31 March 20X0 £	30 April 20X0 £
Raw materials stock	34,400	30,320
Work in progress	11,200	9,500
Finished goods stock	21,000	24,180
Debtors for goods sold	18,400	22,280
Creditors for raw materials	15,200	18,840
Fixed assets at net book value	12,000	11,600

(e) Bank transactions for the month of April 20X0 were as follows.

	£
Bank balance at 31 March	3,000
Receipts from debtors	55,120
Payments made	
Direct labour	12,800
Creditors for raw materials	17,920
Production overhead	10,400
Administration overhead	1,400
Selling and distribution overhead	4,600

(f) Production overhead includes a monthly charge of £400 for depreciation and the opening balance on the production overhead control account each month is nil. Administration, selling and distribution overheads consist entirely of cash items.

Task

Use the information above to write up the following control accounts.

BPP
PUBLISHING

(a) Raw materials stock

(b) Work in progress

(c) Finished goods stock

(d) Production overhead

CHAPTER 8: COSTING METHODS

Practice activity 35

Fill in the missing words

Batch costing is a form of costing that is similar to_____costing except that costs are collected for_____. The cost unit is the_____. A cost per unit is calculated by _____.

Practice activity 36

Suggest appropriate costing methods for the following organisations.

(a) A plumbing business

(b) A clothing manufacturer

(c) A caterer

CHAPTER 9: STANDARD COSTING

Practice activity 37

An employee makes 200 units of product A, 350 units of product B and 300 units of product C. The standard time allowed per unit was:

    A   4 minutes,   B   2 minutes   C   3 minutes

Calculate the standard hours produced by the employee.

Practice activity 38

A standard cost is only a guess at what the cost of something should be. It is of little relevance once the actual cost is known. True or false?

Practice activity 39

Name one advantage and one disadvantage of using an ideal standard.

CHAPTER 10: CALCULATION OF VARIANCES

Practice activity 40

Choose the appropriate words.

The workforce of Casios Ltd have been working at a less efficient rate than standard to produce a given output. The result is a *favourable/adverse* fixed overhead *usage/capacity* variance.

The total number of hours worked was, however, more than was originally budgeted. The effect is measured by a *favourable/adverse* fixed overhead *usage/capacity* variance.

Practice activity 41

How is a usage or efficiency variance calculated?

Practice activity 42

Bryan Limited budgets to produce 500 units of ferginude during August 20X2. The expected time to produce one unit of ferginude is 2.5 hours and the budgeted fixed production overhead is £10,000. Actual fixed production overhead expenditure in August 20X2 turns out to be £10,500 and the labour force manages to produce 600 units in 1,350 hours of work.

Comment on the above information, performing whatever calculations you think are most appropriate.

Practice activity 43
(a)   Who is likely to be responsible for an adverse materials usage variance?
(b)   Who is likely to be responsible for an adverse labour rate variance?

CHAPTER 11: VARIANCE ANALYSIS

Practice activity 44

A direct materials price variance may be calculated and entered in the accounts of a business at either the time of receipt of the stock, or the time of issue from stores to production. Which of the methods is usually regarded as the better, and why?

Practice activity 45

In a particular month production overheads were under absorbed because Excelsior plc had to cut back production due to a lack of orders.
(a)   Which variance account would be affected by this situation?
(b)   What would be the effect on unit costs of production?

Practice activity 46

Explain the meaning of the term 'interdependence of variances'.

Practice activity 47

Jemima Ltd uses a standard costing system and values all of its stocks of raw materials at standard price. Stocks are issued to work in progress at standard price. There is an adverse material price variance during an accounting period. What is the cost accounting entry for the material price variance?

The following data relate to practice activities 48-53.

RFB plc was formed in the early nineteenth century producing wheels for horse-drawn vehicles. Today it is a successful, profitable company which still makes wheels, but for a variety of uses: wheelbarrows, carts, toys etc. The production operation consists of three departments: bending, cutting and assembly. The bending and cutting departments have general purpose machinery which is used to manufacture all the wheels it produces.

Practice activity 48

Complete the form below by analysing the cost items into the appropriate columns and agreeing the balances.

	Total £	Prime cost £	Production expense £	Admin. expense £	Selling and distribution expense £
Wages of assembly employees	6,750				
Wages of stores employees	3,250				
Tyres for toy wheels	1,420				
Safety goggles for operators	810				
Job advert for new employees	84				
Depreciation of salesmen's cars	125				
Depreciation of production machines	264				
Cost of trade exhibition	1,200				
Computer stationery	130				
Course fee for AAT training	295				
Royalty for the design of wheel 1477	240				
	14,568				

Practice activity 49

Extracts from three purchase invoices which have been received for wire, code number 1471 are shown as follows. The invoices have been passed by the purchase department and the standard price is £120 per coil.

(a) (i)   Calculate the standard cost of the actual quantity purchased on each invoice.

    (ii)   Name and calculate the variance, stating whether it is adverse or favourable, in each invoice.

Invoice number 3275	Your order number 57623
Date 1.11.X8	
50 coils @ £132	£6,600
Standard cost of actual quantity	_____
.... variance	_____ ( )

```
Invoice number 4517                    Your order number 58127

Date 17.11.X8

      150 coils @ £108                          £16,200

      Standard cost of actual quantity          _____

      ..................................... variance      _____  ( )
```

```
Invoice number 5178                    Your order number 60173

Date 17.11.X8

      100 coils @ £120                          £12,000

      Standard cost of actual quantity          _____

      ..................................... variance      _____  ( )
```

(b) Enter the individual variances calculated in (a) in the variance account below. Do not calculate the balance on the account.

VARIANCE ACCOUNT

(c) Suggest reasons for the variances in (a), and state what action, if any, needs to be taken. Who would be responsible for taking the action that you recommend?

Practice activity 50

(a) Calculate the standard overhead absorption rates for the three departments below, selecting the appropriate data.

	Bending	Cutting	Assembly
Actual overheads £s	128,000	80,000	64,500
Budgeted overheads £s	120,000	90,000	60,000
Actual machine hours	11,800	2,750	-
Budgeted machine hours	10,000	3,000	-
Actual labour hours	-	-	15,900
Budgeted labour hours	-	-	15,000

(b) Using the information given below and the standard overhead rates calculated in (a), calculate the standard cost of producing 100 wheels for a toy car.

	Bending	Cutting	Assembly
Labour rates of pay per hour £	4	6	5
Labour hours per 100 wheels	0.8	0.5	1.2
Machine hours per 100 wheels	0.4	0.5	-

BPP PUBLISHING

STANDARD COST CARD			
Toy car wheels Part number 5917B			Date:
Standard quantity 100 wheels			
	Performance standard	Standard rate/price	Standard cost £
Direct materials			
Tyres	100	10p each	
Steel strip	50	10.40 per 100	
Wire	1000	2p each	
Direct labour	hours	£	
Bending			
Cutting			
Assembly			
Overheads			
Bending			
Cutting			
Assembly			
TOTAL COST			

Practice activity 51

Using the standard cost card from Practice activity 3, calculate the target selling price per 100 wheels if the company expects a profit of 10% of the target selling price.

Practice activity 52

(a) How would the standard labour hours for producing 100 wheels be determined?

(b) The cost of both the stores and the personnel departments has to be apportioned across the other cost centres. What bases would you recommend?

Practice activity 53

Protective gloves are used in the production departments and are drawn from stores at regular intervals. Records show the following for November:

1.11.X8	Opening stock	100 pairs @ £2 each
7.11.X8	Purchases	200 pairs @ £1.90 each
18.11.X8	Issues	150 pairs

Calculate the value of the closing stock of gloves given that the FIFO system of valuing issues is used.

The following data relate to practice activities 54-62.

AMP plc, a printing company, specialises in producing accounting manuals for several accountancy training companies. The manuals are written by the training companies and passed to AMP. The company uses three main stages in producing the manuals:

(a) The preparation of the text;
(b) The printing of the text;
(c) The assembly and binding of the manuals.

Practice activity 54

Write up the following information on the stores record card given below using weighted average prices to value the issues.

Material: Paper - Code 1564A
Opening stock: 10,000 sheets - value £3,000

Purchases			*Issues*	
3 May	4,000 sheets	£1,600	6 May	7,000 sheets
12 May	10,000 sheets	£3,100	15 May	6,000 sheets
25 May	10,000 sheets	£3,200	22 May	7,200 sheets

(The calculation of the weighted average should be to two decimal places of a £ and that of the value of the issues to the nearest £.)

Stores Record Card

Material: Paper   *Code:* 1564A

		Receipts		Issues			Stock		
Date	Details	Sheets	£	Sheets	Price	£	Sheets	Price	£

Practice activity 55

Calculate the gross wages earned for each of the following employees for week 32. The normal week is 38 hours and an individual production bonus of 10p per 100 sheets produced is paid.

	Singh	Smith
Basic rate per hour	£4.50	£4.00
Total hours worked	$39^1/_2$	41
Overtime hours paid:		
at time plus a third	$1^1/_2$	1
at time plus a half	-	2
Output (sheets)	10,500	10,900

(Calculations should be to two decimal places of a £.)

13

Practice activity 56

There has been some pressure from the employees for a piecework system to be introduced.

What would the piecework price per 100 sheets have to be, to at least equal the gross wages earned by Singh in (a) above, assuming the same output level of 10,500 sheets?

(Calculations should be to two decimal places of a £.)

Practice activity 57

The binding department's output last period consisted of 1,200 copies of one manual 'AATA'. The standard cost of this manual is shown below.

Standard Cost Card

Product: Manual AATA **Date prepared:** June 20X9

Element	Performance Standard	Standard Rate/Price	Std Cost
Direct material	1 unit	90p per unit	0.90
Direct labour	¼ hour	£4 per hour	1.00
Variable overheads	¼ hour	£2 per hour	0.50
Fixed overheads	¼ hour	£6 per hour	1.50
		Cost per manual	£3.90

Complete the following departmental operating account, using the information from the standard cost card above to calculate the standard cost and the total variance for each element of cost. Each variance must be marked 'adverse' (A) or 'favourable' (F).

Departmental Operating Account

Month: May 20X9 **Budget hours:** 320 **Department:** Binding
Date prepared: 10.6.99 **Actual hours:** 290 **Manager:** Mrs Jones

Actual Costs	£	Output (Manuals)	Unit Cost £	Total Cost £	Total Variance £
Direct materials	1,200	1,200			
Direct labour:					
290 hours	1,300	1,200			
Variable overheads	580	1,200			
Fixed overheads	1,920	1,200			
Total	5,000				

Practice activity 58

(a) Analyse the direct labour cost variance in practice activity 17 above into the appropriate sub-variances.

(b) Suggest one reason for each of the sub-variances occurring and outline the corrective action that needs to be taken in each case.

(c) Who would be responsible for taking the corrective action in (b) above?

Practice activity 59

AMP has always held large quantities of paper in stock in case it should become difficult to obtain. Suggest two problems that this could create.

Practice activity 60

The overtime premium paid to Singh and Smith in Practice activity 15(a) could be analysed to direct wages or to departmental overheads. Detail the circumstances which would give rise to these differing treatments.

Practice activity 61

Name one overhead variance from Practice activity 17 that you would expect to find in the binding department. Explain whether it would be adverse or favourable. (Calculations are not required.)

Practice activity 62

When setting the standard cost of the various manuals it produces, the company had to decide whether to use ideal standards or current/expected standards. State which of the two standards you would use and explain why.

The following data relates to practice activities 63-67.

Pears plc manufactures children's clothing. The general manager is concerned about how the costs of the various garments it produces are calculated. The material cost varies from one garment to another and the rates of pay in the various departments also vary to reflect the different skills offered. Both these prime costs are charged direct to individual garments so that any variation is taken into account. It is the overhead cost which has been concerning Pears for some time. The present overhead system uses one overhead rate for the whole company and is absorbed as a percentage of direct labour cost. The accounting department has been examining individual cost items and relating them as closely as possible to the department which incurs them. Some apportionment has also taken place and the forecasted overhead cost and other related information is as follows.

	Overhead cost £'000	Numbers employed	% of floor area	Material issued £'000	Machine hours
Production departments					
Cutting	187	10	40	200	15,000
Sewing	232	15	30	250	25,000
Finishing	106	8	15	100	
Service departments					
Stores	28	2	5	-	
Maintenance	50	3	10	50	

BPP PUBLISHING

Practice activity 63

Using the overhead analysis sheet below, apportion:

(a)   The stores department's costs to the production and maintenance departments;

(b)   The maintenance department's costs to the cutting and sewing departments only.

Select the most suitable base for each apportionment and state the bases used on the overhead analysis sheet. (Calculations should be to the nearest £.)

OVERHEAD ANALYSIS SHEET   DATE

	TOTAL	PRODUCTION			SERVICE	
		Cutting	Sewing	Finishing	Stores	Maintenance
	£	£	£	£	£	£
Overheads	603,000	187,000	232,000	106,000	28,000	50,000
Apportion Stores (Base:)						
Apportion Maintenance (Base:)						

Practice activity 64

Given that 12,000 labour hours will be worked in the finishing department calculate overhead absorption rates for the three production departments using machine hour rates for the cutting and sewing departments, and a labour hour rate for the finishing department. (Calculations should be to two decimal places of the £.)

Practice activity 65

Explain briefly why it is appropriate to use machine hour rates in the cutting and sewing departments.

Practice activity 66

Using the form provided below, calculate the standard cost of a new garment 'XL'. It is established that direct material cost will be £4.32. Direct labour cost is to be based on $\frac{1}{4}$ hour in the cutting department, 1 hour in the sewing department and $\frac{1}{2}$ hour in the finishing department. The standard hourly rates of pay are £4.00 in cutting, £3.00 in sewing and £5.00 in finishing. Overheads are to be included using the hourly rates calculated in Practice activity 30 above and the same hours as used in the labour cost above.

```
                    STANDARD PRODUCT COST SHEET
                           PRODUCT : 'XL'
                                                          Date:

                                                      £            £

Direct Material Cost
                        ┌───────────────┬───────────────┐
                        │    Hours      │     Rate      │
Direct Labour Cost      │               │      £        │
 - cutting              │               │               │
 - sewing               │               │               │
 - finishing            │               │               │
                        └───────────────┴───────────────┘
Total Labour Cost
                        ┌───────────────┬───────────────┐
                        │    Hours      │     Rate      │
Overhead Cost           │               │      £        │
 - cutting              │               │               │
 - sewing               │               │               │
 - finishing            │               │               │
                        └───────────────┴───────────────┘
Total Overhead Cost

TOTAL COST
```

Practice activity 67

Pears plc has obtained 50 metres of a material at a special price of £2.00 per metre as it is slightly substandard. The standard price for this material is £3.00 per metre. From this material 20 garments have been made for which the standard quantity is 2 metres per garment.

(a)   Calculate the following.

    (i)   Material price variance

    (ii)   Material usage variance

    (iii)   Total material cost variance

(b)   List the responsible managers who should be informed of each of these variances as part of the routine reporting procedures.

(c)   Explain whether the decision to buy this material was correct.

The following data relate to practice activities 68-72.

(NB. Answer these activities in sequence as the answers to earlier activities may need to be used later.)

Watkins Ltd produces a single product, the N-17T, which passes through three production processes (forming, colouring and assembly). The output of the forming process becomes the input of the colouring process and the input of the assembly process is the output of the colouring process. There are also two service departments, maintenance and general.

The budgeted overheads for the 12 months to 31 December 20X9 are as follows.

	£	£
Rent and rates		8,000
Power		750
Light, heat		5,000
Repairs, maintenance:		
Forming	800	
Colouring	1,800	
Assembly	300	
Maintenance	200	
General	100	
		3,200
Departmental expenses:		
Forming	1,500	
Colouring	2,300	
Assembly	1,100	
Maintenance	900	
General	1,500	
		7,300
Depreciation:		
Plant		10,000
Fixtures and fittings		250
Insurance:		
Plant		2,000
Buildings		500
Indirect labour:		
Forming	3,000	
Colouring	5,000	
Assembly	1,500	
Maintenance	4,000	
General	2,000	
		15,500
		52,500

Other data are available as follows.

	Floor area sq. ft	Plant value £	Fixtures & fittings £	Effective horse-power	Budget Labour hours	Machine hours
Forming	2,000	25,000	1,000	40	27,400	5,000
Colouring	4,000	60,000	500	90	3,000	14,400
Assembly	3,000	7,500	2,000	15	20,000	2,600
Maintenance	500	7,500	1,000	5	-	-
General	500	-	500	-	-	-
	10,000	100,000	5,000	150	50,400	22,000

	Budget Maintenance work to be provided by maintenance department Hours	General work to be provided by general service department Hours
Forming	2,000	1,200
Colouring	5,000	3,600
Assembly	2,000	600
Maintenance	-	600
General	1,000	-
	10,000	6,000

Practice activity 68

Prepare a table which shows the overheads which can be directly allocated to the five departments.

18

Practice activity 69

Complete the table you started in Practice activity 44 by apportioning the remaining overheads to the five departments, clearly indicating the basis of apportionment that you have used.

Practice activity 70

Apportion the service department overheads to the production departments using the repeated distribution method.

Practice activity 71

Calculate suitable overhead absorption rates for the three production departments.

Practice activity 72

During the year to 31 December 20X9, 30,000 labour hours were worked in the forming department, 3,150 in the colouring department and 18,500 in the assembly department. Machines ran for 4,900 hours in the forming department, 16,000 hours in the colouring department and 3,297 in the assembly department. The overheads actually incurred in the three production departments (after allocation and apportionment) were as follows.

	£
Forming	14,580
Colouring	30,050
Assembly	9,840

Calculate any under- or over-absorbed overhead for the twelve months to 31 December 20X9.

The following data relate to practice activities 73-80.

(NB. Answer these activities in sequence as the answers to earlier activities may need to be used later.)

Jasperino Ltd operates a job costing system which is fully integrated with the financial accounts. The following data relate to May 20X9.

	£
Balances at the beginning of the month	
Stores ledger control account	8,000
Work in progress control account	15,000
Finished goods control account	22,000
Prepayments of production overheads, brought forward from April 20X9	1,000
Transactions during the month	
Materials purchased	75,000
Materials issued to production	34,000
Materials issued to factory maintenance	4,000
Materials transferred between jobs	3,500
Total wages of direct workers	18,000
Recorded non-productive time of direct workers	2,500
Wages of indirect production workers (total)	11,000
Other production overheads incurred	16,000
Selling and distribution overheads incurred	12,000
Sales	110,000
Cost of finished goods sold	65,000
Cost of finished goods damaged and scrapped in the month	2,000
Value of work in progress at 31 May 20X9	18,000

Production overhead absorption rate is 200% of direct wages.

Practice activity 73

Prepare the stores ledger control account.

Practice activity 74

Prepare the work in progress control account.

Practice activity 75

Calculate the under- or over-absorbed overhead in the month.

Practice activity 76

Prepare the finished goods control account.

Practice activity 77

Calculate the profit for May.

Practice activity 78

The ten machines used by Jasperino Ltd are eight years old. They have been depreciated on a straight line basis over 5 years and so depreciation is no longer charged to the production overhead control account.

At the beginning of June 20X9 the company decides to buy a new machine for £17,580. It has not yet been established whether the machine is to be depreciated on a straight line basis over five years or on a 25% reducing balance basis.

Calculate the annual depreciation which would be charged over the next five years under the two methods.

Practice activity 79

On 1 May 20X9, there was only one uncompleted job in Jasperino Ltd's factory. The job card for this work is summarised below.

JOB CARD
Job 212/A

Costs to date	£
Direct materials	7,080
Direct labour	1,314
Production overhead	2,628
Factory cost to date	11,022

During May a number of new jobs were started. The chief cost accountant is exceptionally busy and so you have been asked to prepare job accounts for jobs 212/A and one of the new jobs, 219/C. You have gathered together the following information.

	Direct materials	£
Issued to	212/A	3,122
	219/C	4,003
Transfers from	212/A to 219/C	3,500
Direct labour		
	212/A	1,922
	219/C	7,255

Prepare job accounts for 212/A and 219/C

Practice activity 80

If administration and marketing overheads are added to cost of sales at a rate of 15% of factory cost and invoiced amounts are £20,500 for job 212/A and £28,750 for job 219/C, calculate the profit or loss on the two jobs.

Answers to practice activities

Answer to Practice activity 1

(a) Possible cost units would include a kilogram of crops (such as wheat or barley or oats) or an individual cow/calf/bull.

(b) Possible cost centres include an area (such as a field or an acre), a herd of cattle, the dairy, ploughing activities and harvesting activities.

Answer to Practice activity 2

Strictly speaking this is false. Indirect materials costs are called indirect materials costs! Indirect expenses are indirect costs other than materials or labour. In practice, however, terms like 'cost', 'expense' and 'overhead' are used very loosely.

Answer to Practice activity 3

B

Answer to Practice activity 4

By charging as many costs as possible to cost units rather than treating them as overheads, arbitrary overhead apportionment, resulting in a less accurate cost per unit, is avoided.

Answer to Practice activity 5

(a) A building contractor should treat each contract as a cost unit.
(b) An airline should treat each passenger mile (or 100 or 1,000 passenger miles) as a cost unit.

Answer to Practice activity 6

(a) Cost centres: a ward, an operating theatre, a doctor, a sister, a bed
(b) Cost units: a patient/day, an operation, an outpatient visit

Answer to Practice activity 7

The reorder level is influenced by rate of usage and lead time (delivery time).

Answer to Practice activity 8

Minimum stock levels are established for each type of material in a stock control system to allow for unexpected rises or falls in demand and for severe shortages of supply.

Answer to Practice activity 9

(a) A stores requisition is used to request and authorise an issue of stock from stores to production.

(b) A purchase requisition is used to instruct and authorise the purchasing department to obtain supplies.

Answer to Practice activity 10

In a period of rising prices the LIFO method (c) of pricing issues would place the lowest value on closing stocks, because we assume that the newest stock is used first and the residue is the oldest (and hence cheapest) stock.

Answer to Practice activity 11

Economic order quantity (EOQ) $\qquad = \qquad \sqrt{\dfrac{2cd}{h}}$, where

$c =$ cost of ordering $\quad = \qquad$ £18
$d =$ annual demand $\quad = \qquad$ 200,000
$h =$ cost of carrying one unit in stock for one year $= $ £3.20

$\therefore EOQ = \sqrt{\dfrac{2 \times 18 \times 200,000}{3.20}} = 1,500$ units

Answer to Practice activity 12

(a) Changing from FIFO to LIFO during a period of rapidly rising prices would result in lower stock valuations.

(b) Changing from FIFO to LIFO during a period of rapidly rising prices would result in higher costs of materials charged to production.

Answer to Practice activity 13

When deciding the optimum level of stock of component parts to be held in a store serving a mass production assembly line, the following factors should be considered.

(a) The economic order quantity
(b) Deterioration/obsolescence
(c) Space taken up by stores
(d) Cost of capital tied up in stocks
(e) Continuity of supplies

Answer to Practice activity 14

The reorder level is the level to which stocks should be allowed to fall before an order is placed. The maximum stock level indicates the level above which it becomes wasteful to hold stocks whereas the minimum level indicates the level below which stocks should never be allowed to fall. The reordering level is fixed between the maximum and minimum levels and is usually just slightly higher than the minimum level, to cover such emergencies as abnormal usage of material or unexpected delay in delivery of fresh supplies.

Answer to Practice activity 15

The maximum stock level depends on the reorder level, the reorder quantity, the rate of usage and the delivery time.

Answer to Practice activity 16

The main advantages are:

(a)   the system is unambiguous;

(b)   the system saves time. Descriptions can be time-consuming;

(c)   the chances of issuing the wrong stock are reduced;

(d)   computer processing is made easier;

(e)   the system is designed to be flexible, and can be expanded to include more stock items as necessary.

Answer to Practice activity 17

Piecework is an incentive scheme in that the more output you produce the more you are paid. Differential piecework pays a different rate for different levels of production, for example as follows.

Up to 100 units a day   20p per unit
101 to 150 units a day   22p per unit
151 to 200 units a day   25p per unit
Over 200 units a day   30p per unit

Answer to Practice activity 18

Two advantages of paying employees by the results achieved are as follows.

(a)   Output should be higher.
(b)   Employees can receive higher wages.

Answer to Practice activity 19

The majority of employees are paid on the basis of time rather than by results achieved since it can be difficult to measure work done and because quality can suffer if employees try to rush production.

Answer to Practice activity 20

Additional payments to production workers for weekend working would be treated as a production overhead and not a direct cost since it would be unfair if an item made during overtime hours was more costly just because, by chance, it was made during hours in which employees do not normally work.

Answer to Practice activity 21

(a)   Depreciable amount = £(3,000 – 200) = £2,800.

Expected life = 4 years.

Annual depreciation charge = £2,800/4 = £700.

(b)

	£
Depreciation charged = 3 × £700	2,100
Amount which should have been charged	3,000
Obsolescence charge	900

It is normal practice to charge a loss resulting from obsolescence to the costing profit and loss account.

Answer to Practice activity 22

Significant overhead costs incurred by an international firm of management consultants could include the following.

(a) Rent
(b) Travelling expenses
(c) Support staff (secretaries and so on)
(d) Publicity/advertising
(e) Entertaining
(f) Depreciation of computers, wordprocessors and so on

Answer to Practice activity 23

(a) If overheads are over absorbed, the amount over absorbed should be debited to the cost centre overhead account and credited to the cost profit and loss account

(b) Over-absorbed overhead increases cost profit for a period.

Answer to Practice activity 24

We need to calculate an overhead absorption rate.

$$\text{Absorption rate} = \frac{\text{budgeted overheads}}{\text{budgeted activity level}} = \frac{\text{£5,995}}{\text{550 hrs}}$$

$$= \text{£10.90 per machine hour}$$

	£
Actual overheads	6,500
Absorbed overheads (540 hrs × £10.90)	5,886
Under-absorbed overheads	614

Under-absorbed overheads reduce the profit for the period.

Answer to Practice activity 25

(a) With activity based costing, cost drivers are a means of establishing the overhead cost of activities.

(b) A suitable cost driver for the purchasing department of a large manufacturing company would be the number of orders handled in the period.

Answer to Practice activity 26

Cost pool	*Cost driver*
Production scheduling costs	Number of production runs
Despatch costs	Number of orders delivered

Answer to Practice activity 27

False.

	£
Overheads incurred	9,322
Overheads absorbed (£5 × 1,753)	8,765
Under-absorbed overhead	557

Answer to Practice activity 28

(a) Canteen costs: number of employees per production cost centre or labour hours worked in each production cost centre

(b) Heating and lighting: floor area per production cost centre or volume of space occupied by each cost centre

(c) Building maintenance: valuation of production cost centre building or number of hours spent on maintenance jobs undertaken or actual cost of work undertaken

Answer to Practice activity 29

The overhead absorption rate is calculated by dividing the budgeted/estimated overheads which have been apportioned to the particular production cost centre by the budgeted/estimated number of hours machines in that production cost centre will be running. Each unit of output is therefore charged with overhead on the basis of the number of machine hours it requires in that cost centre. The machine hour basis should be used if production is highly mechanised such that a large proportion of overhead expenditure is likely to be more closely related to machine utilisation than to direct labour input.

Answer to Practice activity 30

Activity based costing, a recent development in cost accounting, attempts to absorb overheads into product costs on a more realistic basis than that used by traditional absorption costing. The basic idea is that instead of arbitrarily choosing an absorption base for all overheads, overhead costs are grouped according to what drives them or causes them to be incurred. These costs drivers are then used as an absorption basis.

For example, costs associated with handling orders are driven by the number of orders. The cost driver for such costs is therefore the number of orders. Costs relating to production run set-ups are driven by the number of set-ups, costs associated with machine activity are driven by the number of machine hours and costs related to labour activity are driven by the number of labour hours.

Answer to Practice activity 31

When using absorption costing, a time-based overhead absorption rate is generally favoured over any other because of the belief that most items of overhead expenditure tend to increase with time. A direct wages percentage rate is to an extent time based, but if differential wage rates exist, this can lead to inequitable overhead absorption. The direct labour hour rate does not suffer from this disadvantage.

Note that ABC is based on the idea that most items of overhead expenditure do not increase with time.

BPP
PUBLISHING

Answer to Practice activity 32

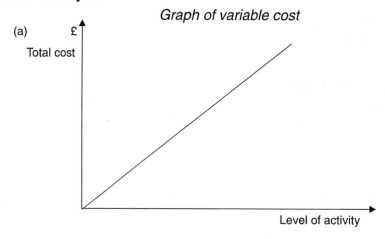

Graph of variable cost

(a) £
Total cost

Level of activity

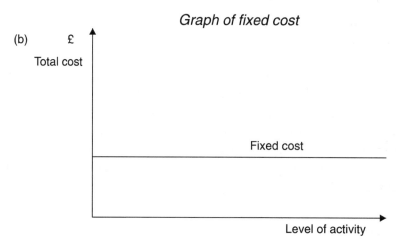

Graph of fixed cost

(b) £
Total cost

Fixed cost

Level of activity

Graph of step cost

(c) £
Total cost

Level of activity

Answer to Practice activity 33

Step 1

Period with highest activity   = year 2
Period with lowest activity   = year 4

Step 2

Total cost at high activity level	=	£1,150,000
Total cost at low activity level	=	£970,000
Total units at high activity level	=	80,000
Total units at low activity level	=	60,000

Step 3

$$\text{Variable cost per unit} = \frac{\text{Total cost at high activity level} - \text{total cost at low activity level}}{\text{Total units at high activity level} - \text{total units at low activity level}}$$

$$= \frac{£(1,150,000 - 970,000)}{80,000 - 60,000} = \frac{£180,000}{20,000} = £9 \text{ per unit}$$

Step 4

Fixed costs = (Total cost at high activity level) – (total units at high activity level × variable cost per unit)

= £1,150,000 – (80,000 × £9) = £1,150,000 – 720,000   = £430,000

Therefore, the costs in year 5 for output of 75,000 units are as follows.

	£
Variable costs (75,000 × £9)	675,000
Fixed costs	430,000
Total costs	1,105,000

Answer to Practice activity 34

(a)
RAW MATERIALS STOCK

	£		£
Opening balance	34,400	Work in progress (bal figure)	25,640
Creditors (W1)	21,560	Balance c/d	30,320
	55,960		55,960
Balance b/d	15,160		

(b)
WORK IN PROGRESS

	£		£
Opening balance	11,200	Finished goods (bal figure)	50,380
Raw materials stock	25,640	Balance c/d	9,500
Direct wages	12,800		
Production overhead (W2)	10,240		
	59,880		59,880
Balance b/d	4,750		

(c)
FINISHED GOODS STOCK

	£		£
Opening balance	21,000	P&L account(Cost of sales)	47,200
Work in progress	50,380	Balance c/d	24,180
	71,380		71,380
Balance b/d	12,090		

Check	£
Production cost of sales	47,200
Profit margin (add 25%)	11,800
Sales	59,000

(d)

PRODUCTION OVERHEAD

	£		£
Cash	10,400	Work in progress	10,240
Depreciation	400	P&L account (under-absorbed)	560
	10,800		10,800

Workings

1

CREDITORS FOR RAW MATERIALS

	£		£
Cash	17,920	Opening balance	15,200
Balance c/f	18,840	Raw materials purchases(bal fig)	21,560
	36,760		36,760

2	Direct labour	£12,800
	Production overhead absorbed (80%)	£10,240

Answer to Practice activity 35

Batch costing is a form of costing that is similar to job costing, except that costs are collected for a batch of items. The cost unit is the batch. A cost per unit is calculated by dividing the total batch cost by the number of units in the batch.

Answer to Practice activity 36

(a)   Job costing
(b)   Batch costing
(c)   Job costing

Answer to Practice activity 37

		Minutes
A	$200 \times 4 =$	800
B	$350 \times 2 =$	700
C	$300 \times 3 =$	900
		2,400

Standard hours produced $= 2,400 \div 60 = 40$ standard hours.

Answer to Practice activity 38

It is true that a standard cost is a 'guess' although it may be a very accurate one determined in a highly scientific manner. It is *not* true that standard costs are not relevant once actual costs are known. Standard costs are used not only for planning in advance, but also for measuring actual performance and deciding whether changes need to be made.

Answer to Practice activity 39

Advantage   Variances from ideal standards are useful for pinpointing areas where a close examination may result in large savings.

Disadvantage   They are likely to have an unfavourable motivational impact. Employees will often feel that the goals are unattainable and not work so hard.

Answer to Practice activity 40

The workforce of Casios Ltd have been working at a less efficient rate than standard to produce a given output. The result is an *adverse* fixed overhead *usage variance*.

The total number of hours worked was, however, more than originally budgeted. The effect is measured by a *favourable* fixed overhead *capacity* variance.

Answer to Practice activity 41

Usage and efficiency variances are quantity variances. They measure the difference between the actual physical quantity of materials used or hours taken and the quantities that should have been used or taken for the actual volume of production. The physical differences are then converted into money values by applying the appropriate standard cost.

Answer to Practice activity 42

The company spent £500 more on fixed production overheads than budgeted, which is probably not very significant. Units were produced in an average of 2.25 hours each which is a good deal faster than standard. The company also managed to operate for 100 hours longer than expected, and produced 100 extra units. Apart from the slight overspending and assuming the extra units can be sold, all of this is good.

If you calculated the variances you should have got the following figures.

	£
Price	500 (A)
Efficiency	1,200 (F)
Capacity	800 (F)
Total	1,500 (F)

Answer to Practice activity 43

(a)   The purchasing manager
(b)   The production manager

Answer to Practice activity 44

It is usually regarded as better to calculate the materials price variance at the time of receipt of stock, so that it can be eliminated and stocks can be valued at standard. The advantage is that this reduces clerical work in issuing stocks. All issues are valued at standard, and it is not necessary to calculate a variance as each issue is made.

Answer to Practice activity 45

(a)   The variance account affected would be the overhead capacity variance account.

(b)   Unit costs of production would increase because costs would have to be spread over a smaller number of units and therefore each unit would have to bear a larger share of the production overhead.

Answer to Practice activity 46

This is term used to express the way in which the cause of one variance may be wholly or partly explained by the cause of another variance. For instance, if the purchasing department buys a cheaper material which is poorer in quality than the expected standard, the material price variance will be favourable, but there may be material wastage and an adverse usage variance.

Answer to Practice activity 47

The cost accounting entry is as follows.

DR   Material price variance account
CR   Stores ledger control account

Answer to Practice activity 48

	Total £	Prime cost £	Production expense £	Admin. expense £	Selling and distribution expense £
Wages of assembly employees	6,750	6,750			
Wages of stores employees	3,250		3,250		
Tyres for toy wheels	1,420	1,420			
Safety goggles for operators	810		810		
Job advert for new employees	84			84	
Depreciation of salesmen's cars	125				125
Depreciation of production machines	264		264		
Cost of trade exhibition	1,200				1,200
Computer stationery	130			130	
Course fee for AAT training	295			295	
Royalty for the design of wheel 1477	240	240			
	14,568	8,410	4,324	509	1,325

Answer to Practice activity 49

(a)   (i) and (ii)

Invoice number 3275	Your order number 57623
Date 1.11.X8	
	£
50 coils @ £132	6,600
Standard cost of actual quantity (50 × £120)	6,000
Material price variance	600 (A)

Invoice number 4517	Your order number 58127
Date 17.11.X8	
	£
150 coils @ £108	16,200
Standard cost of actual quantity (150 × £120)	18,000
Material price variance	1,800 (F)

Invoice number 5178	Your order number 60173
Date 17.11.X8	
	£
100 coils @ £120	12,000
Standard cost of actual quantity (100 × £120)	12,000
Material price variance	- (-)

(b)
VARIANCE ACCOUNT

1.11.X8	Purchase	600	00	17.11.X8	Purchase	1,800	00	

(c) The adverse variance may have been due to careless purchasing by the purchasing department or an unexpected price increase or the loss of a quantity discount because a smaller quantity than standard was purchased. The favourable variance may be due to greater care taken in purchasing by the purchasing department, an unexpected price decrease or an increased quantity discount because a larger quantity than standard was purchased. (The fact that there is no variance when 100 coils are purchased and that there is an adverse variance when less are purchased and a favourable variance when more are purchased implies that the standard purchase quantity is 100 coils and that the variances are the result of changes to quantity discounts.)

To avoid adverse variances, the purchasing manager should ensure that the cheapest price for material is obtained (although quality of material should not be jeopardised). Material should, if at all possible, be purchased in quantities that ensure the standard discount is received, although care must be taken to ensure that the costs of holding stock are not greater than any quantity discounts received. The responsibility for this lies with the purchasing manger and the stores manager.

Answer to Practice activity 50

(a)

	Bending	*Cutting*	*Assembly*
Budgeted overheads	£120,000	£90,000	£60,000
Budgeted activity level	10,000 machine hours	3,000 machine hours	15,000 labour hours
Standard overhead absorption rate	£12 per machine hour	£30 per machine hour	£4 per labour hour

(b)

STANDARD COST CARD				
Toy car wheels	Part number 5917B			Date: X. X. XX
	Standard quantity 100 wheels			
		Performance standard	Standard rate/price	Standard cost £
Direct materials				
Tyres		100	10p each	10.00
Steel strip		50	£10.40 per 100	5.20
Wire		1000	2p each	20.00
				35.20
Direct labour		hours	£	
Bending		0.8	4.00	3.20
Cutting		0.5	6.00	3.00
Assembly		1.2	5.00	6.00
				12.20
Overheads				
Bending		0.4	12.00	4.80
Cutting		0.5	30.00	15.00
Assembly		1.2	4.00	4.80
				24.60
TOTAL COST				72.00

Answer to Practice activity 51

£72.00 = 90%

∴ 100% = £72/90% × 100% = £80

∴ Selling price per 100 wheels = £80

Answer to Practice activity 52

(a) The steps in determining the standard labour hours for producing 100 wheels are as follows.

   (i) Study the operations involved in the task.

   (ii) Establish the most efficient methods of performing the operations.

   (iii) Ascertain the grades of labour and types of machine required to perform the operations.

   (iv) Determine the time for each individual operation, building in allowances for rest, relaxation, calls of nature, fluctuating performance, machine breakdowns and so on.

(b) The costs of the stores department could be apportioned to other cost centres using one of the following bases.

   (i) Number of material requisitions per cost centre

   (ii) Value of requisitions per cost centre

   The costs of the personnel department could be apportioned to other cost centres using the number of employees per cost centre.

Answer to Practice activity 53

Closing stock = 150 pairs × (100 + 200 − 150) × £1.90 (purchase price on 7.11.X8)

= £285

Answer to Practice activity 54

Stores Record Card										
Material: Paper								*Code:* 1564A		
		Receipts		Issues			Stock			
Date	*Details*	*Sheets*	*£*	*Sheets*	*Price*	*£*	*Sheets*	*Price*	*£*	
	Opening stock						10,000	0.30	3,000	
3 May	Purchase	4,000	1,600				14,000	0.33	4,600	
6 May	Issue			7,000	0.33	2,310	7,000	0.33	2,290	
12 May	Purchase	10,000	3,100				17,000	0.32	5,390	
15 May	Issue			6,000	0.32	1,920	11,000	0.32	3,470	
22 May	Issue			7,200	0.32	2,304	3,800	0.32	1,166	
25 May	Purchase	10,000	3,200				13,800	0.32	4,366	

Answer to Practice activity 55

		Singh £	Smith £
Basic pay	(39½ hrs × £4.50)	177.75	
	(41 hrs × £4.00)		164.00
Overtime pay	(1½ × ⅓ × £4.50)	2.25	
	((1 × ⅓ × £4.00) + (2 × ½ × £4.00))		5.33
Production bonus	(£0.10 × (10,500/100))	10.50	
	(£0.10 × (10,900/100))		10.90
Gross wages		190.50	180.23

Answer to Practice activity 56

Gross wages of Singh = £190.50

Piecework rate is per 100 sheets and 10,500 sheets produced.
∴ Piecework rate would be paid 105 (10,500/100) times.

£190.50/105 = £1.81

Piecework rate = £1.81 per 100 sheets

Answer to Practice activity 57

Departmental Operating Account

Month: May 1999
Date prepared: 10.6.X9

Budget hours: 320
Actual hours: 290

Department: Binding
Manager: Mrs Jones

Actual Costs	£	*Output (Manuals)*	*Unit Cost* £	*Total Cost* £	*Total Variance* £
			Standard Costs		
Direct materials	1,200	1,200	0.90	1,080	120 (A)
Direct labour:					
290 hours	1,300	1,200	1.00	1,200	100 (A)
Variable overheads	580	1,200	0.50	600	20 (F)
Fixed overheads	1,920	1,200	1.50	1,800	120 (A)
Total	5,000			4,680	320 (A)

Answer to Practice activity 58

(a)

	£
290 hours should have cost (× £4)	1,160
but did cost	1,300
Direct labour rate variance	140 (A)
1,200 manuals should have taken (× ¼ hr)	300 hrs
but did take	290 hrs
Direct labour efficiency variance (in hours)	10 hrs (F)
× standard rate per hour	× £4
	£40 (F)

Total variance = £140(A) + £40(F) = £100(A)

(b)   The rate variance arose because labour were paid more than the standard £4.00 per hour perhaps because of a wage rate increase following strike action.

The efficiency variance arose because labour worked more efficiently than the rate specified in the standard and hence output was produced more quickly than expected, perhaps because better quality equipment or materials were used than those set in the standard.

If the wage rate has increased and the increase is permanent then the standard needs to be changed to reflect this since variances will always be adverse if it is not.

A favourable variance should be encouraged and the labour force should continue to use higher quality materials and/or equipment unless their use causes, for example, larger adverse material price variances.

(c)   The change of the standard would be the responsibility of the accountant and/or his assistant although wage rates are the responsibility of the personnel department which should feed information about wage rates changes through to the appropriate members of staff.

Answer to Practice activity 59

Holding large quantities of paper in stock could cause the following problems.

(a)   Larger stocks require more storage space and possibly extra staff and equipment to control and handle them.

(b) When material becomes out-of-date and is no longer required, existing stocks must be thrown away and written off to the profit and loss account.

Answer to Practice activity 60

Overtime premium is analysed as departmental overheads except in the following circumstances.

(a) If overtime is worked at the specific request of a customer to get his order completed, the overtime premium is a direct cost of the order.

(b) If overtime is worked regularly by a production department in the normal course of operations, the overtime paid to direct workers could be incorporated into an average direct labour hourly rate (though it does not need to be).

Answer to Practice activity 61

One overhead variance which one would expect to find in the binding department is a fixed overhead expenditure variance. This would be adverse since the budgeted fixed overhead (1,200 × £1.50 = £1,800) is less than the actual overhead (£1,920).

Answer to Practice activity 62

The company should use current/expected standards rather than ideal standards since ideal standards are based on the most favourable operating conditions (no wastage, idle time, breakdowns and so on) and are therefore likely to have an unfavourable motivational impact. Employees will often feel that the goals are unattainable and not work so hard.

Answer to Practice activity 63

OVERHEAD ANALYSIS SHEET   DATE   17.4.X9

	TOTAL	PRODUCTION			SERVICE	
		Cutting	Sewing	Finishing	Stores	Maintenance
	£	£	£	£	£	£
Overheads	603,000	187,000	232,000	106,000	28,000	50,000
(a) Apportion Stores (W1) (Base: Material issued)	-	9,333	11,667	4,667	(28,000)	2,333
(b) Apportion Maintenance (W2) (Base: Machine hours)	-	19,625	32,708	-	-	(52,333)
	603,000	215,958	276,375	110,667		

BPP
PUBLISHING

Workings

1   Total material issued   =   £'000 (200 + 250 + 100 + 50)

                             =   £600,000

Issued to		*% of total*	*Share of overhead* £
Cutting	200/600	$33^1/_3$	9,333
Sewing	250/600	$41^2/_3$	11,667
Finishing	100/600	$16^2/_3$	4,667
Maintenance	50/600	$8^1/_3$	2,333
		100	28,000

2   Total machine hours = 15,000 + 25,000 = 40,000.

Worked in		*% of total*	*Share of overhead* £
Cutting	15,000/40,000	$37^1/_2$	19,625
Sewing	25,000/40,000	$62^1/_2$	32,708
			52,333

Answer to Practice activity 64

Department	*Basis of absorption*	*Hours*	*Overhead* £	Overhead *absorption rate*
Cutting	Machine hours	15,000	215,958	£14.40 per mach hr
Sewing	Machine hours	25,000	276,375	£11.06 per mach hr
Finishing	Labour hours	12,000	110,667	£9.22 per labour hr
			603,000	

Answer to Practice activity 65

Machine hour rates should be used in the cutting and sewing departments because activity levels and output depend on the number of machine hours worked in the department. Absorption rates should therefore be based on machine hours.

Answer to Practice activity 66

STANDARD PRODUCT COST SHEET PRODUCT : 'XL'				
				Date: XX.XX.XX
			£	£
Direct Material Cost				4.32
	Hours	Rate £		
Direct Labour Cost			1.00	
- cutting	¼	4.00	3.00	
- sewing	1	3.00	2.50	
- finishing	½	5.00		
Total Labour Cost				6.50
	Hours	Rate £		
Overhead Cost			3.60	
- cutting	¼	14.40	11.06	
- sewing	1	11.06	4.61	
- finishing	½	9.22		
Total Overhead Cost				19.27
TOTAL COST				30.09

Answer to Practice activity 67

(a) (i) *Material price variance*

	£
50 metres should have cost (× £3.00)	150
but did cost (× £2.00)	100
Material price variance	50 (F)

(ii) *Material usage variance*

20 garments should have used (× 2m)	40 m
but did use	50 m
Material usage variance (in metres)	10 m (A)
× standard cost per metre	× £3
Material usage variance (in £)	£30 (A)

(iii) *Total material cost variance*

	£
20 garments should have cost (× £3.00 × 2m)	120
but did cost	100
Total material cost variance	20 (F)

(b) Price variance - purchasing manager
Usage variance - production manager

(c) Providing the quality of the product was unaffected, the material should have been bought because the overall cost variance was favourable. The adverse variance arising from the use of substandard material was more than compensated for by the favourable price variance arising from the use of cheaper material.

Answer to Practice activity 68

To complete this activity you have to allocate to the five departments those overheads which are directly associated with the departments.

	Forming £	Colouring £	Assembly £	Maintenance £	General £	Total £
Directly allocated overheads:						
Repairs, maintenance	800	1,800	300	200	100	3,200
Departmental expenses	1,500	2,300	1,100	900	1,500	7,300
Indirect labour	3,000	5,000	1,500	4,000	2,000	15,500
	5,300	9,100	2,900	5,100	3,600	26,000

Answer to Practice activity 69

This activity involves apportioning the remaining overheads (those which have not been directly allocated) to the five departments.

		Forming £	Colouring £	Assembly £	Maintenance £	General £	Total £
Directly allocated overheads:							
Repairs, maintenance		800	1,800	300	200	100	3,200
Departmental expenses		1,500	2,300	1,100	900	1,500	7,300
Indirect labour		3,000	5,000	1,500	4,000	2,000	15,500
		5,300	9,100	2,900	5,100	3,600	26,000
Apportionment of other overheads:							
Rent, rates	1	1,600	3,200	2,400	400	400	8,000
Power	2	200	450	75	25	0	750
Light, heat	1	1,000	2,000	1,500	250	250	5,000
Dep'n of plant	3	2,500	6,000	750	750	0	10,000
Dep'n of F & F	4	50	25	100	50	25	250
Insurance of plant	3	500	1,200	150	150	0	2,000
Insurance of buildings	1	100	200	150	25	25	500
		11,250	22,175	8,025	6,750	4,300	52,500

Basis of apportionment:

1 floor area
2 effective horsepower
3 plant value
4 fixtures and fittings

Answer to Practice activity 70

To complete this activity you had to use the information provided on the number of hours work the two service departments are budgeted to do for the other departments (and each other).

	Forming £	Colouring £	Assembly £	Maintenance £	General £	Total £
Allocated and apportioned o'hds	11,250	22,175	8,025	6,750	4,300	52,500
	1,350	3,375	1,350	(6,750)	675	
					4,975	
	995	2,985	498	497	(4,975)	
	99	249	99	(497)	50	
	10	30	5	5	(50)	
	1	3	1	(5)		
	13,705	28,817	9,978			52,500

Answer to Practice activity 71

The forming and assembly departments are labour intensive. The overhead absorption rate for these two departments should therefore be based on labour hours. The colouring department, on the other hand, is machine intensive. Machine hours should therefore be used as the basis of the overhead absorption rate.

Department			OAR
Forming	$\dfrac{£13,705}{27,400}$	=	£0.50 per labour hour
Colouring	$\dfrac{£28,817}{14,400}$	=	£2.00 per machine hour
Assembly	$\dfrac{£9,978}{20,000}$	=	£0.50 per labour hour

Answer to Practice activity 72

The under-/over-absorbed overhead is calculated as the difference between the overhead actually incurred and the overhead absorbed. The overhead absorbed is the OAR × actual number of the basis of the absorption rate.

	Overhead incurred £		Overhead absorbed £	(Under)-/over- absorbed overhead £
Forming	14,580	(30,000 × £0.50)	15,000	420
Colouring	30,050	(16,000 × £2.00)	32,000	1,950
Assembly	9,840	(18,500 × £0.50)	9,250	(590)
Over-absorbed overhead				1,780

Answer to Practice activity 73

STORES LEDGER CONTROL ACCOUNT

	£		£
Balance b/f	8,000	Work in progress a/c	34,000
Cash/creditors	75,000	Production overhead a/c	4,000
		Balance c/f	45,000
	83,000		83,000

Answer to Practice activity 74

WORK IN PROGRESS CONTROL ACCOUNT

	£		£
Balance b/f	15,000	Finished goods control a/c	
Stores ledger control a/c	34,000	(balancing figure)	77,500
Wages control account(18,000 – 2,500)	15,500		
Production overhead account			
(200% of £15,500)	31,000	Balance c/f	18,000
	95,500		95,500

Answer to Practice activity 75

To calculate the under- or over-absorbed overhead we need to prepare a production overhead control account.

PRODUCTION OVERHEAD CONTROL ACCOUNT

	£		£
Prepayments b/f	1,000	Work in progress control a/c	31,000
Stores ledger control a/c	4,000	Under-absorbed overhead a/c	
Wages control a/c		(balancing figure)	3,500
Direct workers	2,500		
Indirect workers	11,000		
Cash/creditors	16,000		
	34,500		34,500

The under-absorbed overhead is £3,500.

Answer to Practice activity 76

FINISHED GOODS CONTROL ACCOUNT

	£		£
Balance b/f	22,000	Cost of goods sold a/c	65,000
Work in progress control a/c	77,500	Scrap - P&L a/c	2,000
		Balance c/f	32,500
	99,500		99,500

Answer to Practice activity 77

PROFIT AND LOSS ACCOUNT

	£		£
Cost of goods sold a/c	65,000	Sales	110,000
Selling and dist'n o'hd	12,000		
Finished goods a/c – scrap	2,000		
Under-absorbed o'hd a/c	3,500		
Profit c/f	27,500		
	110,000		110,000

Answer to Practice activity 78

	Straight-line		Reducing balance
	£		£
Cost	17,580		17,580
Depreciation (year 1) (£17,580 ÷ 5)	(3,516)	(£17,580 × 25%)	(4,395)
	14,064		13,185
Depreciation (year 2)	(3,516)	(£13,185 × 25%)	(3,296)
	10,548		9,889
Depreciation (year 3)	(3,516)	(£9,889 × 25%)	(2,472)
	7,032		7,417
Depreciation (year 4)	(3,516)	(£7,417 × 25%)	(1,854)
	3,516		5,563
Depreciation (year 5)	(3,516)	(£5,563 × 25%)	1,391
	-		4,172

Answer to Practice activity 79

JOB 212/A

	£		£
Balance b/f	11,022	Materials transfer	3,500
Materials	3,122	Cost of sales	16,410
Labour	1,922		
Production overhead			
(200% of direct wages)	3,844		
	19,910		19,910

JOB 219/C

	£		£
Materials	4,003	Cost of sales	29,268
Materials transfer	3,500		
Labour	7,255		
Production overhead			
(200% of direct wages)	14,510		
	29,268		29,268

Answer to Practice activity 80

	212/A	*219/C*
	£	£
Factory cost	16,410	29,268
Administration and marketing overheads	2,462	4,390
Cost of sale	18,872	33,658
Invoice value	20,500	28,750
Profit/(loss)	1,628	(4,908)

PART B

DEVOLVED ASSESSMENTS

Practice Devolved Assessment 1: Country Custom Kitchens (data and tasks)

Practice Devolved Assessment
1 Country Custom Kitchens

Performance criteria

The following performance criteria are covered in this Devolved Assessment.

Element 6.1: Record and analyse information relating to direct costs

1   Direct costs are identified in accordance with the organisation's costing procedures

2   Information relating to direct costs is clearly and correctly coded, analysed and recorded

3   Direct costs are calculated in accordance with the organisation's policies and procedures

4   Standard costs are compared against actual costs and any variances are analysed

5   Information is systematically checked against the overall usage and stock control practices

6   Queries are either resolved or referred to the appropriate person

Notes on completing the Assessment

This Assessment is designed to test your ability to record and analyse information relating to direct costs.

You are provided with data on Pages 52 to 77 which you must use to complete the tasks on Page 52.

You are allowed **three hours** to complete your work.

A high level of accuracy is required. Check your work carefully.

Correcting fluid should not be used. Errors should be crossed out neatly and clearly. You should write in ink - not pencil.

A FULL SUGGESTED ANSWER TO THIS ASSESSMENT IS PROVIDED ON PAGE 208.

Do not turn to the suggested answer until you have completed all parts of the Assessment.

PRACTICE DEVOLVED ASSESSMENT 1: COUNTRY CUSTOM KITCHENS

Data

Following a chip-pan fire in its warehouse showroom, the computerised stock control system of Country Custom Kitchens is out of action. The management of Country Custom Kitchens has called in your firm to help restore the system and you and a number of your colleagues have been delegated the task of keeping the system running manually while the computer system and records are being rebuilt. This is likely to take up to two weeks.

When you arrive on Monday 6 September you find that you are to look after raw materials stocks in the code range A - F (screws and fixings). You are given the A - F part of the daily stock list which was run on the evening before the fire. No transactions have been posted since then. The stock list gives the usual details and also has an 'exceptions' column signalling stocks that need to be reordered. The cost accountant has left you a note about this (she suffered minor burns and is recuperating).

You are handed a pile of documents received or generated that morning. You sort the documents into separate piles and find that you have the following:

(a)   The stock list

(b)   Several invoices

(c)   A number of goods received notes (all of which match their attached purchase orders) for that morning's deliveries

(d)   Some materials requisition notes

(e)   The note from the cost accountant

Tasks

Using the documents and information on the following pages, complete the tasks outlined below.

(a) Make out stores ledger accounts as necessary and write them up in the light of the documents that you have been given. There is no need to enter control levels on the stores ledger accounts, but otherwise see that all documents (including the materials requisitions) are as complete as possible. If you have any queries note them down on a queries schedule.

(b) (i)   Peruse the stock list and make out purchase requisitions for any items that need to be reordered.

     (ii) Suggest a way of ensuring that stocks that you requisition are not ordered again once the computer system is restored.

           Again, if you are unsure of anything make a note of it.

(c) Peruse the stock list generally and note down on your queries schedule any points that you think need to be brought to the attention of the warehouse manager or the chief purchasing officer.

(d) Prepare journal entries for posting the invoices to the integrated accounts. (Do not prepare entries for variances.)

(e) Calculate any variances that have arisen.

(f) Note on your queries schedule any other matters that you think need to be referred to other persons.

(g) Prepare a schedule of materials issued for job costing purposes.

Documents for use in the solution

The documents you will need to prepare a solution are given on Pages 67 to 77 and consist of the following.

(a) Materials requisitions (to be completed)
(b) 12 blank stores ledger accounts
(c) 7 blank purchase requisitions
(d) 1 blank looseleaf journal page

COUNTRY CUSTOM KITCHENS STOCK LIST 03/09/X3   03/09/X3/ 17:52

CODE	DESCRIPTION		FACTOR/UNIT	SUPPLIER	COST	IN	OUT	ORDERED	BALANCE	EXCEPTION	TRANSACTIONS PREV.TOTAL	HISTORY PREV.CUM.	CURRENT.CUM.
A0080	SCREW AND NUT	50mm	5	28043112	0.49				58		562	421	383
A0090	SCREW AND NUT	60mm	5	28043112	0.53				63		668	455	445
A1010	WING NUT	M4	5	27561297	0.40				38		452	263	289
A1020	WING NUT	M5	5	27561297	0.40				68		666	454	363
A1030	WING NUT	M6	5	27561297	0.45				54		523	370	362
A1040	WING NUT	M8	5	27561297	0.50				34		360	236	259
A1050	SUPANUT	M4	10	23344248	0.27				7		166	124	148
A1060	SUPANUT	M5	10	23344248	0.30		20	10	48		571	389	353
A1070	SUPANUT	M6	10	23344248	0.32				95		1007	587	469
A1080	SUPANUT	M8	10	23344248	0.37	80			88		862	587	645
A1090	SUPANUT	M10	5	23344248	0.40	70			86		834	549	439
A2010	WASHER	15mm	50	28043112	0.25	70			82		976	732	717
A2020	WASHER	20mm	50	28043112	0.30	70			32		339	197	157
A2030	WASHER	25mm	50	28043112	0.33				70		679	480	528
A2040	WASHER	30mm	20	28043112	0.37				99		1049	715	650
A2050	WASHER	35mm	10	28043112	0.30	80			59		578	380	456
A2060	WASHER	15mm	10	28043112	0.40				1		740	493	487
A2070	WASHER	20mm	5	27561247	0.45		60		13		605	393	399
A2080	WASHER	25mm	5	27561247	0.50		30		62		607	429	343
A2090	WASHER BRASS	30mm	5	27561247	0.55				86	***	1023	596	655
A3010	SELF-TAP BRASS	15mm	10	23344248	0.21	80			16	***	170	127	115
A3020	SELF-TAP BRASS	20mm	10	23344248	0.24				17		148	100	98
A3030	SELF-TAP BRASS	25mm	10	23344248	0.27			15	52		509	335	368
A3040	SELF-TAP	30mm	10	23344248	0.30				74		647	441	529
A3050	SELF-TAP	35mm	10		0.33				18		1166	680	618
A3060	SELF-TAP	40mm	5		0.30			80	40		350	247	242
A3070		45mm	5		0.33				72		698	523	271
A3080		50mm	5		0.36				61		647	425	510
A3090		60mm	5	23344248	0.39				21		183	124	136
A4010		15mm	10	23344248	0.22				61		591	344	337
A4020	SELF-TAP	20mm	10	23344248	0.24				57		678	480	528
A4030	SELF-TAP	25mm	10	23344248	0.26				74		725	477	434
A4040	SELF-TAP	30mm	10	23344248	0.28		50		13		760	500	475
	ROUNDHEAD			28043112									
	ROUNDHEAD			28043112						***			
	ROUNDHEAD			28043112									
	ROUNDHEAD			28043112									

COUNTRY CUSTOM KITCHENS STOCK LIST 03/09/X3 — 03/09/X3 / 17:52

CODE	DESCRIPTION		FACTOR/UNIT	SUPPLIER	COST	IN	OUT	ORDERED	BALANCE	EXCE-PTION	TRANSACTIONS PREV.TOTAL	HISTORY PREV.CUM.	CURRENT.CUM.
A4050	ROUNDHEAD	35mm	10	28043112	0.30				78		827	544	533
A4060	ROUNDHEAD	40mm	5	23344248	0.20			30	10		372	279	223
A4070	ROUNDHEAD	45mm	5	23344248	0.24			75	50		892	520	572
A4080	ROUNDHEAD	50mm	5	23344248	0.28		50		12	***	800	520	533
A4090	ROUNDHEAD	60mm	5	23344248	0.32				15		481	316	309
A5010	CROSSHEAD	15mm	10	27561297	0.18			40	66		785	535	588
A5020	CROSSHEAD	20mm	10	27561297	0.19				80		784	555	505
A5030	CROSSHEAD	25mm	10	27561297	0.20				131		1389	914	895
A5040	CROSSHEAD	30mm	10	27561297	0.21				84		823	617	678
A5050	CROSSHEAD	35mm	10	27561297	0.23				76		737	429	343
A5060	CROSSHEAD	40mm	5	28043112	0.17				25		298	211	232
A5070	CROSSHEAD	45mm	5	28043112	0.20	100			21		205	134	107
A5080	CROSSHEAD	50mm	5	28043112	0.24				96		840	572	632
A5090	CROSSHEAD	60mm	5	28043112	0.30				93		985	544	1182
A6010	BRASS	15mm	10	29295001	0.35				96		940	705	641
A6020	BRASS	20mm	10	29295001	0.39				32		310	204	199
A6030	BRASS	25mm	10	29295001	0.41				36		428	303	333
A6040	BRASS	30mm	10	29295001	0.43				96		941	548	438
A6050	BRASS	35mm	10	29295001	0.46				57		552	376	342
A6060	BRASS	40mm	5	29295001	0.46			40	21		492	340	341
A6070	BRASS	45mm	10	29295001	0.56			50	29		610	400	417
A6080	BRASS	50mm	5	29295001	0.62				77		916	603	482
A6090	BRASS	60mm	5	29295001	0.74				72		705	480	436
*****													
B0010	RLH NAILS	20mm	1kg	23344248	2.69				74		148	148	0
B0020	RLH NAILS	25mm	1kg	23344248	2.69				51		153	153	0
B0030	RLH NAILS	30mm	1kg	23344248	2.69		4	10	0		107	72	79
B0040	RLH NAILS	35mm	1kg	23344248	2.79				24		235	154	150
B0050	RLH NAILS	40mm	1kg	23344248	2.79		6		16		155	109	186
B0060	RLH NAILS	45mm	1kg	23344248	2.99				56		666	388	353
B0070	RLH NAILS	50mm	1kg	23344248	2.99				27		264	173	138
B0080	N/A												
B0090	N/A												

BPP PUBLISHING

COUNTRY CUSTOM KITCHENS STOCK LIST 03/09/X3   03/09/X3/ 17:52

CODE	DESCRIPTION		FACTOR/UNIT	SUPPLIER	COST	IN	OUT	ORDERED	BALANCE	EXCEPTION	TRANSACTIONS PREV.TOTAL	HISTORY PREV.CUM	CURRENT CUM
B1010	RW NAILS	15mm	1kg	27314295	2.60				40		424	280	130
B1020	RW NAILS	20mm	1kg	27314295	2.60				49		568	520	212
B1030	RW NAILS	25mm	1kg	27314295	2.60				19		186	139	136
B1040	RW NAILS	30mm	1kg	27314295	2.60				29		281	184	167
B1050	RW NAILS	35mm	1kg	27314295	2.90				22		262	152	314
B1060	RW NAILS	40mm	1kg	27314295	2.90		5		12		105	74	81
B1070	RW NAILS	45mm	1kg	27314295	2.99		5	60	11		695	457	447
				27314295								83	14
B1080	RW NAILS	50mm	1kg	27314295	3.05				61		85	179	7
B1090	RW NAILS	60mm	1kg	27314295	3.15				93		200	266	292
B2010	PANEL PINS	15mm	500g	27561297	1.89				34		405	101	111
B2020	PANEL PINS	20mm	500g	27561297	1.89				14		135	250	268
B2030	PANEL PINS	25mm	500g	27561297	1.99		35		42		403	249	273
B2040	PANEL PINS	30mm	500g	27561297	1.99				49		428	243	238
B2050	PANEL PINS	35mm	500g	27314295	1.99				30		357	69	75
B2060	PANEL PINS	40mm	500g	27314295	2.15		4		11		106	157	125
B2070	PANEL PINS	45mm	500g	27314295	2.15				2		222	45	54
B2080	PANEL PINS	50mm	500g	27314295	2.40			20	7		61	242	266
B2090	PANEL PINS	60mm	500g	27314295	2.40				31		369	118	54
*****													
D0010	BUTT HINGE	40mm	5PR	26134906	1.89				89		180	16	1
D0020	BUTT HINGE	50mm	5PR	26134906	2.70				0		16	18	0
D0030	BUTT HINGE	65mm	5PR	26134096	3.45	15			2	***	19	171	155
D0040	BUTT HINGE	75mm	5PR	26134096	5.27				26	***	252	167	163
D0050	BUTT HINGE	100mm	5PR	26134096	9.99				26		254	92	104
D0060	BUTT CHR	40mm	5PR	23344248	3.14				11		131	146	143
D0070	BUTT CHR	50mm	5PR	23344248	3.73				22		192	265	241
D0080	BUTT CHR	75mm	5PR	23344248	6.84				38		403	118	141
D0090	BUTT CHR	100mm	5PR		11.87				8		174	45	49
D1010	RISING BUTT	40mm	5PR		1.70		10		8		78	29	0
	RISING BUTT	50mm	5PR	23344248	2.20				3		38	43	2
	RISING BUTT	65mm	5PR	26134906	2.56			10	2	***	47	109	119
D1020	RISING BUTT	75mm	5PR	26134906	4.32				19	***	166	75	73
D1030	RISING BUTT	100mm	5PR	26134906	8.87				9		107		
D1040	RISING BUTT			26134906									
D1050	RISING BUTT			26134906									

COUNTRY CUSTOM KITCHENS STOCK LIST 03/09/X3 — 03/09/X3/ 17:52

CODE	DESCRIPTION		FACTOR/UNIT	SUPPLIER	COST	IN	OUT	ORDERED	BALANCE	EXCE-PTION	TRANSACTIONS PREV.TOTAL	HISTORY PREV.CUM	HISTORY CURRENT CUM
D1060	RIS BUTT CHR	40mm	5PR	23344248	2.99				14		148	111	133
D1070	RIS BUTT CHR	50mm	5PR	23344248	3.49				17		164	107	97
D1080	RIS.BUTT CHR	75mm	5PR	23344248	7.50				17		166	113	110
D1090	RIS BUTT CHR	100mm	5PR	23344248	12.00				15		131	76	83
D2010	LIFT OFF BUTT	40mm	5PR	21840027	3.07	10			30		357	267	213
D2020	LIFT OFF BUTT	50mm	5PR	21840027	3.99				38		368	242	237
D2030	LIFT OFF BUTT	65mm	5PR	21840027	4.58				2		204	130	140
D2040	LIFT OFF BUTT	75mm	5PR	21840027	6.90		20		19	***	201	137	124
D2050	LIFT OFF BUTT	100mm	5PR	21840027	12.00				13		127	74	72
D2060	L/O BUTT CHROME	40mm	5PR	23344248	4.05				8		214	151	166
D2070	L/O BUTT CHROME	50mm	5PR	23344248	6.07			10	4		122	80	96
D2080	L/O BUTT CHROME	75mm	5PR	23344248	8.17			10	4		137	102	81
D2090	L/O BUTT CHROME	100mm	5PR	23344248	14.92			10	6		64	37	40
D3010	CRANKED LIFT OFF	38mm	1PR	27561297	1.35		3		8		77	54	52
D3020	EASY HANG	50mm	1PR	29295001	1.45				22		262	172	156
D3030	EASY FIX ANTIQUE	50mm	1PR	27314295	0.99		20	35	0		417	274	328
D3040	CONCEALED	26mm	1PR	28043112	2.59	50			64		627	427	341
D3050	CONCEALED	35mm	1PR	28043112	3.35	75			85		901	593	652
D3060	CONCEALED	170*	1PR	28043112	8.95	50			75		656	464	371
D3070	PIANO	350mm	1	25567840	2.12				33		323	188	184
D3080	PIANO	700mm	1	25567840	3.99				26		309	203	184
D3090	PIANO	900mm	1	25567840	4.35		1		13		126	85	102
*****													
F0010	CAVITY FIXINGS	C23	12	27314295	2.89	60			78		827	563	450
F0020	CAVITY FIXINGS	C29	12	26134906	1.24				30		294	193	212
F0030	CAVITY FIXINGS	H54	12	29295001	1.99				51		607	354	346
F0040	CAVITY FIXINGS	F42	12	25567840	1.59	50		50	73		638	451	410
F0050	PLASTIC PLUGS	25mm	100	27561297	1.19				76		737	485	582
F0060	PLASTIC PLUGS	35mm	100	27561297	1.49	75			90		954	715	786
F0070	PLASTIC PLUGS	40mm	100	27561297	1.99				71		695	405	396
F0080	PLASTIC PLUGS	45mm	100	27561297	2.05				32		361	246	196
F0090	PLASTIC PLUGS	50mm	100	27561297	2.47				50		437	287	287
F1010	END BRACKETS	19mm	1PR	27314295	2.29		4		10		97	68	74

BPP PUBLISHING

COUNTRY CUSTOM KITCHENS STOCK LIST 03/09/X3 — 03/09/X3/ 17:52

CODE	DESCRIPTION		FACTOR/UNIT	SUPPLIER	COST	IN	OUT	ORDERED	BALANCE	EXCE-PTION	TRANSACTIONS PREV.TOTAL	PREV.CUM.	HISTORY CURRENT CUM.
F1020	END BRACKETS	25mm	1PR	27314295	2.47				0	***	148	97	17
F1030	END BRACKETS	25mm	1PR	27314295	2.47			10	4		6	3	90
F1040	CENTRE BRACKET	19mm	1	27314295	1.79		1		2		20	11	10
F1050	CENTRE BRACKET	25mm	1	27314295	2.20		2		2		23	17	20
F1060	STEEL TUBE	19mm	2m	28043112	5.59				2		19	12	10
F1070	STEEL TUBE	25mm	2m	28043112	7.07		1		1	***	14	9	9
F1080	BRASS TUBE	19mm	2m	28043112	8.23				5		43	24	26
F1090	BRASS TUBE	25mm	2m	28043112	10.00				8		85	60	58
F2010	DRAWER RUNNERS		1PR	29295001	2.49				122		1452	955	764
F2020	CORNER FITTINGS		4	29295001	3.29				79		774	527	579
F2030	EXTERNAL ANGLE		2m	23344248	1.65				50		485	282	256
F2040	EXTERNAL ANGLE	19mm	2m	23344248	1.99			200	113		2028	1436	1723
F2050	CLIPON EDGING	25mm	2m	26134906	2.49	300			350		3710	2782	3060
F2060	FLAT EDGING		2m	26134906	1.35				167		1987	1308	1046
F2070	LIPPED EDGING		2m	26134906	1.55				105		1029	728	662
F2080	DOOR TRACK		2m	26134906	11.79				140		1225	714	785
F2090	SINGLE CHANNEL	17mm	2m	26134906	2.29		20		185		1961	1336	1309
F3010	SINGLE CHANNEL	6mm	2m	26134906	1.15				216		2116	1587	1904
F3020	SINGLE CHANNEL	W	2m	27314295	1.50				175		2083	1371	1247
F3030	S/A TRIM		2m	27314295	1.50				220		2620	1747	1654
F3040	S/A TRIM	B	2m	27314295	1.50		25	125	27		1611	939	1032
F3050	S/A TRIM		4	25567840	1.65				67		649	459	550
F3060	DEC. MOULDINGS		4	25567840	2.29				35		417	274	268
F3070	DEC. CORNERS		4	25567840	4.79			10	7		148	111	101
	DEC. CROWNS			25567840									
F3080	DEC. BRACKET		4	25567840	3.75				0	***	5	5	1
F3090	DEC. TRIM		2m	28043112	3.99				0	***	12	12	2
F4010	BICYCLE HOOKS		1PR	28043112	0.99				55		533	310	341
F4020	UNIV. HOOKS		1PR	28043112	1.49				46		450	306	244
F4030	CUP HOOKS		4	28043112	0.45				89		778	512	614
F4040	CUP HOOKS BRASSED		4	28043112	0.28				70		679	480	528
F4050	HOOK AND EYES		1	28043112	0.41				923		10984	7231	5073
F4060	SCREW HOOK		1	28043112	0.77	800	400		360		4284	3213	2923
F4070	VINE EYES		10	28043112	1.89		50		40		350	204	199

COUNTRY CUSTOM KITCHENS STOCK LIST 03/09/X3

03/09/X3 / 17:52

CODE	DESCRIPTION		FACTOR/UNIT	SUPPLIER	COST	IN	OUT	ORDERED	BALANCE	EXCE-PTION	TRANSACTIONS PREV.TOTAL	HISTORY PREV.CUM.	HISTORY CURRENT CUM.
F4080	SCREWEYES	19mm	25	27314295	0.76			60	12		763	520	624
F4090	SCREWEYES	25mm	25	27314295	0.89				12		116	82	90
F5010	MAGN.CATCH	W	1	27561297	3.99				45		441	300	240
F5020	MAGN.CATCH	B	1	27561297	3.99				44		385	253	229
F5030	MAGN.CATCH	S	1	27561297	3.99				43		512	384	376
F5040	SLIDELATCH	W	1	23344248	4.79				40		388	226	271
F5050	SLIDELATCH	B	1	23344248	4.79			40	7		460	325	357
F5060	THUMBLATCH	W	1	23344248	3.99				36		315	214	194
F5070	THUMBLATCH	B	1	23344248	3.99				37		358	208	166
F5080	AUTOLATCH	W	1	23344248	2.69				36		428	281	275
F5090	AUTOLATCH	B	1	23344248	2.69				68		595	446	490
F6010	PEGCASTORS	$\frac{3}{4}$"	4	26134906	2.39				32		310	219	250
F6020	PEGCASTORS	$\frac{3}{4}$"	4	26134906	2.56				8		85	57	51
F6030	PEGCASTORS	1"	4	26134906	2.78				7		61	40	32
F6040	PLATECASTORS	$1\frac{1}{4}$"	4	26134906	2.39				9		78	53	51
F6050	PLATECASTORS	$\frac{3}{4}$"	4	26134906	2.56				5		58	33	36
F6060	PLATECASTORS	1"	4	26134906	2.78				5		48	36	43
F6070	BUGGYWHEEL	$1\frac{1}{4}$"	4	25567840	1.45				9		78	51	46
F6080	BUGGYWHEEL	$1\frac{1}{2}$"	4	25567840	1.99			4	5		53	37	29
F6090		2"	4	25567840	3.50			4	6		58	39	42
F7010			1	29295001	0.35				10		118	77	92
F7020	DEC. CASTORS		1	29295001	0.50				35		306	208	189
F7030	TOOLCLIP	20mm	1	29295001	0.46				78		764	445	489
F7040	TOOLCLIP	38mm	1	29295001	0.46				89		943	667	653
F7050	HOSECLIP	20mm	1	29295001	0.53				20		194	127	101
F7060	HOSECLIP	38mm	1		0.18	60			41		401	300	273
F7070	HOSECLIP	50mm	1		0.20				60		525	306	336
	G.CLIP	15mm	1	28043112	0.23				68		809	573	687
	G.CLIP	20mm	1	28043112	0.25				48		465	306	278
F7080	G.CLIP	25mm	1	28043112	0.66				25		245	167	133
F7090	G.CLIP	30mm	2	28043112	1.29				19		166	117	128
F8010	DOORSTOP-CONC		1	21840027	0.75				37		392	258	252
F8020	DOORSTOP-FLEX			21840027									
F8030	DOORSTOP-RUB			21840027									

CHIPPIES
Veneers
Splinter's Yard, Glue Street
Deighton

Country Custom
Kitchens
Brightwell Road
Croydon

INVOICE

Order N./Ref 2073   Inv. No. 76298   Date 03.09.X3

Quantity	Description	Unit Price		Total	
		£	p	£	p
1000	Ash veneer 500cm panels	4	70	4,700	00
		Sub-total		4,700	00
		VAT @ 17.5%		822	50
		Invoice total		5,522	50

VAT Reg: 88458485

PERKALLS FIXINGS

Pink Street, Dartford, Kent

Country Custom
Kitchens
Brightwell Road
Croydon

INVOICE

Order No./Ref 2072   Inv. No. 1187   Date 03.09.X3

Quantity	Description	Unit Price		Total	
		£	p	£	p
50	F42 R/P	1	68	84	00
4	Buggy wheel	2	07	8	28
	Sub-total			92	28
	VAT @ 17.5%			16	15
	Invoice total			108	43

VAT Reg No: 17128987

KEWANBY SUPPLIES
THE EDGE, OFTOWN, WARE

┌   ┐
Country Custom
Kitchens
Brightwell Road
Croydon
└   ┘

INVOICE

O/N - 2178   Inv. No. 87/61743   Date 03.09.X3

Quantity	Description	Unit Price		Total	
		£	p	£	p
15	Self-tap 20mm	0	24	3	60
75	Roundhead 45mm	0	24	18	00
40	Roundhead 60mm	0	35	14	00
80	Self-tap 35mm	0	35	28	00
10	Round lost heads 30mm	2	72	27	20
40	Slide latch (black)	4	95	198	00
10	Chromium lift off 50mm	6	20	62	00
	Sub-total			350	80
	VAT @ 17.5%			61	39
	Invoice total			412	19

VAT Reg No: 09347219

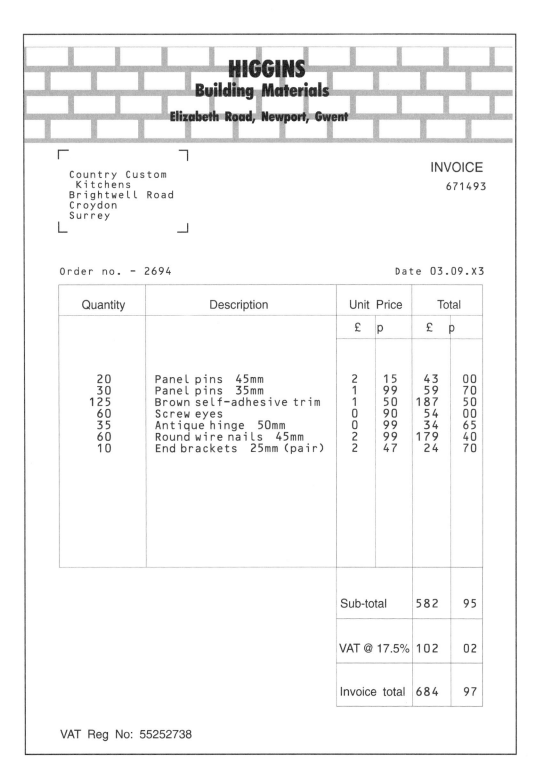

HIGGINS
Building Materials
Elizabeth Road, Newport, Gwent

Country Custom
Kitchens
Brightwell Road
Croydon
Surrey

INVOICE
671493

Order no. - 2694   Date 03.09.X3

Quantity	Description	Unit Price £	Unit Price p	Total £	Total p
20	Panel pins 45mm	2	15	43	00
30	Panel pins 35mm	1	99	59	70
125	Brown self-adhesive trim	1	50	187	50
60	Screw eyes	0	90	54	00
35	Antique hinge 50mm	0	99	34	65
60	Round wire nails 45mm	2	99	179	40
10	End brackets 25mm (pair)	2	47	24	70
	Sub-total			582	95
	VAT @ 17.5%			102	02
	Invoice total			684	97

VAT Reg No: 55252738

GOODS RECEIVED NOTE WAREHOUSE COPY

DATE: 6.9.X3   TIME: 9.15   NO 24638

ORDER NO: 2164

SUPPLIER'S ADVICE NOTE NO: AN067

QUANTITY	CAT NO	DESCRIPTION
10		Chrome hinges 75mm

| | Stock code | D2080 |

RECEIVED IN GOOD CONDITION: JB   (INITIALS)

GOODS RECEIVED NOTE WAREHOUSE COPY

DATE: 6.9.X3   TIME: 9.25   NO 24639

ORDER NO: 2170

SUPPLIER'S ADVICE NOTE NO: PRB/73

QUANTITY	CAT NO	DESCRIPTION
50 (5 packs)		Brass screws 45mm

| | Stock code | A6070 |

RECEIVED IN GOOD CONDITION: JB   (INITIALS)

GOODS RECEIVED NOTE WAREHOUSE COPY

DATE: 6.9.X3   TIME: 10.10   NO 24670

ORDER NO: 2154

SUPPLIER'S ADVICE NOTE NO: 10423

QUANTITY	CAT NO	DESCRIPTION
10 (4 pkt)		Decorative crowns

| | Stock code | ? |

RECEIVED IN GOOD CONDITION: JB   (INITIALS)

GOODS RECEIVED NOTE WAREHOUSE COPY

DATE: 6.9.X3   TIME: 11.05   NO 24671

ORDER NO: 2184

SUPPLIER'S ADVICE NOTE NO: NONE

QUANTITY	CAT NO	DESCRIPTION
10 (10 pkt)		Super Nut M4

| | Stock code | A1050 |

RECEIVED IN GOOD CONDITION: JB   (INITIALS)

GOODS RECEIVED NOTE WAREHOUSE COPY

DATE: _6.9.X3_   TIME: _11.05_   NO **24672**

ORDER NO: _2184_

SUPPLIER'S ADVICE NOTE NO: _NONE_

QUANTITY	CAT NO	DESCRIPTION
200 (2m lengths)	—	Angle 19mm

	Stock code	F2040

RECEIVED IN GOOD CONDITION: _JB_   (INITIALS)

GOODS RECEIVED NOTE WAREHOUSE COPY

DATE: _6.9.X3_   TIME: _11.05_   NO **24673**

ORDER NO: _2184_

SUPPLIER'S ADVICE NOTE NO: _NONE_

QUANTITY	CAT NO	DESCRIPTION
30 (5 pkt)	—	Roundhead screws 40mm

	Stock code	

RECEIVED IN GOOD CONDITION: _JB_   (INITIALS)

MATERIALS REQUISITION

Material Required for: *K309/93*
(Job or Overhead Account)

No. 0914

Date: *6.9.X3*

Quantity	Description	Code No.	Factor/ Unit	Rate	£	Notes
15	Steel washer 30mm					

Foreman: *Vlad Kopeii*   Costed and Coded:

MATERIALS REQUISITION

Material Required for: *K309/93*
(Job or Overhead Account)

No. 0915

Date: *6.9.X3*

Quantity	Description	Code No.	Factor/ Unit	Rate	£	Notes
10	R/Hd 30mm					

Foreman: *Vlad Kopeii*   Costed and Coded:

MATERIALS REQUISITION

Material Required for: *K312/93*
(Job or Overhead Account)

No. 0916

Date: *6.9.X3*

Quantity	Description	Code No.	Factor/ Unit	Rate	£	Notes
10 chrome	Butt hinges 40mm					

Foreman: *VK*   Costed and Coded:

BPP PUBLISHING

MATERIALS REQUISITION

Material Required for: *K313/93*   No. 0917
(Job or Overhead Account)
                                          Date: *6.9.X3*

Quantity	Description	Code No.	Factor/Unit	Rate	£	Notes
8	*Drawer runners*					

Foreman: *UK*   Costed and Coded:

MATERIALS REQUISITION

Material Required for: *K313/93*   No. 0918
(Job or Overhead Account)
                                          Date: *6.9.X3*

Quantity	Description	Code No.	Factor/Unit	Rate	£	Notes
20	*White magnetic catches*					

Foreman: *Vlad*   Costed and Coded:

MATERIALS REQUISITION

Material Required for: *K309/93*   No. 0919
(Job or Overhead Account)
                                          Date: *6.9.X3*

Quantity	Description	Code No.	Factor/Unit	Rate	£	Notes
2	*Panel pins 35mm*					

Foreman: *UK*   Costed and Coded:

STORES LEDGER ACCOUNT

Material: .... Maximum Quantity: ....

Code: .... Minimum Quantity: ....

Date	Receipts				Issues				Stock		
	G.R.N. No.	Quantity	Unit Price £	Amount £	Stores Req. No.	Quantity	Unit Price £	Amount £	Quantity	Unit Price £	Amount £

STORES LEDGER ACCOUNT

Material: .... Maximum Quantity: ....

Code: .... Minimum Quantity: ....

Date	Receipts				Issues				Stock		
	G.R.N. No.	Quantity	Unit Price £	Amount £	Stores Req. No.	Quantity	Unit Price £	Amount £	Quantity	Unit Price £	Amount £

STORES LEDGER ACCOUNT

Material: .... Maximum Quantity: ....

Code: .... Minimum Quantity: ....

Date	Receipts				Issues				Stock		
	G.R.N. No.	Quantity	Unit Price £	Amount £	Stores Req. No.	Quantity	Unit Price £	Amount £	Quantity	Unit Price £	Amount £

STORES LEDGER ACCOUNT

Material: ....   Maximum Quantity: ....

Code: ....   Minimum Quantity: ....

Date	Receipts				Issues				Stock		
	G.R.N. No.	Quantity	Unit Price £	Amount £	Stores Req. No.	Quantity	Unit Price £	Amount £	Quantity	Unit Price £	Amount £

STORES LEDGER ACCOUNT

Material: ....   Maximum Quantity: ....

Code: ....   Minimum Quantity: ....

Date	Receipts				Issues				Stock		
	G.R.N. No.	Quantity	Unit Price £	Amount £	Stores Req. No.	Quantity	Unit Price £	Amount £	Quantity	Unit Price £	Amount £

STORES LEDGER ACCOUNT

Material: ....   Maximum Quantity: ....

Code: ....   Minimum Quantity: ....

Date	Receipts				Issues				Stock		
	G.R.N. No.	Quantity	Unit Price £	Amount £	Stores Req. No.	Quantity	Unit Price £	Amount £	Quantity	Unit Price £	Amount £

STORES LEDGER ACCOUNT

Material: .... Maximum Quantity: ....

Code: .... Minimum Quantity: ....

Date	Receipts				Issues				Stock		
	G.R.N. No.	Quantity	Unit Price £	Amount £	Stores Req. No.	Quantity	Unit Price £	Amount £	Quantity	Unit Price £	Amount £

STORES LEDGER ACCOUNT

Material: .... Maximum Quantity: ....

Code: .... Minimum Quantity: ....

Date	Receipts				Issues				Stock		
	G.R.N. No.	Quantity	Unit Price £	Amount £	Stores Req. No.	Quantity	Unit Price £	Amount £	Quantity	Unit Price £	Amount £

STORES LEDGER ACCOUNT

Material: .... Maximum Quantity: ....

Code: .... Minimum Quantity: ....

Date	Receipts				Issues				Stock		
	G.R.N. No.	Quantity	Unit Price £	Amount £	Stores Req. No.	Quantity	Unit Price £	Amount £	Quantity	Unit Price £	Amount £

BPP PUBLISHING

STORES LEDGER ACCOUNT

Material: ....   Maximum Quantity: ....

Code: ....   Minimum Quantity: ....

Date	Receipts				Issues				Stock		
	G.R.N. No.	Quantity	Unit Price £	Amount £	Stores Req. No.	Quantity	Unit Price £	Amount £	Quantity	Unit Price £	Amount £

STORES LEDGER ACCOUNT

Material: ....   Maximum Quantity: ....

Code: ....   Minimum Quantity: ....

Date	Receipts				Issues				Stock		
	G.R.N. No.	Quantity	Unit Price £	Amount £	Stores Req. No.	Quantity	Unit Price £	Amount £	Quantity	Unit Price £	Amount £

STORES LEDGER ACCOUNT

Material: ....   Maximum Quantity: ....

Code: ....   Minimum Quantity: ....

Date	Receipts				Issues				Stock		
	G.R.N. No.	Quantity	Unit Price £	Amount £	Stores Req. No.	Quantity	Unit Price £	Amount £	Quantity	Unit Price £	Amount £

PURCHASE REQUISITION   Req. No.   10427

Department _____

Suggested Supplier:

Date

Requested by:

Quantity	Code	Description	Estimated Cost	
			Unit	£

Authorised signature:

PURCHASE REQUISITION   Req. No.   10428

Department _____

Suggested Supplier:

Date

Requested by:

Quantity	Code	Description	Estimated Cost	
			Unit	£

Authorised signature:

BPP PUBLISHING

PURCHASE REQUISITION   Req. No.   10429

Department _____

Suggested Supplier:

Date

Requested by:

Quantity	Code	Description	Estimated Cost	
			Unit	£

Authorised signature:

PURCHASE REQUISITION   Req. No.   10430

Department _____

Suggested Supplier:

Date

Requested by:

Quantity	Code	Description	Estimated Cost	
			Unit	£

Authorised signature:

PURCHASE REQUISITION   Req. No.   10431

Department _____

Date

Suggested Supplier:

Requested by:

Quantity	Code	Description	Estimated Cost	
			Unit	£

Authorised signature:

PURCHASE REQUISITION   Req. No.   10432

Department _____

Date

Suggested Supplier:

Requested by:

Quantity	Code	Description	Estimated Cost	
			Unit	£

Authorised signature:

BPP PUBLISHING

PURCHASE REQUISITION   Req. No.   10433

Department _____   Date   .
Suggested Supplier:

                                        Requested by:

Quantity	Code	Description	Estimated Cost	
			Unit	£

Authorised signature:

Notes from cost accountant on stock list

'Cost' is Standard cost per packet of 10 (or whatever) as shown in the factor column.

In/Out/Balance etc is number of packets (etc) not number of individual items.

Exceptions: - Stock needing re-ordering

- re-order signalled when less than 1 month's stock on the basis of last year's usage

- re-order qty roughly 1 month's stock (to the nearest five)

- computer over-ridden for slow-moving stock

Prev. total = number of items issued last year

Slow moving stock   - we classify stock as slow moving if the current cumulative number of items issued is significantly lower than the previous year's cumulative

NB Friday's deliveries are all posted but system does not up-date 'ordered' column until next morning (helps with matching invoices)

Otherwise self explanatory

Journal No. _ _ _ _ _ _ _ _ _ _ _

Date	Customer/supplier code	Invoice	Order No.	Stock code	Quantity	Net £	VAT (17.5%) £

BPP PUBLISHING

Practice Devolved Assessment 2: Stancourt Motors (data and tasks)

Practice Devolved Assessment
2   *Stancourt Motors*

Performance criteria

The following performance criteria are covered in this Devolved Assessment.

Element 6.1: Record and analyse information relating to direct costs

1   Direct costs are identified in accordance with the organisation's costing procedures

2   Information relating to direct costs is clearly and correctly coded, analysed and recorded

3   Direct costs are calculated in accordance with the organisation's policies and procedures

6   Queries are either resolved or referred to the appropriate person

---

Notes on completing the Assessment

This Assessment is designed to test your ability to operate and maintain a system of accounting for labour costs.

You are provided with data on Pages 82 to 94 which you must use to complete the task on Page 82.

You are allowed **two hours** to complete your work.

A high level of accuracy is required. Check your work carefully.

Correcting fluid should not be used. Errors should be crossed out neatly and clearly. You should write in ink - not pencil.

A FULL SUGGESTED ANSWER TO THIS ASSESSMENT IS PROVIDED ON PAGE 224.

Do not turn to the suggested answer until you have completed all parts of the Assessment.

BPP
PUBLISHING

PRACTICE DEVOLVED ASSESSMENT 2: STANCOURT MOTORS

Data

Stancourt Motors is a small car dealer in Birmingham selling new and used cars and repairing and servicing cars of all makes. Your name is Doris and you started work as an accounts assistant in the accounts department just over a week ago.

Late on Tuesday afternoon you learn that you are to be sent over to the repairs and services department because Rex Davison, the costing clerk, has been called away suddenly. There are four job cost cards to be prepared prior to producing invoices for customers due to collect their cars on Wednesday morning.

By the time you arrive in Rex Davison's office he has gone, but there is a sheaf of papers underneath a paperweight and a scribbled note saying 'Doris this is all you need'.

You find the following documents.

(a)   A computer produced summary of the original estimates prepared for all customers collecting tomorrow

(b)   Four job cards stamped with times, in the style of a clock card

(c)   Numerous tear off slips which, on closer examination, turn out to be materials issue slips generated by the computer. These appear to have originally been stapled to the job cards, but in such a way that they have had to be removed so that the details can be read. They have been helpfully rearranged in issue note number order.

(d)   A handwritten invoice

Otherwise all you have is your wits and the small amount of knowledge you have gained in your short time working for Stancourt Motors. You know, for example, that the mechanics and body repairers work a 40 hour week, that they are paid weekly and that, if they complete a job in less than the estimated time, they get a bonus equal to the time saved at their standard rate of pay. These bonuses are included in the job costs. You know that there are two cost centres, A for mechanical repairs and B for bodywork.

There is a file of completed job cost cards on Rex's desk. These are very difficult to read, but you manage to establish that indirect expenses seemed to be charged at a rate of £3.50 for every labour hour worked in cost centre A and £2.50 for every labour hour worked in cost centre B. After some study, you deduce that quotations are given on the basis of labour at £18 per hour plus parts at cost. This is the invoiced price unless cost plus 10% is greater.

You also obtain a copy of last week's payroll for the repairs and services department.

Task

Complete the four job cost cards required using the documents on the following pages.

The four blank job cost cards that you will need to prepare your answer are given on Pages 84 to 87.

ESTIMATE SUMMARY - CARS GOING OUT 14.6.X3

Estimate No.	Detail	Hours
2574	Remove nearside rear vent. Fit new vent. Flat down near side rear vent. Prime and prepare, respray in colour. Fit new parts as listed below. Refit all removed parts.	4
2583	Investigate knocking thought to be faulty distributor shaft. Re-align centre bearing. Carry out repairs as necessary, but advise customer when fault is known.	2
2589	Repairs to distributor and commutator end frame pursuant to 2583.	3
2594	Remove clutch master cylinder. Clean and replace parts as necessary. Refit. Check and adjust brakes as necessary.	2 1
2599	Remove off-side front door furniture and drop glass. Beat out and reshape off-side front door. Fit new drop glass. Flat down off-side front door and blend to rear wing. Prime and prepare. Respray in colour. Fit new parts as listed below. Refit all removed parts.	10

BPP PUBLISHING

JOB COST CARD

Job No.	

Customer	Customer's Order No.	Vehicle make
Job Description		
Estimate Ref.	Invoice No.	Vehicle reg. no.
Quoted price	Invoice price	Date to collect

Material

Date	Req. No.	Qty.	Price	Cost £	Cost p
Total C/F					

Labour

Date	Employee	Cost Ctre	Hrs.	Rate	Bonus	Cost £	Cost p
Total C/F							

Overheads

Hrs	OAR	Cost £	Cost p
Total C/F			

Expenses

Date	Ref.	Description	Cost £	Cost p
Total C/F				

Job Cost Summary

	Actual £	Actual p	Estimate £	Estimate p
Direct Materials B/F				
Direct Expenses B/F				
Direct Labour B/F				
Direct Cost				
Overheads B/F				
Admin overhead (add 10%)				
= Total Cost				
Invoice Price				
Job Profit/Loss				

Comments

Job Cost Card Completed by ....

JOB COST CARD

		Job No.
Customer	Customer's Order No.	Vehicle make
Job Description		
Estimate Ref.	Invoice No.	Vehicle reg. no.
Quoted price	Invoice price	Date to collect

Material

Date	Req. No.	Qty.	Price	Cost £	Cost p
Total C/F					

Labour

Date	Emp-loyee	Cost Ctre	Hrs.	Rate	Bonus	Cost £	Cost p
Total C/F							

Overheads

Hrs	OAR	Cost £	Cost p
Total C/F			

Expenses

Date	Ref.	Description	Cost £	Cost p
Total C/F				

Job Cost Summary

	Actual £	Actual p	Estimate £	Estimate p
Direct Materials B/F				
Direct Expenses B/F				
Direct Labour B/F				
Direct Cost Overheads B/F				
Admin overhead (add 10%)				
= Total Cost				
Invoice Price				
Job Profit/Loss				

Comments

Job Cost Card Completed by ....

BPP PUBLISHING

JOB COST CARD

	Job No.

Customer	Customer's Order No.	Vehicle make
Job Description		
Estimate Ref.	Invoice No.	Vehicle reg. no.
Quoted price	Invoice price	Date to collect

Material						Labour								Overheads			
				Cost							Bonus	Cost				Cost	
Date	Req. No.	Qty.	Price	£	p	Date	Emp-loyee	Cost Ctre	Hrs.	Rate		£	p	Hrs	OAR	£	p
Total C/F							Total C/F							Total C/F			

Expenses						Job Cost Summary	Actual		Estimate	
				Cost			£	p	£	p
Date	Ref.	Description		£	p					
						Direct Materials B/F				
						Direct Expenses B/F				
						Direct Labour B/F				
						Direct Cost				
						Overheads B/F				
						Admin overhead (add 10%)				
						= Total Cost				
						Invoice Price				
Total C/F						Job Profit/Loss				

Comments

Job Cost Card Completed by ....

JOB COST CARD			Job No.	
Customer		Customer's Order No.	Vehicle make	
Job Description			Vehicle reg. no.	
Estimate Ref.		Invoice No.		
Quoted price		Invoice price	Date to collect	

Material						Labour								Overheads			
Date	Req. No.	Qty.	Price	Cost		Date	Emp-loyee	Cost Ctre	Hrs.	Rate	Bonus	Cost		Hrs	OAR	Cost	
				£	p							£	p			£	p
Total C/F						Total C/F								Total C/F			

Expenses						Job Cost Summary	Actual		Estimate	
							£	p	£	p
Date	Ref.	Description	Cost			Direct Materials B/F				
			£	p		Direct Expenses B/F				
						Direct Labour B/F				
						Direct Cost Overheads B/F				
						Admin overhead (add 10%)				
						= Total Cost				
						Invoice Price				
Total C/F						Job Profit/Loss				

Comments

Job Cost Card Completed by ....

BPP PUBLISHING

JOB CARD				A926
Customer	Mrs Crankley			
Vehicle	Metro			
Reg. no.	A 987 OPB			
Estimate ref.	2583 and 2589			
Name	John Moore/Tony Booth			
Employee ref.	012/007			
Date commenced	11.6.X3/12.6.X3			

WORK DONE	MINS	ON	OFF
Examine distributor, centre bearing and ascertain reason for knocking		11.15 14.00	12.00 15.15
Work agreed and done by Tony:			
Dismantle distributor, replace parts and reassemble		08.15	09.27
Ditto commutator end frame		09.27	10.50
Realign centre bearing		10.55	11.30
TOTAL (or c/fwd)			

JOB CARD				A930
Customer	Mr F Jenkins			
Vehicle	Sierra			
Reg. no.	F109 HEV			
Estimate ref.	2594			
Name	Ed Murray			
Employee ref.	009			
Date commenced	13.6.X3			

WORK DONE	MINS	ON	OFF
Remove clutch master cylinder		09.15	09.45
Dismantle and inspect for wear		09.45	10.25
Replace parts as necessary and refit		12.00	12.30
Check brakes and adjust as necessary		14.45	15.32
TOTAL (or c/fwd)			

JOB CARD				B638
Customer		Mr Robert		
Vehicle		TR7		
Reg. no.		RGY 367W		
Estimate ref.		2574		
Name		Dave Bishop		
Employee ref.		016		
Date commenced		13.6.X3		

WORK DONE	MINS	ON	OFF
Remove damaged vent and fit new vent		9.11	11.00
Mask up and spray etc		11.15	12.00
Spray 2nd coat		14.37	15.03
Remove masking and finish off		15.30	16.15
TOTAL (or c/fwd)			

JOB CARD				B641
Customer		Mr J White		
Vehicle		Peugeot 205 GTi		
Reg. no.		G 614 SOX		
Estimate ref.		2599		
Name		Jeff Wilson		
Employee ref.		018		
Date commenced		12.6.X3		

WORK DONE	MINS	ON	OFF
Remove off-side front door furniture and drop glass		08.00	09.47
		15.25	15.37
Beat out and reshape off-side front door		09.24	11.31
Fit new drop glass. Flat down off-side front door and blend to rear wing		11.07	12.58
Prime and prepare. Respray in colour			
Fit new parts and refit removed parts		14.10	16.07
TOTAL (or c/fwd)			

BPP PUBLISHING

Part B: Devolved Assessments

ISSUE NOTE	36807		12:06:X3	08:30
QTY	PART NO.		UNIT COST	TOTAL COST
1	T265347		7.18	7.18
		DISRIBUTOR CLAMP		
	JOB: A926			REF: 007

ISSUE NOTE	36808		12:06:X3	08:31
QTY	PART NO.		UNIT COST	TOTAL COST
2	T386434		1.24	2.48
		SPRING CLIP		
	JOB: A926			REF: 007

ISSUE NOTE	36815		12:06:X3	08:40
QTY	PART NO.		UNIT COST	TOTAL COST
1	T68111		75.49	75.49
		DROP GLASS		
	JOB: B641			REF: 018

ISSUE NOTE	36816		12:06:X3	08:41
QTY	PART NO.		UNIT COST	TOTAL COST
1	T75710		33.19	33.19
		MOULDING		
	JOB: B641			REF: 018

ISSUE NOTE	36821		12:06:X3	09:38
QTY	PART NO.		UNIT COST	TOTAL COST
1	T839849		88.40	88.40
		FIELD COIL		
	JOB: A926			REF: 007

○ ISSUE NOTE 36830   12:06:X3   11.05 ○
○
○ QTY   PART NO.   UNIT COST   TOTAL COST ○
○
○   1   T437105   61.90   61.90 ○
○
○   CENTRE BEARING   ○
○   JOB: A926   REF: 007 ○

○ ISSUE NOTE 36842   12:06:X3   15:27 ○
○
○ QTY   PART NO.   UNIT COST   TOTAL COST ○
○
○   5   T057897   6.01   30.05 ○
○
○   BODY FILLER   ○
○   JOB: B641   REF: 018 ○

○ ISSUE NOTE 36861   13:06:X3   09:58 ○
○
○ QTY   PART NO.   UNIT COST   TOTAL COST ○
○
○   1   T999636   45.20   45.20 ○
○
○   PUSHROD CLEVIS   ○
○   JOB: A930   REF: 009 ○

○ ISSUE NOTE 36867   13:06:X3   10:14 ○
○
○ QTY   PART NO.   UNIT COST   TOTAL COST ○
○
○   1   T62908   72.56   72.56 ○
○
○   VENT   ○
○   JOB: B638   REF: 016 ○

○ ISSUE NOTE 36868   13:06:X3   10:15 ○
○
○ QTY   PART NO.   UNIT COST   TOTAL COST ○
○
○   1   T765354   3.03   3.03 ○
○
○   VENT FITTINGS PACK   ○
○   JOB: B638   REF: 016 ○

Part B: Devolved Assessments

ISSUE NOTE	36874		13:06:X3		10:20
QTY		PART NO.		UNIT COST	TOTAL COST
1		T759251		6.95	6.95
		HOLE SNAP RING			
	JOB: A930			REF: 009	

ISSUE NOTE	36881		13:06:X3		11:20
QTY		PART NO.		UNIT COST	TOTAL COST
5		T889388		3.99	19,95
		RED PAINT			
	JOB: B641			REF: 018	

ISSUE NOTE	36885		13:06:X3		12:04
QTY		PART NO.		UNIT COST	TOTAL COST
1		T680538		8.75	8.75
		COMPRESSION SPRING			
	JOB: A930			REF: 009	

ISSUE NOTE	36894		13:06:X3		14.38
QTY		PART NO.		UNIT COST	TOTAL COST
3		T889386		3.99	11.97
		BLUE PAINT			
	JOB: B638			REF: 016	

ISSUE NOTE	36902		13:06:X3		15:02
QTY		PART NO.		UNIT COST	TOTAL COST
2		T498204		35.80	71.60
		BRAKE SHOE			
	JOB: A930			REF: 009	

NORMAN JOLLEY

"Expert panel beating"
47 Thump Street, Little Wallop, LW14 9QT

To/

2 hours work on
Peugeot 205 GTI   50.00

Job B641

_____

                                         50.00

_____

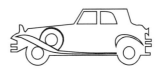

Received with thanks Norm

PAYROLL SUMMARY - W/E 9.6.X3

NAME	NO.	BASIC	BONUS	TOTAL	PAYE	EMPLOYEE NI	OTHER DEDS	NET	EMPLOYER NI
COST CENTRE A									
BOOTH, A	007	240.00	15.00	255.00	46.17	22.95	5.00	180.88	26.65
DUNCAN, R	008	260.00	30.00	290.00	54.60	24.94	-	210.46	30.17
MURRAY, E	009	260.00	24.00	284.00	52.95	24.50	10.00	196.55	29.65
BOOTH, T	010	280.00	-	280.00	49.35	24.36	-	206.29	29.23
LINCOLN, T	011	280.00	-	280.00	48.36	24.36	-	207.28	29.23
MOORE, J	012	280.00	19.50	299.50	59.20	26.05	10.00	204.25	31.27
COST CENTRE B									
BISHOP, D	016	240.00	13.00	253.00	39.50	20.24	-	193.26	26.41
SMITH, P	017	280.00	-	280.00	49.35	24.36	-	206.29	29.23
WILSON, J	018	260.00	20.00	280.00	47.50	24.36	-	208.14	29.23
		2,380.00	121.50	2,501.50	446.98	216.12	25.00	1,813.40	261.07

BPP PUBLISHING

Practice Devolved Assessment 3: Strange (Properties) Ltd (data and tasks)

Practice Devolved Assessment
3 Strange (Properties) Ltd

Performance criteria

The following performance criteria are covered in this Devolved Assessment.

Element 6.1: Record and analyse information relating to direct costs

1   Direct costs are identified in accordance with the organisation's costing procedures

2   Information relating to direct costs is clearly and correctly coded, analysed and recorded

3   Direct costs are calculated in accordance with the organisation's policies and procedures

6   Queries are either resolved or referred to the appropriate person

Element 6.2: Record and analyse information relating to the allocation, apportionment and absorption of overhead costs

1   Data are correctly coded, analysed and recorded

2   Overhead costs are established in accordance with the organisation's procedures

3   Information relating to overhead costs is accurately and clearly recorded

4   Overhead costs are correctly attributed to producing and service cost centres in accordance with agreed methods of allocation, apportionment and absorption

5   Adjustments for under or over recovered overhead costs are made in accordance with established procedures

7   Methods of allocation, apportionment and absorption are revised at regular intervals in discussion with senior staff and agreed changes to methods implemented

8   Staff working in operational departments are consulted to resolve any queries in the data

Notes on completing the Assessment

This Assessment is designed to test your ability to operate and maintain a system of accounting for expenses and a system for the apportionment and absorption of indirect costs.

You are provided with data on Pages 98 to 109 which you must use to complete the tasks on Pages 106 and 109.

You are allowed **three hours** to complete your work.

A high level of accuracy is required. Check your work carefully.

Correcting fluid should not be used. Errors should be crossed out neatly and clearly. You should write in ink - not pencil.

A FULL SUGGESTED ANSWER TO THIS ASSESSMENT IS PROVIDED ON PAGE 230.

Do not turn to the suggested answer until you have completed all parts of the Assessment.

PRACTICE DEVOLVED ASSESSMENT 3: STRANGE (PROPERTIES) LTD

Data

Your name is John Vernon and you joined Strange (Properties) Ltd at the beginning of November, taking over as head of the accounts department on the retirement of Brian Dimple who had occupied the post for many years.

Strange (Properties) Ltd is a property management company headed by Edward Strange, a solicitor, and his brother Victor, a chartered surveyor. The company looks after all of the affairs of around thirty blocks of flats or estates in the surrounding area. This involves company secretarial services, conveyancing, dealing with disputes, regular inspections of sites, obtaining tenders for repairs and maintenance contracts, bookkeeping, cash management and so on - a huge variety of tasks in fact.

During your first month you have spent most of your time chasing debtors, since there are many long-outstanding debts and a large bank overdraft as a consequence. You have left the day to day cash management to your two assistants. However, you have just received the following memo and attachments from Edward Strange.

MEMO

To: John Vernon
From: Edward Strange
Date: 1 December 20X2
Subject: Charges to clients

A number of our clients have complained recently about the way our charges fluctuate from month to month. Have you seen this list that the auditors did for July to September? I vaguely remember that your predecessor, Brian Dimple, used to say something about costing, and things not balancing, and fictional whatnots, but this was in the days before we bought the computer. Perhaps things are different now.

I was talking to an accountant at the golf club the other night and he started on about various different sorts of costing. 'Standard costing' was mentioned and 'absorbent costing'. One I thought might be appropriate to Strange (Properties) was 'process costing': I've heard you talk about processing invoices and data processing and the like.

Could you have a think about this and let me have a suggestion. I'll grin and bear it if 'notional thingummies' really are too bothersome, but I would like to appease our uppity paymasters if it does no harm to our business.

Enc. List of client charges; letter to Loudwater Place, copy invoices.

Client charges
July to September 20X2

	July £	August £	September £
Ashby Mansions, Harlington	2,336	2,705	2,220
Burgess Court, Southall	2,580	3,425	2,716
Clerk Court, Ealing	3,112	2,913	2,580
Clift Flats, Heston	2,656	3,233	2,959
Clifton Gardens, Hounslow	2,761	2,705	2,875
Coomer Place, Putney	2,730	2,705	2,142
Davison Close, Acton	2,200	3,215	2,330
De Beauvoir Buildings, Chiswick	2,807	4,171	2,975
Endymion Place, Hammersmith	3,230	2,705	2,721
Frampton Court, Fulham	5,185	3,429	2,142
Gibbs House, Hounslow	2,586	2,847	2,850
Glebe Gardens, Perivale	2,200	2,705	2,455
Grasmere Mansion, Isleworth	2,943	3,131	2,142
Hennigan House, Wembley	2,544	3,482	2,562
Jones Court, Fulham	2,338	2,705	5,740
Ketley Close, Sheen	6,905	2,705	3,909
Kings Buildings, Petersham	2,596	2,962	2,462
Laine House, Hanwell	2,806	2,765	2,804
Loudwater Place, Kew	2,200	8,983	3,858
Matkins Gardens, Hounslow	2,751	2,910	2,142
Mallow Close, Ealing	2,531	3,554	2,458
Neville House, Acton	3,463	2,961	2,791
Oakwood Buildings, Roehampton	2,580	2,864	2,304
Queen's Court, Isleworth	2,479	2,705	3,102
Rhodes Close, Sheen	3,177	3,655	2,142
Rodway House, Chiswick	2,200	3,023	2,284
Seymour Manor, Hammersmith	2,891	2,705	2,538
Tilbury Tower, Wembley	3,448	2,846	2,403
Undercliff Gardens, Richmond	2,652	2,917	3,392
Wyndham Rise, Southall	2,549	3,454	2,142

BPP PUBLISHING

STRANGE
(Properties)
LTD
Wyrde Street, Brentford
London W13

Peter Purviss
17, Loudwater Place
Kew
London

1 December 20X2

Dear Peter,

<u>Monthly Fees</u>

Thank you for your letter of 24 November.

I note what you say about your cash flow and your difficulty in knowing what level of service charges to set your fellow residents. Indeed, this is a matter of concern to us too especially where we (in theory) hold cash on behalf of our clients. I have already instructed our staff to look into our costing procedures to see if anything can be done and I am hoping that a solution that is not too much of an administrative burden can be arrived at.

With best wishes for Christmas and the New Year

Yours sincerely

Edward

E. Strange

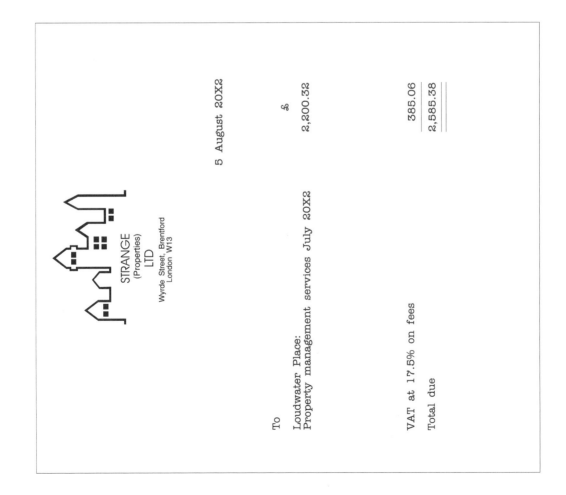

STRANGE (Properties) LTD
Wyrde Street, Brentford
London W13

6 September 20X2

£

To
Loudwater Place:
Property management services August 20X2   8,983.17

VAT at 17.5% on fees   1,572.05

Total due   10,555.22

STRANGE (Properties) LTD
Wyrde Street, Brentford
London W13

5 August 20X2

£

To
Loudwater Place:
Property management services July 20X2   2,200.32

VAT at 17.5% on fees   385.06

Total due   2,585.38

Part B: Devolved Assessments

You are aware that clients' monthly charges are made up as follows.

	£
Direct expenses paid by Strange (Properties) Ltd	X
Fixed fee	1,500.00
One-thirtieth share of overheads incurred in the month	X
	X

The treatment of overheads seems reasonable as far as your own department's services are concerned, because you and your staff do indeed seem to spend a roughly equal amount of time on each client. However you are not sure how fair it is with respect to other work.

In any case you decide to see what the charges for November will be on this basis. You have the cash book for November but this has not yet been coded up for posting. You also have a list of account codes.

Account codes

Range	Sub-account	Name
100		STAFF COSTS
	/001	Wages
	/002	Salaries
	/003	PAYE and NI
	/010	Staff welfare
	/020	Employer's liability insurance
200		TRAVEL COSTS
	/001	Petrol
	/002	Motor insurance
	/003	Fares and taxis
300		BUILDINGS COSTS
	/001	Heat and light
	/002	Buildings insurance
	/003	Rates
	/004	Repairs and maintenance
	/005	Cleaning
400		COMMUNICATIONS
	/001	Postage
	/002	Telephone
	/003	Stationery
	/004	Computer sundries
500		PROFESSIONAL FEES
	/001	Auditors
	/002	Public liability insurance
	/003	Subscriptions
600		FINANCE CHARGES
	/001	Bank interest
	/002	Bank charges

Range	Sub-account	Name
700		PUBLICITY
	/001	Advertising
	/002	Entertaining
800		CLIENT CODES
	/001	Rodway House
	/100	Matkins Gardens
	/101	Glebe Gardens
	/105	Gibbs House
	/110	Grasmere Mansion
	/189	Seymour Manor
	/225	Queen's Court
	/250	Loudwater Place
	/261	De Beauvoir Buildings
	/274	Jones Court
	/301	Ashby Mansions
	/325	Kings Buildings
	/350	Clift Flats
	/376	Neville House
	/401	Frampton Court
	/429	Hennigan House
	/430	Wyndham Rise
	/450	Coomer Place
	/501	Laine House
	/525	Undercliff Gardens
	/555	Burgess Court
	/556	Ketley Close
	/605	Mallow Close
	/620	Clifton Gardens
	/675	Endymion Place
	/750	Oakwood Buildings
	/801	Davison Close
	/890	Tilbury Tower
	/914	Rhodes Close
	/999	Clerk Court
900		SUNDRIES
	/001	E S expenses
	/002	V S expenses
	/003	General sundries

No.	Date	Description	Code	Total
	November			
1	1	Caretaker - Clerk Court		76.50
2	1	Sankey Builders, Sheen - Ketley		600.00
3	1	Post Office		3.61
4	1	Sundries - Gibbs Ho		52.80
5	1	Perivale Glass Co.		317.00
6	3	Motor Mower - Burgess Ct		263.00
7	4	Electricity - Ketley Cl, (to 28,10)		355.84
8	4	Water rates - Q.C		92.00
9	4	Inst, Ch, Surveyors		515.00
10	5	Hanwell DIY		69.10
11	8	Law Society (subs)		742.00
12	8	Inland Revenue		8,437.50
13	8	Gas - Mallow Cl, (to 5.11)		81.50
14	9	Cleaners - Seymour M.		390.01
15	10	Power Drill - Laine Ho.		48.90
16	13	Perivale Roofing		4,720.00
17	17	Dentone (sols) - re Ashby M.		723.37
18	17	Coomer PL - Caretaker		226.00
19	17	Kew Electrics		590.72
20	17	Southern Electricity (to 15.11)		1,110.43
21	17	Wyrde St Computer Supplies		33.00
22	18	Brentford Advertiser		66.50
23	19	Rentokil - Jones Co.		856.06
24	21	Nevill Ho - Skip Hire (17.10-19.11)		32.40
25	21	Hanwell Timber		236.00
26	21	Sankeys - Ketley Clo.		1,800.00
27	24	Heston Service Station		8.81
28	24	Bldgs Ins - Oakwood B		408.00
29	24	Plumbing Supplies (Petersham) Ltd - Kings		426.80
30	24	Wages - Grasmere Caretaker		279.19
31	25	BACS - Salaries		12,187.89
32	25	British Gas - Tilbury		35.60

No.	Date	Description	Code	Total
	November			
1	26	Hall Hire - Wyndham AGM		32.50
2	26	Sainsbury's		19.50
3	28	Caretaker - Rodway Ho.		438.00
4	28	Property Management News		18.40
5	28	British Telecom		475.70
6	28	Co. House - Wyndham		32.00
7	28	Concrete repairs - Tilbury T		2,250.00
8	28	Acton Skip Hire - 1.11-30.11 - Davison		32.40
9	28	Brentford Cleaning		183.00
10	28	Wages - Davison Clo. C/T		66.10
11	28	Wages - Endymion Pl. C/T		64.50
12	28	Middlesex Gazette		22.22
13	28	Ben Smith Stationery Supplies		178.57
14	28	Electricity - Hennigan Ho. (to 25.11)		568.35
15	28	Guardian Royal Exchange - Pub. Liab		970.00
16	28	Guardian Royal Exchange - Richm.. Bldgs		1,630.00
17	28	E Strange Exps		88.90
18	28	Non-Dom Rates DD		271.25
19	28	GRE - Jaguar		1,315.50
20	28	Bank - charges		70.90
21	28	Bank - interest		949.93
22				
23				
24				
25				
26				
27				
28				
29				
30				
31				
32				

Tasks

Task 1

(a)   Code up the entries in the cash book, allocating the payments either directly to clients or to the appropriate Strange (Properties) Ltd account.

(*Note.* You can assume that geographical references in a cash book entry mean that the cost should be allocated to the buildings in the same location.)

(b)   Prepare a schedule of client charges using the current basis for allocating charges. Ignore VAT for the purposes of this part of the exercise.

If any matters occur to you at this stage for your reply to Mr Strange's memo, make rough notes. (You will be writing your reply later.)

Task 2

Amongst the debtors you have been pursuing are five former clients who dispensed with Strange (Properties) Ltd's services earlier in the year. The telephone conversations and letters that you have had have contained comments like 'I don't see why we should subsidise your business!'; 'You do next to nothing for us as far as we know'; 'Why are we paying for building works on your other clients' properties?' and so on.

You decide to see if you can find a way of charging each client a fair proportion of the overheads incurred and to do this you collect or compile the following materials:

(a)   A rough plan of the building
(b)   An organisation chart
(c)   A copy of Strange (Properties) Ltd's accounts for the year ended 30 September 20X2
(d)   A summary of the timesheets of Edward Strange and Victor Strange for the year 20X1/20X2

These documents, or extracts from them, are shown below.

Floor plan

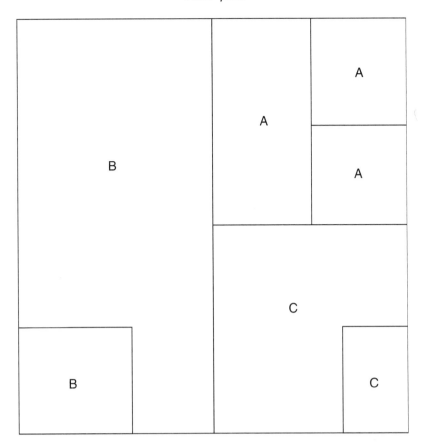

A = Solicitors staff
B = Surveying staff
C = Accounts staff

Organisation chart

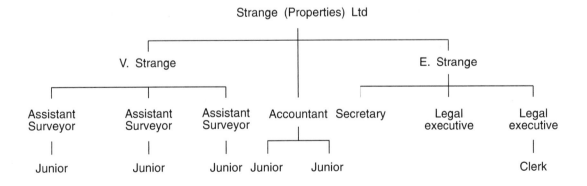

STRANGE (PROPERTIES) LTD
PROFIT AND LOSS ACCOUNT FOR THE YEAR ENDED
30 SEPTEMBER 20X2

	£	£
Fees		1,333,838
Less direct expenses		352,187
		981,651
Less costs of administration		
Wages and salaries	272,255	
Business rates	3,524	
Insurance	7,600	
Heat and light	4,775	
Depreciation of motor vehicles	7,500	
Depreciation of office equipment	1,752	
Repairs and maintenance	834	
Cleaning	6,584	
Depreciation of buildings	4,000	
Staff welfare	1,538	
Telecommunications	1,908	
Printing, postage and stationery	3,975	
Subscriptions	1,131	
Audit and accountancy fees	4,500	
Bank charges	862	
Advertising	1,973	
		324,711
		656,940
Interest payable		10,121
Profit before tax		646,819
Taxation		159,680
Profit for the financial year		487,139
Dividends		475,320
Retained profit transferred to reserves		11,819

STRANGE (PROPERTIES) LTD
BALANCE SHEET AS AT 30 SEPTEMBER 20X2

Fixed assets	*Leased buildings* £	*Motor vehicles* £	*Office equipment* £	*Total* £
Cost	80,000	30,000	17,520	127,520
Depreciation	48,000	22,500	7,008	77,508
	32,000	7,500	10,512	50,012
Current assets				
Debtors			309,060	
Prepayments			5,296	
			314,356	
Creditors				
Bank overdraft		113,880		
Other creditors		47,294		
Dividends		50,000		
			211,174	
				103,182
				153,194
Share capital				20,000
Profit and loss account				133,194
				153,194

(*Note.* The motor vehicles are the two second-hand Jaguars used by the Strange brothers. Both cost £15,000.)

TIME SHEET SUMMARY 20X1/X2

Current clients	Edward Strange Hours	Victor Strange Hours
Ashby Mansions	43	20
Burgess Court	71	82
Clerk Court	62	34
Clift Flats	15	113
Clifton Gardens	25	64
Coomer Place	60	80
Davison Close	49	52
De Beauvoir Buildings	74	38
Endymion Place	33	51
Frampton Court	16	73
Gibbs House	51	21
Glebe Gardens	81	60
Grasmere Mansion	84	30
Hennigan House	76	94
Jones Court	61	66
Ketley Close	49	36
Kings Buildings	63	57
Laine House	45	77
Loudwater Place	73	48
Matkins Gardens	76	35
Mallow Close	57	61
Neville House	24	92
Oakwood Buildings	117	40
Queen's Court	51	18

	Edward Strange Hours	Victor Strange Hours
Rhodes Close	82	97
Rodway House	64	88
Seymour Manor	23	64
Tilbury Tower	29	59
Undercliff Gardens	80	71
Wyndham Rise	75	28

Ex-clients		
Anderson Place	14	8
Jacques Court	25	12
Oxford Gardens	22	14
Robin House	20	15
Williams Close	30	22

Your task is to apportion the administrative and selling expenses and interest shown in the accounts as you think appropriate and to calculate how much should have been charged to each of Strange (Properties) Ltd's current clients.

Task 3

Reply to Mr Strange's memo, offering a solution to his problem. You may, of course, give him a copy of the calculations that you have already done. It would also be helpful to explain to him briefly about different methods of costing, but bear in mind that he has a very limited understanding of accountancy jargon.

Practice Devolved Assessment 4: Stately Hotels plc (data and tasks)

Practice Devolved Assessment
4 Stately Hotels plc

Performance criteria

The following performance criteria are covered in this Devolved Assessment.

Element 6.1: Record and analyse information relating to direct costs

4   Standard costs are compared against actual costs and any variances are analysed

Element 6.2: Record and analyse information relating to the allocation, apportionment and absorption of overhead costs

6   Standard costs are compared against actual costs and any variances are analysed

Element 6.3: Prepare and present standard cost reports

1   Standard cost reports with variances clearly identified are presented in an intelligible form

2   Unusual or unexpected results are identified and reported to managers

3   Any reasons for significant variances from standard are identified and the explanations presented to management

4   The results of the analysis and explanations of specific variances are produced for management

5   Staff working in operational departments are consulted to resolve any queries in the data

Notes on completing the Assessment

This Assessment is designed to test your ability to prepare and present standard cost reports.

You are provided with data on Pages 114 to 116 which you must use to complete the tasks on Pages 115 to 117.

You are allowed **three hours** to complete your work.

A high level of accuracy is required. Check your work carefully.

Correcting fluid should not be used. Errors should be crossed out neatly and clearly. You should write in ink - not pencil.

A FULL SUGGESTED ANSWER TO THIS ASSESSMENT IS PROVIDED ON PAGE 238.

Do not turn to the suggested answer until you have completed all parts of the Assessment.

BPP
PUBLISHING

SECTION 1

PRACTICE DEVOLVED ASSESSMENT 4: STATELY HOTELS PLC

Data

You work as the assistant to the management accountant for a major hotel chain, Stately Hotels plc. The new manager of one of the largest hotels in the chain, The Regent Hotel, is experimenting with the use of standard costing to plan and control the costs of preparing and cleaning the hotel bedrooms.

Two of the costs involved in this activity are cleaning labour and the supply of presentation soap packs.

Cleaning labour

Part-time staff are employed to clean and prepare the bedrooms for customers. The employees are paid for the number of hours that they work, which fluctuates on a daily basis depending on how many rooms need to be prepared each day.

The employees are paid a standard hourly rate for weekday work and a higher hourly rate at the weekend. The standard cost control system is based on an average of these two rates at £3.60 per hour.

The standard time allowed for cleaning and preparing a bedroom is fifteen minutes.

Presentation soap packs

A presentation soap pack is left in each room every night. The packs contain soap, bubble bath, shower gel, hand lotion etc. Most customers use the packs or take them home with them, but many do not. The standard usage of packs used for planning and control purposes is one pack per room per night.

The packs are purchased from a number of different suppliers and the standard price is £1.20 per pack. Stocks of packs are valued in the accounts at standard price.

Actual results for May

During May, 8,400 rooms were cleaned and prepared. The following data was recorded for cleaning labour and soap packs.

Cleaning labour paid for:

Weekday labour	1,850	hours @ £3 per hour
Weekend labour	700	hours @ £4.50 per hour
	2,550	

Presentation soap packs purchased and used:

6,530	packs @ £1.20 each
920	packs @ £1.30 each
1,130	packs @ £1.40 each
8,580	

Tasks

1   Using the data above, calculate the following cost variances for May:

    (a) Soap pack price
    (b) Soap pack usage
    (c) Cleaning labour rate
    (d) Cleaning labour utilisation or efficiency

2   Suggest one possible cause for each of the variances which you have calculated.

SECTION 2

Data

You are employed as the assistant management accountant to Albion Ltd. Albion Ltd manufactures a single product, the Xtra, an ingredient used in food processing. The basic raw material in Xtra production is material X. The average unit prices for material X in each quarter last year are reproduced below.

	Quarter 1	Quarter 2	Quarter 3	Quarter 4
Average unit price of X	£10	£11	£16	£19

Albion Ltd operates a standard absorption costing system. Standards are established at the beginning of each year. Each week the management accounting section prepares a statement for the production director reconciling the actual cost of production with its standard cost. Standard costing data for week 8 of quarter 4 in the current year is given below.

Standard costing and budget data for week 8 of quarter 4			
	Quantity	*Unit price*	*Cost per unit*
Material (kilograms)	3	£23.00	£69
Labour (hours)	2	£20.00	£40
Fixed overheads (hours)	2	£60.00	£120
Standard unit cost			£229
Budgeted production for week 8	*Budgeted units*	*Standard cost per unit*	*Standard cost of production*
	10,000	£229	£2,290,000

During week 8, production of Xtra totalled 9,000 units and the actual costs for that week were:

Inputs	*Units*	*Total cost*
Materials (kilograms)	26,500	£662,500
Labour (hours)	18,400	£349,600
Fixed overheads (hours)	18,400	£1,500,000

Using this data, a colleague has already calculated the fixed overhead variances. These were as follows:

- Fixed overhead expenditure (or price) variance   £300,000 adverse
- Efficiency (or usage) variance   £24,000 adverse
- Capacity variance   £96,000 adverse

Tasks

Your colleague asks you to:

1   Calculate the following variances:

    (a)   material price;

    (b)   material usage;

    (c)   labour rate;

    (d)   labour efficiency (sometimes called utilisation).

2   Prepare a statement listing all of the cost variances.

SECTION 3

Data

You are employed as part of the management accounting team in a large industrial company which operates a four-weekly system of management reporting. Your division makes a single product, the Alpha, and, because of the nature of the production process, there is no work in progress at any time.

The group management accountant has completed the calculation of the material and labour standard costing variances for the current period to 1 December but has not had the time to complete any other variances. Details of the variances already calculated are produced in the working papers below, along with other standard costing data.

Standard costing and budget data - four weeks ended 1 December			
	Quantity	*Unit price*	*Cost per unit*
Material (litres)	40	£4.00	£160
Labour (hours)	10	£8.40	£84
Fixed overheads (hours)	10	£6.70	£67
Standard cost per unit			£311
	Units	*Standard unit cost*	*Standard cost of production*
Budgeted production	12,000	£311	£3,732,000

Working papers:

Actual production and expenditure for the four weeks ended 1 December

Units produced	11,200
Cost of 470,000 litres of materials consumed	£1,974,000
Cost of 110,000 labour hours worked	£935,000
Expenditure on fixed overheads	£824,000

Material and labour variances

Material price variance	£94,000	(A)
Materials usage variance	£88,000	(A)
Labour rate variance	£11,000	(A)
Labour efficiency variance	£16,800	(F)

Tasks

1   Calculate the following variances.

    (a)   The fixed overhead expenditure variance
    (b)   The fixed overhead volume variance
    (c)   The fixed overhead capacity variance
    (d)   The fixed overhead efficiency variance

2   Prepare a report for presentation to the production director showing the cost variances for the 4 weeks ended 1 December.

3   The production director, who has only recently been appointed, is unfamiliar with fixed overhead variances. Because of this, the group management accountant has asked you to prepare a *brief* memo to the production director.

    Your memo should do the following:

    (a)   Explain what is meant by fixed overhead expenditure, volume, capacity and efficiency variances.

    (b)   Suggest one possible cause for each of the variances that you have calculated.

BPP
PUBLISHING

TRIAL RUN DEVOLVED ASSESSMENT 1

INTERMEDIATE STAGE - NVQ/SVQ3

Unit 6

Recording Cost Information

The purpose of this Trial Run Devolved Assessment is to give you an idea of what a Devolved Assessment could be like. It is not intended as a definitive guide to the tasks you may be required to perform.

The suggested time allowance for this Assessment is **four hours**.

Calculators may be used but no reference material is permitted.

**DO NOT OPEN THIS PAPER UNTIL YOU ARE READY TO START
UNDER TIMED CONDITIONS**

INSTRUCTIONS

This Assessment is designed to test your ability to record cost information.

Background information is provided on Page 121.

The tasks you are to perform are set out on Page 122.

You are provided with data on Pages 123 to 136 which you must use to complete the tasks.

Your answers should be set out in the answer booklet on Pages 139 to 144 using the documents provided. You may require additional answer pages.

You are allowed **four hours** to complete your work.

A high level of accuracy is required. Check your work carefully.

Correcting fluid may not be used. Errors should be crossed out neatly and clearly. You should write in black ink, not pencil.

You are advised to read the whole of the Assessment before commencing as all of the information may be of value and is not necessarily supplied in the sequence in which you might wish to deal with it.

A FULL SUGGESTED ANSWER TO THIS ASSESSMENT IS PROVIDED ON PAGE 244.

THE SITUATION

It is your first day at your new job. You should have started as the accountant at Food with a Bite Ltd four weeks ago (1 March 20X3), the company's first day of business. A broken leg from a rather nasty fall on the Matterhorn during a skiing holiday has, however, delayed your joining the company.

You arrive on Monday 29 March knowing that you have four weeks work to catch up on but nobody seems to be around the factory or offices apart from Fred and Ali, the two production line workers. They explain that their supervisor is dealing with a delivery, the storeman won't be starting for another week (his wife has had a baby and so Harry Jordan, the General Manager, has given him five weeks paternity leave) and that Harry Jordan himself is out of the office for the day. All that you need has, however, been left on your desk, which they point you in the direction of.

On your desk you find three piles of documents marked financial accounts, management accounts and cost accounts and a note from Harry Jordan.

It seems as if you are going to have to cope on your own for the day and you quickly try to assemble in your mind all that you know about Food with a Bite Ltd from your conversations with Harry Jordan at your interviews.

(a) The company began trading on 1 March 20X3.

(b) It makes two products, a hot vegetarian chilli in the chilli production department and a spicy vegetarian curry in the curry production department.

(c) Two production line workers are employed. Ali is initially working on the chilli production line and Fred is initially working on the curry production line. Eventually they will both work on either production line as demand dictates. They are overseen by a supervisor. A storekeeper (when he finally begins working) will look after the stores area (the company's other department). He will spend half of his time controlling the chilli ingredients and half of his time controlling the curry ingredients.

(d) The company's year is divided into 13 four-week periods.

(e) There is a great demand for the two products. Sam's Supermarkets have agreed to take (on a Friday) whatever has been produced during the week.

You pick up Harry's note.

Friday 26 March

Sorry to leave you in the lurch! Hope I've left everything you're going to need on your desk.
Can you start with cost accounting because I desperately need your help for the board meeting on Friday. I've got to take standard cost cards for our two products with me and give them some idea about how efficiently Fred has been working over the last four weeks. The board also want to know how efficiently he's been using the vegetables in the curry.
Do you think you can prepare the cards (I don't know what they are but the board gave me a couple of blanks) and find out about Fred and the vegetables? The board also expect to see updated stores ledger accounts (whatever they are) for lentils and vegetables. Again, they've given me a couple of blanks.
Thanks very much. See you on Wednesday.

Harry

BPP
PUBLISHING

TASKS TO BE COMPLETED

In the answer booklet on Pages 139 to 144 complete the tasks outlined below. Data for this assessment is provided on Pages 123 to 136.

As you complete each of the tasks you should note any matters which need discussing with members of staff on a schedule of queries indicating who you will need to speak to and any action which may be necessary. You should ignore VAT and employer's National Insurance contributions and work to two decimal places.

(a) Calculate standard material costs for a vegetarian chilli and a vegetarian curry, basing the standard quantities on the information provided by Delia Craddock and the standard prices on the expected prices at 1 September 20X3. (Materials includes cartons.)

Fill in the details of the standard quantities and standard prices, and hence the standard material costs, on each of the standard cost cards.

(b) Calculate standard labour costs for a vegetarian chilli and a vegetarian curry using information from the business plan and the offers of employment.

Fill in the details of the standard times and standard wage rates, and hence the standard labour costs, on each of the standard cost cards.

(c) Calculate standard variable overhead costs for a vegetarian chilli and a vegetarian curry using information provided by Oly from Oly's Oils.

Fill in the details of the standard quantity and standard price, and hence the standard overhead cost, on each of the standard cost cards.

(d) (i) Calculate the budgeted annual fixed overheads, fixed overheads being the salaries of the supervisor and storekeeper, the cost of cleaners, heat and light and overtime.

(ii) Allocate (if possible) overheads direct to departments.

(iii) Apportion the remaining overheads between the three departments using suitable bases (budgeted direct labour hours, floor area and overtime hours).

(iv) Apportion the service department overheads to the two production departments.

(v) Calculate departmental overhead absorption rates based on direct labour hours.

Fill in the details of the standard overhead absorbed into each product on the standard cost card. You should now have two completed standard cost cards.

(e) Calculate a labour efficiency variance for the curry department for the four-week period using details from the clock cards and standard cost cards and the fact that 5,000 portions of curry were made.

(f) Complete (as fully as possible, given the available information) stores ledger accounts for the four-week period for lentils and vegetables using the information provided in the list of what was taken from the storeroom and the two Exotic Foods Emporium invoices. Use the stock valuation method recommended in the business plan.

(g) Calculate a usage variance for the vegetables used during the four-week period using information on the appropriate stores ledger account and standard cost card.

(h) Calculate any under or over absorption of fixed overhead during the four-week period. To determine the overtime cost incurred you need to know, in addition to the information you already have, that 5,300 portions of chilli were made and that Ali worked 171.25 hours.

DATA

(a)   The following letter and list of ingredients were received from Delia Craddock.

Mr H. Jordan
Food With a Bite Ltd
Spicy Court
Riceford

Apple Cottage
Rose Lane
Little Smedlingford

23rd February 20X3

Dear Harry

What a lovely surprise hearing from you after so many years. Yes, of course I remember
our days at University together. How could I forget!! Do you remember that poem
you recited to me as we punted down the river?

I'm so pleased your business empire is expanding and I'd love to help in any way I can.
I enclose a list of the standard ingredients for vegatarian chilli and vegetarian curry. I hope
it's what you needed.

I look forward to seeing you on the 29 March. I'll be in black!

Enclosed

Delia Craddock

Standard ingredients for one portion
Vegetarian chilli
0.125 kg rice
0.0625 kg lentils
0.167 kg tinned tomatoes
0.167 kg mushroom/onion/pepper mixture
0.167 kg kidney beans
0.025 kg dried chillies

Vegetarian curry
0.125 kg rice
0.167 litres coconut oil
0.005 kg spices
0.167 kg vegetables

(b)   The following compliments slip and current price list were received from Exotic Foods Emporium.

xotic Foods Emporium

Please find enclosed current price list. As to your enquiry, our prices have increased by 10% since 1.3.X2. It is likely that our prices will increase by a similar percentage during the coming year.

With Compliments

xotic Foods Emporium
The Industrial Estate
Riceford
0321 909 698

PRICE LIST at 1.3.X3

	£
Chillis - 50 kg drum	86.50
Coconut oil - 100 l drum	115.00
Kidney beans - 50 kg drum	44.00
Lentils - 100 kg sack	84.00
Mushroom/onion/pepper - 50 kg drum	58.00
Rice - 100 kg sack	130.00
Spices - 10 kg drum	92.00
Tomatoes - 50 kg drum	35.00
Vegetables - 50 kg drum	53.50

(c)   The following quotation was received from a carton manufacturer.

   The Container Company   Matfield Road   Riceford

QUOTATION

25/2/X3

Plastic food containers (1 portion) with appropriate design on cardboard lid: unit price 4p.

Price increase to 5p from 1.4.X3. Fixed for 12 months.

(d) The following extract from the Business Plan for Food With a Bite Ltd was prepared by Smethick & Co (Management Consultants).

Extracts from Business Plan
for
Food with a Bite Ltd
by
Smethick & Co
(Management Consultants)

Expected production for 12 months (13 periods) to 28.2.X4

Vegetarian chilli - 78,000 portions
Vegetarian curry - 66,300 portions

Expected labour time to produce 1 portion

Vegetarian chilli - 1.5 minutes
Vegetarian curry - 2 minutes

Per discussion with National Electricity

Likely charge per annum for heat and light £5,000

Recommendations

Initially, value issues and stock using weighted average method. Standard costing will be used once the company and its operations are established.

Asborb overheads on basis of direct labour hours.

Do not allow annual overtime to exceed 100 hours in total for both production line workers. Overtime should not be regular occurrence once system established.

(e)   The following offers of employment were sent out in the middle of February.

Food with a Bite

Spicy Court
Riceford

Mr A Khan   20 February 20X3
132 The Drive
Riceford

Dear Mr Khan

I have great pleasure in offering you the position of production line worker (chilli) at Food with a Bite.

Your basic rate of pay will be £4.00 per hour. Any hours worked over and above the basic time of eight hours a day will be paid at time and a half. During your first year of service you are entitled to one day's holiday. This will be increased to four weeks in your second year of service.

I look forward to hearing from you in the very near future.

Yours sincerely

Harry Jordan

Harry Jordan

Food with a Bite

Spicy Court
Riceford

Mr F Jarvis   20 February 20X3
44 The Close
Riceford

Dear Mr Jarvis

I have great pleasure in offering you the position of
production line worker (curry) at Food with a Bite.

Your basic rate of pay will be £4.00 per hour. Any hours
worked over and above the basic time of eight hours a day
will be paid at time and a half. During your first year of
employment you are entitled to one day's holiday. This will
be increased to four weeks in your second year of service.

I look forward to hearing from you in the very near future.

Yours sincerely

Harry Jordan

Harry Jordan

Food with a Bite

Spicy Court
Riceford

Mr J Simpson   20 February 20X3
4 The Street
Riceford

Dear Mr Simpson

I have great pleasure in offering you the position of
production line supervisor at Food with a Bite.

Your starting salary will be £16,000 per annum with an annual
review on 1 April 20X4 and every April thereafter. You are
entitled to four weeks' holiday per annum.

I look forward to hearing from you in the very near future.

Yours sincerely

Harry Jordan

Harry Jordan

Food with a Bite

Spicy Court
Riceford

Mr K Sampson   20 February 20X3
2 The Road
Riceford

Dear Mr Sampson

I have great pleasure in offering you the position of
Storekeeper at Food with a Bite.

Your starting salary will be £12,000 per annum with an annual
review on 1 April 20X4 and every April thereafter. You are
entitled to four weeks' holiday per annum.

I look forward to hearing from you in the very near future.

Yours sincerely

Harry Jordan

Harry Jordan

BPP PUBLISHING

(f)   The following telephone message was taken on the 15th March 20X3.

Telephone Message

Mr Jordan

while you were out

Oly from Oly's Oils ....called

at ......9.00...... on ......15/3/X3......

Message ....

line machines @ £17.50 per 10 litre drum. Said to tell you

price hasn't changed for last 4 years and unlikely to in

future. You'll probably need to use 1 litre of oil per

machine for every 100 portions produced by machine.

(g)   The following contract is for cleaning the factory and stores of Food With a Bite Ltd.

Mrs Mopp Cleaners

Contract

With:

Food with a Bite Ltd
Spicy Court
Riceford

From: 1/3/X3

To: 28/2/X4

For: 2 hours cleaning per night
               (factory and stores areas)

At: £10 per hour

For Mrs Mopp Cleaners: _____V. Rix_____ (Director)

For: Food with a Bite Ltd   _____N. Richards_____ (Director)

(h)   The following floor plan shows the factory and stores area.

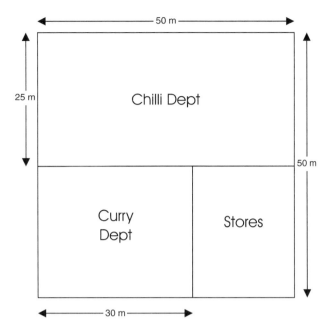

(i)   The following electricity bill was received at the end of March 20X3.

NATIONAL ELECTRICITY

YOUR CUSTOMER SERVICES OFFICE IS:	YOU CAN PHONE US ON:
POWER ROAD RICEFORD	0321 949 494

FOOD WITH A BITE LTD
SPICY COURT
RICEFORD

WHEN TELEPHONING
We have a call queuing
system. When you hear
the ringing tone please
wait for a reply as calls
are answered in strict
rotation.
BUSY TIMES
Please try to avoid
9-30AM - 10-30 AM
and 2 PM to 3 PM

METER READING		UNITS USED	UNIT PRICE (pence)	V.A.T code	AMOUNT £
PRESENT	PREVIOUS				
2359 E	-	2359	17.470	1	412.12
STANDING CHARGE				1	217.50
TOTAL CHARGE (EXCLUDING VAT)					629.62
VAT 1 629.62 @ 17.5% COMMERCIAL					110.18

MAKE YOUR BILLS EASIER TO SWALLOW - SEE PAGE 4 OF 'SOURCE'
FOR BUDGET SCHEME APPLICATION

E=Estimated reading. Please read carefully the advice given on the back of this bill
C=Your own reading

BALANCE TO PAY			739.80
VAT CHARGE THIS BILL			110.18
YOUR ACCOUNT NUMBER	BILL DATE/TAX POINT	READING DATE	NON-DOMESTIC USE
34721193672	26.03.X3	26.03.X3	100%

Part B: Devolved Assessments

(j)   The following four clock cards cover the weeks ending 5 March 20X3 and 12 March 20X3.

No 101				Ending 5/3/X3	
Name *Fred Jarvis*					
HOURS	**RATE**	**AMOUNT**	**DEDUCTIONS**		
Basic			Income Tax		
O/T			NI		
Others			Other		
			Total deduction		
Total					
Less deductions					
Net due					

Time	Day	Basic time	Overtime
1630	F		
1330	F		
1230	F		
0800	F		
1700	T		
1330	T		
1230	T		
0830	T		
1830	W		
1330	W		
1300	W		
0800	W		
1700	T		
1330	T		
1230	T		
0830	T		
1700	M		
1330	M		
1230	M		
0830	M		

Signature

No 101				Ending 12/3/X3	
Name *Fred Jarvis*					
HOURS	**RATE**	**AMOUNT**	**DEDUCTIONS**		
Basic			Income Tax		
O/T			NI		
Others			Other		
			Total deduction		
Total					
Less deductions					
Net due					

Time	Day	Basic time	Overtime
1630	F		
1330	F		
1200	F		
0800	F		
1800	T		
1330	T		
1230	T		
0800	T		
1630	W		
1330	W		
1230	W		
0730	W		
1630	T		
1330	T		
1230	T		
0730	T		
1630	M		
1330	M		
1230	M		
0730	M		

Signature

No	101			Ending	19/3/X3

	HOURS	RATE	AMOUNT	DEDUCTIONS	
Basic				Income Tax	
O/T				NI	
Others				Other	
				Total deduction	
Total					
Less deductions					
Net due					

Name *Fred Jarvis*

Time	Day	Basic time	Overtime
1700	F		
1330	F		
1230	F		
0830	F		
1730	T		
1330	T		
1300	T		
0800	T		
1730	W		
1330	W		
1300	W		
0730	W		
1800	T		
1400	T		
1330	T		
0700	T		
1700	M		
1330	M		
1230	M		
0830	M		

Signature ....

No	101			Ending	26/3/X3

Name *Fred Jarvis*

	HOURS	RATE	AMOUNT	DEDUCTIONS	
Basic				Income Tax	
O/T				NI	
Others				Other	
				Total deduction	
Total					
Less deductions					
Net due					

Time	Day	Basic time	Overtime
1800	F		
1400	F		
1330	F		
0730	F		
1830	T		
1430	T		
1400	T		
0800	T		
1730	W		
1330	W		
1230	W		
0830	W		
1730	T		
1330	T		
1300	T		
0800	T		
1800	M		
1330	M		
1230	M		
0730	M		

Signature ....

BPP PUBLISHING

(k)   The following list shows what Fred and Ali took from stores.

What we took from storeroom

Mon 1 March
  - 1 sack/drum of each food stuff
  - 2,000 cartons

Wed 3 March
  - 2 rice
  - 3 toms
  - 3 mush
  - 3 kidney
  - 2,000 cartons
  - 1 coconut
  - 3 veg

Mon 8 March
  - 5 veg
  - 5 rice
  - 1 lentil
  - 5 toms
  - 5 mush
  - 5 kidney
  - 3,000 cartons
  - 2 coconut
  - 1 spice

Mon 15 March
  - 2 rice
  - 1 lentil
  - 4 toms
  - 4 mush
  - 4 kidneys
  - 2,000 cartons
  - 2 coconut
  - 1 spice
  - 4 veg
  - 1 chilli

Mon 22 March
  - 3 rice
  - 1 lentil
  - 1 chilli
  - 5 toms
  - 5 kidney
  - 5 mush
  - 3,000 cartons
  - 3 coconut
  - 5 veg

Fri 26 March
no stock left in production
line area

Whenever we took rice or cartons, I had half
for chilli and Fred took half for curry

BPP PUBLISHING

(1)   The following two invoices were received from Exotic Foods Emporium.

---

xotic Foods Emporium
The Industrial Estate
Riceford
0321 909 698

Food with a Bite Ltd
Spicy Court
Riceford

INVOICE

Order no: 0001   Del date: 1/3/X3   Invoice no: 7164   Date: 1/3/X3

Quantity	Description	Unit price £	Total £
10	Rice - 100 kg sack	130.00	1,300.00
4	Lentils - 100 kg sack	84.00	336.00
10	Tomatoes - 50 kg drum	35.00	350.00
10	Mushs etc - 50 kg drum	58.00	580.00
10	Vegetables - 50 kg drum	53.50	535.00
6	Coconut oil - 100 l drum	115.00	690.00
3	Spice - 10 kg tin	92.00	276.00
10	Kidney beans - 50 kg drum	44.00	440.00
2	Chillis - 50 kg drum	86.50	173.00
		Total	4,680.00

This agrees with what
was delivered
Fred Jarvis
1/3/X3

BPP
PUBLISHING

xotic Foods Emporium
The Industrial Estate
Riceford
0321 909 698

Food with a Bite Ltd
Spicy Court
Riceford

INVOICE

Order no: 003   Del date: 12/3/X3 Invoice no: 7321   Date: 12/3/X3

Quantity	Description	Unit price £	Total £
4	Rice - 100 kg sack	131.00	524.00
10	Tomatoes - 50 kg drum	35.00	350.00
10	Mushs etc - 50 kg drum	58.50	585.00
11	Vegetables - 50 kg drum	53.75	591.25
4	Coconut oil - 100 l drum	118.00	472.00
12	Kidney beans - 50 kg drum	44.00	528.00
3	Chillis - 50 kg drum	86.50	259.50
		Total	3,309.75

Only 2 drums of chillis delivered
but 5 sacks of rice came
Fred Jarus
12/3/X3

TRIAL RUN DEVOLVED ASSESSMENT 1

Recording Cost Information

ANSWER BOOKLET

Documents for use in this Assessment

The documents you will need to prepare the solution are given on Pages 139 to 141 and consist of two blank standard cost cards and two blank stores ledger accounts. Pages 142 to 144 are blank and can be used for any written solutions, calculations or workings.

Standard cost cards

STANDARD COST CARD
PRODUCT Veg Chilli

DESCRIPTION	QUANTITY	COST PER KG/HOUR/ETC	EXTENSION	TOTAL
Materials		£	£	£
Rice.	0.125	1.37	0.17	
Lentils.	0.0625	0.88	0.06	
Toms.	0.167	0.74	0.12	
Mush.	0.167	1.22	0.20	
K. Beans	0.167	0.92	0.15	
Chillies.	0.025	1.82	0.05	
Cartons.	1	0.05	0.05	
SUB-TOTAL				0.80
Labour				
Direct.	1.5 mins	4.00/u	0.10	
SUB-TOTAL				0.10
Direct cost				0.90
Variable o/h	0.01 LH.	1.75		0.02
Standard variable cost				0.92
Fixed o/h	0.025			
Standard cost of sale				0.98

STANDARD COST CARD

PRODUCT ....Veg Curry....

DESCRIPTION	QUANTITY	COST PER KG/HOUR/ETC	EXTENSION	TOTAL
Materials		£	£	£
Rice·	0.125	1.37		
Oil·	0.167	1.21		
Spice·	0.005	9.66		
Veg.	0.167	1.12		
Cartons	1	0.05		
SUB-TOTAL				
Labour				
	2mins	4.00	.13	
SUB-TOTAL				
Direct cost				
Variable o/h				
Standard variable cost				
Fixed o/h	0.033			
Standard cost of sale				

Stores ledger accounts

STORES LEDGER ACCOUNT

Material: .... Maximum Quantity: ....

Code: .... Minimum Quantity: ....

Date	Receipts				Issues				Stock		
	G.R.N. No.	Quantity	Unit Price £	Amount £	Stores Req. No.	Quantity	Unit Price £	Amount £	Quantity	Unit Price £	Amount £

STORES LEDGER ACCOUNT

Material: .... Maximum Quantity: ....

Code: .... Minimum Quantity: ....

Date	Receipts				Issues				Stock		
	G.R.N. No.	Quantity	Unit Price £	Amount £	Stores Req. No.	Quantity	Unit Price £	Amount £	Quantity	Unit Price £	Amount £

BPP PUBLISHING

Blank 1

Blank 2

Blank 3

TRIAL RUN DEVOLVED ASSESSMENT 2

INTERMEDIATE STAGE - NVQ/SVQ3

Unit 6

Recording cost information

The purpose of this Trial Run Devolved Assessment is to give you an idea of what a Devolved Assessment could be like. It is not intended as a definitive guide to the tasks you may be required to perform.

The suggested time allowance for this Assessment is **four hours**.

Calculators may be used but no reference material is permitted.

**DO NOT OPEN THIS PAPER UNTIL YOU ARE READY TO START
UNDER TIMED CONDITIONS**

INSTRUCTIONS

This simulation is designed to test your ability to record cost information.

The situation is provided on page 147.

The tasks you are required to complete are set out on pages 148 and 149.

This booklet also contains data that you will need to complete the tasks. You should read the whole simulation before commencing work so as to gain an overall picture of what is required.

Your answers should be set out in the answer booklet provided. You may require additional pages.

You are allowed **four hours** to complete your work.

A high level of accuracy is required. Check your work carefully.

Correcting fluid may be used but it should be used in moderation. Errors should be crossed out neatly and clearly. You should write in black ink, not pencil.

A FULL SUGGESTED ANSWER TO THIS ASSESSMENT IS PROVIDED ON PAGE 252.

THE SITUATION

Introduction

Your name is Louise Chandler. It is eight o'clock in the morning of 12 June 20X8 and you receive a phone call from your Aunt Leanne. She is in hospital, having broken her leg, which means that she is unable to get into work to prepare the cost accounts for her company's first month of trading. Despite the fact that you are on holiday, she knows that you won't mind going into Leanne's Orthodontic Soothers Ltd (her company) and using the knowledge you have acquired during your AAT studies to draw up the company's first month's cost accounts.

Not having seen or spoken to you Aunt recently you don't know much about Leanne's Orthodontic Soothers Ltd and so she fills you in with a few details.

Production

The business began trading a month ago (1 May) producing babies' orthodontic soothers. The soothers are made of a plastic which is soaked in natural food extracts to give it a taste and smell which babies will like. It is anticipated that soothers with various tastes and smells will be made in a variety of different shapes and colours once the company has established a market for its products (your aunt thinks this will be after about twelve months of trading), but so far only teddy bear-shaped white soothers infused with strawberry essence have been produced in department 1 and daisy-shaped yellow soothers infused with vanilla essence in department 2.

The soothers are made using a very simple technique which involves identical machines in departments 1 and 2.

Personnel

The company employs three workers, John, Julie and Darryl. Julie works in department 1, John in department 2 and Darryl is the maintenance and repairs engineer.

General

In this simulation you will have to deal with transactions which occur during May 20X8. You are likely to need to prepare rough workings on a spare piece of paper.

TASKS TO BE PERFORMED

As you complete each of the following tasks you should note any matters which need discussing with members of staff on a schedule of queries, indicating who you will need to speak to and any action which may be necessary, using page 172 of the answer booklet.

You should ignore VAT and employer's National Insurance contributions and work to three decimal places.

Standard cost cards and overhead absorption

1 On page 165 of the answer booklet, design a standard cost card that can be used for any shape, colour and smell/taste of soother. The standard cost should incorporate the costs of direct materials, direct labour and overheads.

2 Using the summary product specification on page 150, the invoices, compliment slips, delivery note, price list and personnel record card on pages 150 to 155, complete the labour and materials section of your standard cost card for the type of soother made in department 1.

3 Information about the company's *annual* overhead costs is provided on pages 157 to 160. Apportion these overheads to the company's three departments, using the information on page 160 to determine suitable apportionment bases. Use page 166 of the answer booklet for your calculations.

4 Apportion the service department overheads to the two production departments based on the assumption that the work done by Darryl during May (see page 160) is likely to reflect his work patterns in future months. Use page 166 of the answer booklet.

5 Given that overheads are absorbed on the basis of direct labour hours, calculate a suitable overhead absorption rate for each production department. Use page 167 of the answer booklet. You will need to refer back to the summary product specification.

6 Insert the appropriate standard overhead cost and complete all necessary details on the standard cost card your prepared for department 1.

7 Using the information contained in Leanne's scribbled note about John and Julie's hours on page 161, calculate any under-/over-absorbed overhead which may have arisen during May and explain possible reasons for its occurrence. You will need to refer back to some of the information used in task 3 and the summary design specification. Use page 168 of the answer booklet.

Labour and materials

8 You are not impressed with the control over labour and material costs at Leanne's Orthodontic Soothers Ltd. Write a memo to your Aunt Leanne in hospital which covers the following points.

(a) A description of a more effective way of recording the labour time of John and Julie

(b) Descriptions of the two documents that your aunt should consider introducing which would assist in the control over the ordering and the delivery of stock

(c) A brief description of the stock control documentation which provides evidence of stock movements

(d) A monthly stock report (completed for May) which incorporates a logical stock coding system and which shows raw materials stock movements and values. You will need to refer to the invoices, delivery notes and price list on pages 151 to 154, and the memo on page 149.

Use the blank memo form on page 169 of the answer booklet and date your memo 20 June 20X8.

Variance analysis

9 Using the information contained in the monthly production control report on page 161 and your completed stock control report and standard cost card, calculate material usage, labour efficiency and overhead efficiency variances for department 1 in May 20X8. Use page 170 of the answer booklet.

10 Using the blank memo form on page 171 of the answer booklet, write a memo to your Aunt Leanne suggesting reasons why the variances calculated in Task 9 might have arisen and describing any action which might be necessary. Date your memo 26 June 20X8.

BRIAN CATSON

Product design engineer

Summary product specification

Product name

Orthodontic Soother

General product specification

Plastic known as jenjam to be infused with food essence and then moulded into shape.

Materials specification

Each soother will require 0.25kg of one of a number of different colours of jenjam and 0.1kg of one of a number of different essences.

Labour specification

Each soother will require direct labour time depending on shape as follows.

Teddy Bear	6.0 minutes
Daisy	7.2 minutes

Projected output

Until market share has been established just two variations (white/strawberry/teddy bear and yellow/vanilla/daisy) should be produced.

Projected demand

Projected demand for the above two products in first year of trading is as follows.

White/strawberry/teddy bear	15,000
Yellow/vanilla/daisy	18,000

Essence Of The Matter Ltd

Cot Court, Cryton, 01525 113752

Please find enclosed our current price list.
As to your enquiry, we do not anticipate price changes during the next twelve months.

With compliments

Essence Of The Matter Ltd

Cot Court, Cryton, 01525 113752

Price List

at 1.5.X8

	Price per Kg £
Tropical banana essence	10.50
Smooth vanilla essence	8.00
Fruity strawberry essence	8.00
Ripe apple essence	3.50
Tangy orange essence	11.20
Warm milk chocolate essence	9.30

Perfect Plastics Ltd

**The Industrial Estate
Cryton
Tel: 01525 720121**

Re your enquiry - anticipate prices will be as per invoice dated 3.5.X8 for the next twelve months

With compliments

Perfect Plastics Ltd

The Industrial Estate
Cryton
Tel: 01525 720121

Leanne's Othodontic Soothers Ltd
Pram Road
Cryton

Order no: 7411   **Del date:** 1/5/X8   **Invoice no:** I72143   **Date:** 3/5/X8

Quantity	Description	Unit price £	Total £
300 Kgs	Jenjam - soft white	1.50	450.00
300 Kgs	Jenjam - blush pink	1.40	420.00
300 Kgs	Jenjam - pale blue	1.65	495.00
300 Kgs	Jenjam - spring yellow	1.00	300.00
300 Kgs	Jenjam - mint green	2.10	630.00
		Total	2,295.00

Only 250 Kgs of pink delivered Julie 1/5/X8

Perfect Plastics Ltd

The Industrial Estate
Cryton
Tel: 01525 720121

Leanne's Othodontic Soothers Ltd
Pram Road
Cryton

Order no: 7499   **Del date:** 23/5/X8   **Invoice no:** I72893   **Date:** 28/5/X8

Quantity	Description	Unit price £	Total £
50 Kgs	Jenjam – soft white	1.50	75.00
150 Kgs	Jenjam – spring yellow	1.00	150.00
		Total	225.00

This agrees with what was delivered John 28/5/X8

Essence Of The Matter Ltd

Cot Court, Cryton, 01525 113752
Delivery note

Leanne's Orthodontic Soothers Ltd
Pram Road
Cryton

Order No:	513
Account No:	L727L
Del note No:	EM567

Product	Quantity Kgs
Fruity Strawberry Essence	100
Smooth Vanilla Essence	100
Tropical Banana Essence	100
Warm Milk Chocolate Essence	100

Del Date: 1 May 20X8

All delivered OK! Julie 1/5/X8

PERSONNEL RECORD CARD

NUMBER

NAME JONES, JULIE

PERSONAL DETAILS

| SURNAME | JONES |
| FORENAMES | JULIE |

| SEX | Nationality | British |
| M (F) | Social Security Number | RR 35 66 21D |

Date of Birth   31 October 20V0

Marital Status   Single Married Separated (Divorced) Widowed

Dependants   1

Disabilities   None

Professional Qualifications   None

Educational Details

Higher Education

A levels

BTec

GCSE

O levels   8

CSEs

Other

ADDRESS
1 Rattle Road,
Cryton

Telephone   01525 674333

ADDRESS   1ST CHANGE

Telephone

ADDRESS   2ND CHANGE

Telephone

IN EMERGENCY CONTACT

| Name | Jones, Muriel | Mother |
| Address | As above | |

Telephone (h)   As above
Telephone (wk)   01525 444333

EMPLOYMENT HISTORY

Years of Service (12 months to 31 December)

1 2 3 4 5 6 7 8 9 10 11 12 13 14 15 16 17 18 19 20 21 22

FROM	TO	TITLE	DEPT	REASON	PAY
1/5/X8		Production line worker	1	1st job here	£6.50 an hour

Training History

Course Code	

Special Details

Leave Entitlement   20 days

Barney Woofton Holdings Ltd

Rental Agreement

With:

> Leanne's Othodontic Soothers Ltd
> Pram Road
> Cryton

From: 1/5/X8

To: 30/4/X9

For: Rental of premises at Pram Road

At: £1,000 per month

For Barney Woofton Ltd: **B. Woofton** (Director)

For: Leanne's Orthodontic Soothers Ltd   *L. Zealand* (Director)

CENTRAL ELECTRICITY

QUARTERLY BILL

YOUR CUSTOMER SERVICES OFFICE IS:	YOU CAN PHONE US ON:
LIGHT STREET, CRYTON	01525 721312

LEANNE'S ORTHODONTIC SOOTHERS LTD
PRAM ROAD
CRYTON

I anticipate the same charge will be incurred each month.
Leanne

WHEN TELEPHONING
We have a call queuing system. When you hear the ringing tone please wait for a reply as calls are answered in strict rotation.
BUSY TIMES
Please try to avoid 9-30AM - 10-30 AM and 2 PM to 3 PM

METER READING		UNITS USED	UNIT PRICE (pence)	AMOUNT £
PRESENT	PREVIOUS			
1488 E	-	1488	16.80	249.98
STANDING CHARGE				102.02
TOTAL CHARGE				352.00

MAKE YOUR BILLS EASIER TO SWALLOW - SEE PAGE 4 OF 'SOURCE' FOR BUDGET SCHEME APPLICATION

E=Estimated reading. Please read carefully the advice given on the back of this bill
C=Your own reading

BALANCE TO PAY	352.00

YOUR ACCOUNT NUMBER	BILL DATE/TAX POINT	READING DATE	NON-DOMESTIC USE
56329999887	31.05.X8	31.05.X8	100%

BPP PUBLISHING

PERSONNEL RECORD CARD

NAME JEPSON, DARRYL

NUMBER

PERSONAL DETAILS

SURNAME	JEPSON		
FORENAMES	DARRYL		

SEX	Nationality	Irish
(M) F	Social Security Number	NF 39 06 780

Date of Birth	23 June 20U7

Marital Status	Single (Married) Separated Divorced Widowed

Dependants	2

Disabilities	None

ADDRESS
5 Shawl Street,
Cryton

Telephone 01525 223490

ADDRESS   1ST CHANGE

Telephone

ADDRESS   2ND CHANGE

Telephone

Professional Qualifications
None

Educational Details

Higher Education

A levels Engineering

BTec	
GCSE	6
O levels	
CSEs	
Other	

IN EMERGENCY CONTACT

Name	Jepson, Mavis	Wife
Address	As above	

Telephone (h) As above
Telephone (wk) 01678 101912

EMPLOYMENT HISTORY

Years of Service (12 months to 31 December)
1 2 3 4 5 6 7 8 9 10 11 12 13 14 15 16 17 18 19 20 21 22

FROM	TO	TITLE	DEPT	REASON	PAY
1/5/X8		Maintenance and repairs engineer	Maintenance and repairs	1st job here	£13,000 pa

Training History

Course Code								

Special Details

Leave Entitlement	20 days

CLIVE D✲GLEY LTD

Suppliers of Machines
The Industrial Estate, Cryton, 01525 221217

Invoice to :   Leanne's Orthodontic Soothers Ltd, Pram Road, Cryton

Order No :   7NJF   Account No : LTS1   Invoice No :   C9412

Delivery date :   28 April X8   Invoice date :   2 May X8

Invoice for :

2	N53 * 67P Plastic moulding machines at £7,500 each	£15,000

Amount due   £15,000

Telephone Message

Leanne

while you were out

Your friend Milly ....called

at ......3.15...... on 23/5/X8

Message ...Her company uses very similar machines to ours and their depreciation policy is 20% per annum on a straight line basis. They think the machines have a useful life of 5 years.

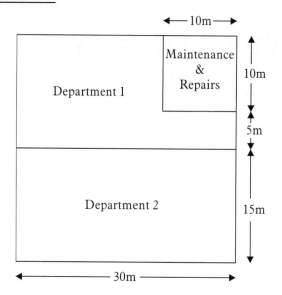

Date	Time	Dept.	Nature of work
Time log for maintenance and repairs engineer			
1 May	9 – 10	1	Check machine OK to start production
1 May	10 – 11.30	2	Check machine OK to start production
4 May	2 – 5.30	2	Ram driver broken, needed replacing
5 May	9 – 1, 2 – 5.30	2	Ram driver broken, needed replacing
6 May	9 – 1	2	Ram driver broken, needed replacing
17 May	10 – 1, 2 – 4	1	Fuse in fillup socket blew
23 May	4.30 – 5.30	2	Ram driver broken, needed replacing
24 May	9 – 1	2	Ram driver broken, needed replacing
28 May	9.30–12, 1–5.30	1	Monthly overhaul
29 May	10–12, 1–3.30	1	Monthly overhaul
30 May	9 – 12	2	Monthly overhaul

Julie's hours in May
6 6 6 6 6 6 8 6 6 7 7 8 7½
7½ 8 8 8 8 7 7½ 7 7 14

John's hours in May
7 7 7 7 7 7 7 7 7 7
7 7 7 7 7 7 7 7 7
7 7

Memo

To: Leanne
From: John
Date: 1 June X8
Subject: Stores check

As you asked, I looked through the stores and noted down what was there first thing this morning

Yellow	30 Kgs
Blue	300 Kgs
Green	250 Kgs
Pink	250 Kgs
White	nothing
Chocolate	100 Kgs
Banana	100 Kgs
Vanilla	1 Kg
Strawberry	nothing

MONTHLY PRODUCTION REPORT
May 20X8

	Department 1 Units	Department 2 Units
Transfers to finished goods stock	950	1,050

TRIAL RUN DEVOLVED ASSESSMENT 2

Recording Cost Information

ANSWER BOOKLET

Task 1

Standard cost card

Tasks 3 and 4

Overhead apportionment and absorption

Task 5

Overhead absorption rates

BPP PUBLISHING

Task 7

Under/over absorption of overhead

Task 8

MEMORANDUM

To:
From:
Date:
Subject:

Variance calculations

Task 10

MEMORANDUM

To:
From:
Date:
Subject:

BPP
PUBLISHING

Schedule of queries

AAT Sample
Simulation

SAMPLE SIMULATION

INTERMEDIATE STAGE - NVQ/SVQ3

Unit 6

Recording Cost Information
(AAT Sample)

This Sample Simulation is the AAT's Sample Simulation for Unit 6. Its purpose is to give you an idea of what an AAT simulation looks like. It is not intended as a definitive guide to the tasks you may be required to perform.

The suggested time allowance for this Assessment is four hours. Up to 30 minutes extra time may be permitted in an AAT simulation. Breaks in assessment may be allowed in the AAT simulation, but it must normally be completed in one day.

Calculators may be used but no reference material is permitted.

**DO NOT OPEN THIS PAPER UNTIL YOU ARE READY TO START
UNDER TIMED CONDITIONS**

INSTRUCTIONS

This Simulation is designed to test your ability to record cost information.

Background information is provided on Page 177.

The tasks you are to perform are set out on Pages 178 to 179.

You are provided with data on Pages 180 to 189 which you must use to complete the tasks.

Your answers should be set out in the answer booklet on Pages 193 to 206 using the documents provided. You may require additional answer pages.

You are allowed **four hours** to complete your work.

A high level of accuracy is required. Check your work carefully.

Correcting fluid may not be used. Errors should be crossed out neatly and clearly. You should write in black ink, not pencil.

You are advised to read the whole of the Simulation before commencing as all of the information may be of value and is not necessarily supplied in the sequence in which you might wish to deal with it.

A FULL SUGGESTED ANSWER TO THIS SIMULATION IS PROVIDED IN THIS KIT ON PAGES 267.

THE SITUATION

Introduction

Your name is Lesley Hunt and you work as an accounts assistant for Polycot Ltd, a manufacturer of cotton duvet covers.

Cost centres

The production cost centres in Polycot Ltd are a cutting department, a finishing department and a packing department.

- Work in the cutting department is machine-intensive. The machines are operated by a number of direct employees.

- Work in the finishing department and packing department is labour-intensive, and is carried out entirely by direct employees of Polycot Ltd.

In addition to the production cost centres there is also a stores department.

Cost accounting records

Polycot Ltd uses the FIFO method for valuing issues of materials to production and stocks of materials.

The company is registered for VAT and all of its outputs are standard-rated. This means that VAT on its purchases can always be reclaimed and should therefore be ignored in the cost records.

The accounts code list for the company includes the following codes:

Cost centre codes		*Expenditure codes*	
C100	Cutting department	E200	Direct materials
C200	Finishing department	E210	Indirect materials
C300	Packing department	E300	Direct wages
C400	Stores	E310	Indirect wages
		E410	Indirect revenue expenses
		E500	Depreciation - production equipment

Until now, the company has absorbed all production overheads on the basis of a percentage of direct labour costs. However, as you will see, a change is proposed in this area for the coming year. Whatever method of overhead absorption is used, any under or over absorption is transferred to the profit and loss account at the end of each quarter.

Personnel

The personnel involved in the simulation are as follows:

Production manager	Jim Stubbs
General manager	Patrick McGrath

In the simulation you will begin by dealing with certain transactions in the month of March 1998, and you will then be involved in forecasting outcomes for the company's financial year ending 31 March 1999. Finally, you will use your results to account for transactions in July 1998. Note that for many of the tasks you will need to prepare rough workings; you should use the paper provided for this purpose on Page 206 of the answer booklet.

TASKS TO BE COMPLETED

Part 1: Transactions in March 1998

1   Refer to the invoices and materials requisitions on Pages 180 - 184. Using this information you are required to complete the stores ledger accounts on Pages 193 and 194 of the answer booklet for the month of March 1998. You are reminded that the company uses the FIFO method. You may assume that suppliers raise invoices on the same day as goods are delivered.

2   You are required to prepare a memo for the general manager, Patrick McGrath, drawing attention to any unusual matters concerning stock levels of the items dealt with in task 1 above. Use the blank memo form on Page 195 of the answer booklet and date your memo 3 April 1998.

3   Timesheets for two employees of Polycot Ltd are shown on Pages 196 and 197 of the answer booklet. These employees work on production of duvet covers. Using the information contained in the internal policy document on Page 185 of this booklet, you are required to analyse their wages for the week ending 6 March 1998, as follows:

   •   Complete the total column in each timesheet.

   •   Check for discrepancies and make any necessary adjustments.

   •   Calculate the bonus earned by each employee on each day and in total for the week, and enter the appropriate amounts on the timesheets.

   •   Complete the analysis at the bottom of each timesheet.

   •   Enter the appropriate figures on the cost ledger data entry sheet on Page 198 of the answer booklet.

4   Prepare a memo to the production manager, Jim Stubbs, outlining any discrepancies in the wages data for these two employees for the week and requesting assistance in resolving your queries. Use the blank memo form on Page 199 of the answer booklet and date your memo 10 March 1998.

Part 2: Overhead absorption for 1998/99

5   The company at present absorbs all production overheads as a percentage of direct labour costs. The company is considering a revision in this policy for the accounting year 1998/99. Under the proposed new policy, a machine hour rate would be used in the cutting department, and direct labour hour rates in the finishing and packing departments. You are required to write a memo to the production manager, Jim Stubbs, explaining why this proposal is appropriate. Use the blank memo form on Page 200 of the answer booklet and date your memo 10 March 1998.

6   Refer to the information given on Page 186. Using this information, you are required to calculate 1998/99 overhead absorption rates for each production department: cutting (machine hour rate), finishing (direct labour hour rate) and packing (direct labour hour rate). Use the analysis sheet on Page 201 of the answer booklet.

7   Refer to the memo on Page 187. You are required to use the information in this memo to perform the following tasks:

(a) Write a memo to the production manager, Jim Stubbs, concerning the query on the wages for the temporary employee. Explain precisely and clearly what information you would need to be able to fully analyse and classify the hours worked by the employee and the wages paid. Use the blank memo form on Page 202 of the answer booklet and date your memo 6 July 1998.

For the remainder of this task, you are required to ignore the pending query concerning the temporary employee.

(b) Using the overhead absorption rate that you calculated in task 6 and the information contained in the labour hours analysis, calculate the production overhead absorbed in the packing department during the quarter ending 30 June 1998. Insert your result in the working sheet on Page 203 of the answer booklet.

(c) Using the information on the costs charged to cost centre code C300, determine the total actual production overhead cost for the packing department for the quarter ending 30 June 1998. Insert your result in the working sheet on Page 203 of the answer booklet.

(d) Determine the amount to be transferred to the profit and loss account for the quarter ending 30 June 1998, in respect of under or over absorbed production overheads for the packing department. Indicate clearly whether the overheads are under or over absorbed for the quarter.

Part 3: Standard costs and variances, July 1998

8   Refer to the information on Page 188. Using this information you are required to complete the standard cost card on Page 204 of the answer booklet. Note that you may need to refer to the following information: your completed stores ledger accounts on Pages 193 and 194 of the answer booklet; the direct labour hour rates on Page 185; and the overhead absorption rates that you calculated in task 6.

9   Refer to the memo on Page 189. You are required to prepare a memo, addressed to the general manager, Patrick McGrath, analysing all of the variances arising during the week ended 8 July 1998 in the cutting department and suggesting possible reasons for the main variances. You should date your report 13 July 1998. Use the memo form on Page 205 of the answer booklet.

Note. In addition to the information referred to above, you will also need to refer to the overhead absorption rates that you calculated in task 6 and the standard cost card that you prepared in task 8.

SALES INVOICE

Kenilworth Limited

VAT registration: 291 8753 42

12 Luton Road, Mapleton, Bedfordshire LU4 8EN

Telephone: 01582 622411

Date/tax point: 2 March 1998

Invoice to:

Invoice number: 2078

Polycot Limited

17 Hightown Road

Your order: 3901

Branston BN4 3EW

Item description	Quantity	Unit price £	Trade discount @ 30% £	Net price £	Total £
Plastic poppers (100 in each box)	100 boxes	91.00	27.30	63.70	6,370.00

Total	6,370.00
VAT @ 17.5%	1,114.75
Total due	7,484.75

Terms: net 30 days

SALES INVOICE

Baxter Limited

VAT registration: 215 8761 34

39 Langdale Avenue, Bisham MW3 9TY

Telephone: 01693 77612

Date/tax point: 6 March 1998

Invoice to:

Polycot Limited

Invoice number: 7123

17 Hightown Road

Branston BN4 3EW

Your order: 3889

Item description	Quantity £	Unit price £	Trade discount @ 30% £	Net price £	Total £
Cotton - 50 metre rolls	90	124.00	37.20	86.80	7,812.00

Total	7,812.00
VAT @ 17.5%	1,367.10
Total due	9,179.10

Terms: net 30 days

SALES INVOICE

Kenilworth Limited

VAT registration: 291 8753 42

12 Luton Road, Mapleton, Bedfordshire LU4 8EN

Telephone: 01582 622411

Date/tax point: 9 March 1998

Invoice to:

Polycot Limited

Invoice number: 2115

17 Hightown Road

Branston BN4 3EW

Your order: 3912

Item description	Quantity £	Unit price £	Trade discount @ 30% £	Net price £	Total £
Plastic poppers (100 in each box)	100 boxes	91.00	27.60	64.40	6,440.00

Total	6,440.00
VAT @ 17.5%	1,127.00
Total due	7,567.00

Terms: net 30 days

SALES INVOICE

Hartston Limited

VAT registration: 214 5143 28

55 Parlour Street, Jamestown, FE6 8UR

Telephone: 01225 67124

Date/tax point: 12 March 1998

Invoice to:

Polycot Limited

Invoice number: 34415

17 Hightown Road

Branston BN4 3EW

Your order: 3932

Item description	Quantity £	Unit price £	Trade discount @ 30% £	Net price £	Total £
Plastic poppers (100 in each box)	100 boxes	95.00	28.50	66.50	6,650.00

Total	6,650.00
VAT @ 17.5%	1,163.75
Total due	7,813.75

Terms: net 30 days

181

SALES INVOICE					

Baxter Limited

VAT registration: 215 8761 34

39 Langdale Avenue, Bisham MW3 9TY

Telephone: 01693 77612

Date/tax point: 12 March 1998

Invoice to:

Polycot Limited

Invoice number: 7249

17 Hightown Road

Branston BN4 3EW

Your order: 3917

Item description	Quantity £	Unit price £	Trade discount @ 30% £	Net price £	Total £
Cotton - 50 metre rolls	90	126.00	37.80	88.20	7,938.00
Total					7,938.00
VAT @ 17.5%					1,389.15
Total due					9,327.15
Terms: net 30 days					

MATERIALS REQUISITION

DATE 6 March 1998   NUMBER   944

DEPARTMENT   Finishing

QUANTITY	CODE	DESCRIPTION
90	PP29	Plastic poppers

SIGNATURE   Jim Stubbs

MATERIALS REQUISITION

DATE 10 March 1998   NUMBER   948

DEPARTMENT   Cutting

QUANTITY	CODE	DESCRIPTION
50	C733	Cotton, 50 metre rolls

SIGNATURE   Jim Stubbs

MATERIALS REQUISITION

DATE 18 March 1998   NUMBER   959

DEPARTMENT   Cutting

QUANTITY	CODE	DESCRIPTION
40	C733	Cotton, 50 metre rolls

SIGNATURE   Jim Stubbs

BPP PUBLISHING

MATERIALS REQUISITION

DATE *20 March 1998*   NUMBER   *961*

DEPARTMENT   *Finishing*

QUANTITY	CODE	DESCRIPTION
110	*PP29*	*Plastic poppers*

SIGNATURE   *Jim Stubbs*

MATERIALS REQUISITION

DATE *30 March 1998*   NUMBER   *984*

DEPARTMENT   *Cutting*

QUANTITY	CODE	DESCRIPTION
30	*C733*	*Cotton, 50 metre rolls*

SIGNATURE   *Jim Stubbs*

INTERNAL POLICY DOCUMENT

Document no.   15
Subject: Wages
Issued: December 1997

Direct labour rates to be paid

Employee grade	£ per hour
1	4.00
2	3.00
3	2.50

The above rates are also payable for any hours spent on indirect work.

Direct employees work an eight hour day.

Overtime (any hours worked in excess of eight per day): employees are to be paid for one and a half hours for every hour of overtime that they work.

Employees will be paid a bonus of £0.15 for every duvet cover produced in excess of 60 in any single day. No in lieu bonuses are paid for idle time, training etc.

Employees are to be credited with eight hours for any full days when they are sick, on holiday, or engaged in training activities. Half or part days are credited on a pro rata basis. These hours are to be paid at the basic rate.

Analysis of wages

The following are to be treated as direct labour costs:

* Payment for hours spent on direct tasks
* The basic pay for overtime spent on direct tasks

The following are to be treated as indirect labour costs:

* Overtime premium payments
* Bonus payments
* Idle time payments
* Holiday pay, sick pay and training pay

Discrepancies on time sheets

The company wishes to facilitate the prompt payment of wages and early reporting of labour costs to management. Employees will initially be paid for the total number of hours shown at the bottom of their time sheet, plus appropriate bonuses and overtime premiums.

Any discrepancies on time sheets are to be temporarily adjusted within direct labour hours, pending the outcome of enquiries.

BPP
PUBLISHING

Production overheads for the year to 31 March 1999

Polycot Ltd rents its production premises. The rent and rates for the year to 31 March 1999 will amount to £79,500.

Catering facilities for production staff are limited to a number of vending machines dispensing drinks and snacks. The rent for these machines during the year ending 31 March 1999 will be £100 per month.

Machinery and equipment owned by Polycot is subject to a maintenance contract covering preventive and urgent maintenance, parts, labour and call out charges. For the year to 31 March 1999 the maintenance company will charge £25,250 in respect of the machinery in the cutting department, £5,600 in respect of machinery in the finishing department, £11,000 in respect of machinery in the packing department and £4,000 in respect of machinery in the stores department. Depreciation on all machinery will total £13,490.

The production manager's salary will be £21,000 for the year; he divides his time about equally between the three production departments. The storekeeper's salary will be £14,000.

Other production overheads for the year are estimated at £40,000. The general manager has suggested that this should be divided evenly across the four departments.

The following data is also available.

	Cutting	Finishing	Packing	Stores
Floor area (sq metres)	1,900	2,650	1,900	1,125
Number of employees	20	68	40	3
Cost of machinery	£74,125	£16,625	£32,300	£11,850
Direct labour hours	5,125	129,750	67,500	
Machine hours	30,750	28,350	10,750	
Number of materials requisitions	21,175	17,675	14,100	

MEMO

To: Lesley Hunt
From: Patrick McGrath, General Manager
Date: 3 July 1998
Subject: Overhead absorption, quarter ending 30 June 1998

Your colleague in the accounts department had almost completed the task of calculating the production overheads under or over absorbed for the last quarter. Unfortunately she was not able to complete the task before leaving for her summer holiday. She has asked me to pass on the following information, and assures me that you will know what to do in order to complete the calculations.

Thanks for your help.

Information attached to the memo:

Amounts charged to cost centre code C300 - Packing department: quarter ending 30 June 1998

Cost centre code	Expenditure code	Amount charged £
C300	E200	8,020
C300	E210	855
C300	E300	48,345
C300	E310	4,045
C300	E410	10,800
C300	E500	800

Labour hours analysis - quarter ending 30 June 1998

	Cutting department hours	Finishing department hours	Packing department hours
Direct labour hours	1,200	38,800	18,300
Indirect labour hours	890	1,250	1,830
Total labour hours	2,090	40,050	20,130

Note. The above tables do not include a payment that I still have to enquire about, as follows.

• Wages paid to temporary employee for 320 hours worked during the quarter ending 30 June 1998: £1,920.

Standard costs for 1998/99

The general manager, Patrick McGrath, has informed you of the following decisions relating to standard costs for double duvet covers for the year ending 31 March 1999.

Cotton prices
Assume a 5 per cent increase over the highest price paid in March 1998. (Refer back to the relevant stores ledger card for this information.)

Plastic poppers
Assume a price of £67 per box of 100.

Thread
Assume a price of £14.20 per 10,000 metres.

Packing cartons
Assume a price of £0.25 per box, each box being large enough for 6 double covers.

Direct labour
Assume a 5 per cent increase over current rates for all grades.

MEMO

To: Lesley Hunt
From: Patrick McGrath
Date: 12 July 1998
Subject: Standard cost report for double duvet covers in Cutting department

I have collated some of the data you will need for the standard cost report for week ended 8 July - see below.

Please could you let me have an analysis of all the cost variances that you can calculate from this, with explanations of any significant ones. I'd be grateful if you could let me have this by close of business tomorrow.

Cost data for week ended 8 July 1998 - double duvet covers in Cutting department

Output
Budgeted double covers produced in the week = 1,900; actual double covers produced in the week = 1,760.

Materials
Cotton used = 11,350 metres, costing £21,565.

Direct labour
Cutting department = 90 hours of Grade 1 labour, costing £402.

Machine hours
Cutting department = 560 machine hours

Overhead
Production overhead charged to Cutting department = £1,650.

SAMPLE SIMULATION

Recording Cost Information

ANSWER BOOKLET

Task 1

STORES LEDGER ACCOUNT

Material description: *Plastic poppers, boxes of 100*

Code no: *PP29*

Maximum quantity:	*180*
Minimum quantity:	*62*
Reorder level:	*95*
Reorder quantity:	*100*

Date	Receipts			Issues			Stock balance		
	Quantity	Price per box £	Total £	Quantity	Price per box £	Total £	Quantity	Price per box £	Total £
1 March							*75*	*62.50*	*4,687.50*

BPP PUBLISHING

STORES LEDGER ACCOUNT

Material description: *Cotton, 50m rolls*

Code no: *C733*

Maximum quantity: 175
Minimum quantity: 55
Reorder level: 75
Reorder quantity: 90

Date	Receipts			Issues			Stock balance		
	Quantity	Price per box £	Total £	Quantity	Price per box £	Total £	Quantity	Price per box £	Total £
1 March							65	85.50	5,557.50

Task 2

MEMO

To:

From:

Date:

Subject:

BPP PUBLISHING

Task 3

TIMESHEET

Week ending   *6 March 1998*

Employee name   *Amy Harding*   **Employee number**   *2173*

Department   *Finishing*   **Employee grade**   *2*

Activity	Monday	Tuesday	Wednes-day	Thursday	Friday	Total
	Hours	Hours	Hours	Hours	Hours	Hours
Machining	7	10	4		4	
Holiday			4	8		
Waiting for work	1					
Training					4	
Total hours payable for day	8	10	8	8	8	
Number of covers produced	65	72	30	0	32	

Bonus payable @ £0.15 per cover above 60 per day

Signed   *Amy Harding*   **Manager**   *Jim Stubbs*

- -

Analysis for week	Hours	Rate per hour £	Wages cost £
Direct wages			
Indirect wages			
Basic hours			
Overtime premium			
Bonus			
	_____		_____
	_____		_____

Task 3, continued

TIMESHEET

Week ending   *6 March 1998*

Employee name   *Jane Amber*   **Employee number**   *2487*

Department   *Cutting*   **Employee grade**   *1*

Activity	Monday	Tuesday	Wednes-day	Thursday	Friday	Total
	Hours	Hours	Hours	Hours	Hours	Hours
Cutting	*10*	*6*	*6*		*8*	
Waiting for work		*3*	*2*			
Sick				*8*		
Training					*2*	
Total hours payable for day	*10*	*8*	*8*	*8*	*10*	
Number of covers produced	*70*	*51*	*62*	*0*	*62*	

Bonus payable @ £0.15 per cover above 60 per day

Signed   *Jane Amber*   **Manager**   *Jim Stubbs*

Analysis for week	Hours	Rate per hour £	Wages cost £
Direct wages			
Indirect wages			
Basic hours			
Overtime premium			
Bonus			
	_____		_____
	_____		_____

Task 3, continued

COST LEDGER DATA ENTRY SHEET

Week ending

Debit accounts

Cost centre code	Expenditure code	Amount to be debited £
C100	E300	
C200	E300	
C300	E300	
C400	E300	
C100	E310	
C200	E310	
C300	E310	
C400	E310	

Check total: total wages for the two employees

Task 4

MEMO

To:

From:

Date:

Subject:

BPP PUBLISHING

Task 5

MEMO

To:

From:

Date:

Subject:

Task 6

OVERHEAD ANALYSIS SHEET: 1998/99						
Overhead expense: primary apportionments and allocations	Basis of allocation/ apportionment	Total £	Cutting dept £	Finishing dept £	Packing dept £	Stores £
Total of primary allocations						
Re-apportion stores						
Total production cost centre overhead						
Machine hours						
Direct labour hours						
Overhead absorption rate for 1998/99						

BPP
PUBLISHING

Task 7a

MEMO

To:

From:

Date:

Subject:

Task 7b, c, d

Working sheet for calculation of overhead under/over absorbed

Packing department, quarter ending 30 June 1998

7(b) Production overhead absorbed   £ _____

7(c) Actual production overhead incurred   £ _____

7(d) Production overhead under or over absorbed, to be
transferred to profit and loss account   £ _____

Task 8

STANDARD COST CARD 1998/99

Product: Box of 6 double duvet covers
Product code no: 00214

Description	Material code no/direct labour grade	Quantity	Std price £ per metre/ hour etc	Total £
Direct materials				
Cotton fabric	CT33	38.2 metres		
Plastic poppers	PP29	60		
Polyester thread	TP72	22 metres		
Packing - cardboard box	PB03	1 box		
Other materials	Various	-	-	0.81
Subtotal, direct materials			(A)	
Direct labour				
Cutting	Grade 1	0.35 hours		
Finishing	Grade 1	4.10 hours		
Packing	Grade 3	0.50 hours		
Subtotal, direct labour			(B)	
Production overhead				
Cutting department		1.80 machine hours		
Finishing department		4.10 labour hours		
Packing department		0.50 labour hours		
Subtotal, production overhead			(C)	
Total standard production cost			(A + B + C)	

Task 9

MEMO

To:
From:
Date:
Subject:

Workings

Answers to Practice Devolved Assessment 1: Country Custom Kitchens

ANSWERS TO PRACTICE DEVOLVED ASSESSMENT 1: COUNTRY CUSTOM KITCHENS

Tutorial note. This is not a difficult assignment, but you could go hopelessly wrong if you don't keep your head and approach it in a methodical manner. It is vital that you study the cost accountant's note carefully before you start. Then see that you understand how the stock list is arranged and what the mass of figures mean.

Answer

(a)

STORES LEDGER ACCOUNT

Material: Supanut M4   Maximum Quantity: _____

Code: A1050   Minimum Quantity: _____

Date	Receipts				Issues				Stock		
	G.R.N. No.	Quantity	Unit Price £	Amount £	Stores Req. No.	Quantity	Unit Price £	Amount £	Quantity	Unit Price £	Amount £
Sept X3	b/f								7	0.27	1.89
6	24671	10	0.27	2.70					17	0.27	4.59

STORES LEDGER ACCOUNT

Material: Washer 30mm   Maximum Quantity: _____

Code: A2040   Minimum Quantity: _____

Date	Receipts				Issues				Stock		
	G.R.N. No.	Quantity	Unit Price £	Amount £	Stores Req. No.	Quantity	Unit Price £	Amount £	Quantity	Unit Price £	Amount £
Sept X3	b/f								99	0.37	36.63
6					0914	15	0.37	5.55	84	0.37	31.08

STORES LEDGER ACCOUNT

Material: Roundhead screws 30mm   Maximum Quantity: ....

Code: A4040   Minimum Quantity: ....

Date	Receipts				Issues				Stock		
	G.R.N. No.	Quantity	Unit Price £	Amount £	Stores Req. No.	Quantity	Unit Price £	Amount £	Quantity	Unit Price £	Amount £
Sept X3 6	b/f				0915	10	0.28	2.80	13 3	0.28 0.28	3.64 0.84

STORES LEDGER ACCOUNT

Material: Roundhead screws 40mm   Maximum Quantity: ....

Code: A4060   Minimum Quantity: ....

Date	Receipts				Issues				Stock		
	G.R.N. No.	Quantity	Unit Price £	Amount £	Stores Req. No.	Quantity	Unit Price £	Amount £	Quantity	Unit Price £	Amount £
Sept X3 6	b/f 24673	30	0.20	6.00					10 40	0.20 0.20	2.00 8.00

STORES LEDGER ACCOUNT

Material: Brass screw 45mm   Maximum Quantity: ....

Code: A6070   Minimum Quantity: ....

Date	Receipts				Issues				Stock		
	G.R.N. No.	Quantity	Unit Price £	Amount £	Stores Req. No.	Quantity	Unit Price £	Amount £	Quantity	Unit Price £	Amount £
Sept X3 6	b/f 24639	50	0.56	28.00					29 79	0.56 0.56	16.24 44.24

STORES LEDGER ACCOUNT

Material: Panel pins 35mm   Maximum Quantity: ....

Code: B2050   Minimum Quantity: ....

Date	Receipts				Issues				Stock		
	G.R.N. No.	Quantity	Unit Price £	Amount £	Stores Req. No.	Quantity	Unit Price £	Amount £	Quantity	Unit Price £	Amount £
Sept X3 6	b/f				0919	2	1.99	3.98	30 28	1.99 1.99	59.70 55.72

STORES LEDGER ACCOUNT

Material: ...... Butt Hinge-chromium 40mm ...... Maximum Quantity: ....

Code: ...... D0060 ...... Minimum Quantity: ....

Date	Receipts				Issues				Stock		
	G.R.N. No.	Quantity	Unit Price £	Amount £	Stores Req. No.	Quantity	Unit Price £	Amount £	Quantity	Unit Price £	Amount £
Sept X3 6	b/f				0916	10	3.14	31.40	11 1	3.14 3.14	34.54 3.14

STORES LEDGER ACCOUNT

Material: ...... Drawer runners ...... Maximum Quantity: ....

Code: ...... F2010 ...... Minimum Quantity: ....

Date	Receipts				Issues				Stock		
	G.R.N. No.	Quantity	Unit Price £	Amount £	Stores Req. No.	Quantity	Unit Price £	Amount £	Quantity	Unit Price £	Amount £
Sept X3 6	b/f				0917	8	2.49	19.92	122 114	2.49 2.49	303.78 283.86

STORES LEDGER ACCOUNT

Material: Lift off butt hinge - chromium 75mm   Maximum Quantity: ....

Code: D2080   Minimum Quantity: ....

Date	Receipts				Issues				Stock		
	G.R.N. No.	Quantity	Unit Price £	Amount £	Stores Req. No.	Quantity	Unit Price £	Amount £	Quantity	Unit Price £	Amount £
Sept X3	b/f								4	8.17	32.68
6	24638	10	8.17	81.70					14	8.17	114.38

STORES LEDGER ACCOUNT

Material: External Angle 19mm   Maximum Quantity: ....

Code: F2040   Minimum Quantity: ....

Date	Receipts				Issues				Stock		
	G.R.N. No.	Quantity	Unit Price £	Amount £	Stores Req. No.	Quantity	Unit Price £	Amount £	Quantity	Unit Price £	Amount £
Sept X3	b/f								113	1.99	224.87
6	24672	200	1.99	398.00					313	1.99	622.87

STORES LEDGER ACCOUNT

Material: Decorative Crowns   Maximum Quantity: ....

Code: F3070   Minimum Quantity: ....

Date	Receipts				Issues				Stock		
	G.R.N. No.	Quantity	Unit Price £	Amount £	Stores Req. No.	Quantity	Unit Price £	Amount £	Quantity	Unit Price £	Amount £
Sept X3 6	b/f 24670	10	4.79	47.90					7 17	4.79 4.79	33.53 81.43

STORES LEDGER ACCOUNT

Material: Magnetic catch (white)   Maximum Quantity: ....

Code: F5010   Minimum Quantity: ....

Date	Receipts				Issues				Stock		
	G.R.N. No.	Quantity	Unit Price £	Amount £	Stores Req. No.	Quantity	Unit Price £	Amount £	Quantity	Unit Price £	Amount £
Sept X3 6	b/f				0918	20	3.99	79.80	45 25	3.99 3.99	179.55 99.75

BPP PUBLISHING

Part B: Devolved Assessments

MATERIALS REQUISITION

Material Required for: *K309/93*   No. 0914
(Job or Overhead Account)

Date: *6.9.X3*

Quantity	Description	Code No.	Factor/ Unit	Rate	£	Notes
15	Steel washer 30mm	A2040	Pack 20	0.37	5.55	—

Foreman: *Vlad Kopeii*   Costed and Coded: AAT

MATERIALS REQUISITION

Material Required for: *K309/93*   No. 0915
(Job or Overhead Account)

Date: *6.9.X3*

Quantity	Description	Code No.	Factor/ Unit	Rate	£	Notes
10	R/Hd 30mm	A4040	Pack 10	0.28	2.80	Reorder 10429

Foreman: *Vlad Kopeii*   Costed and Coded: AAT

MATERIALS REQUISITION

Material Required for: *K312/93*   No. 0916
(Job or Overhead Account)

Date: *6.9.X3*

Quantity	Description	Code No.	Factor/ Unit	Rate	£	Notes
10 chrome	Butt hinges 40mm	D0060	5 pairs	3.14	31.40	Reorder 10433

Foreman: *VK*   Costed and Coded: AAT

MATERIALS REQUISITION

Material Required for: *K313/93*
(Job or Overhead Account)

No. 0917

Date: *6.9.X3*

Quantity	Description	Code No.	Factor/ Unit	Rate	£	Notes
8	Drawer runners	F2010	1 pair	2.49	19.92	/

Foreman: *VK* Costed and Coded: AAT

MATERIALS REQUISITION

Material Required for: *K313/93*
(Job or Overhead Account)

No. 0918

Date: *6.9.X3*

Quantity	Description	Code No.	Factor/ Unit	Rate	£	Notes
20	White magnetic catches	F5010	1	3.99	79.80	/

Foreman: *Vlad* Costed and Coded: AAT

MATERIALS REQUISITION

Material Required for: *K309/93*
(Job or Overhead Account)

No. 0919

Date: *6.9.X3*

Quantity	Description	Code No.	Factor/ Unit	Rate	£	Notes
2	Panel pins 35mm	B2050	0.5kg	1.99	3.98	/

Foreman: *VK* Costed and Coded: AAT

> **Tutorial note.** Materials requisitions 0915 and 0916 relate to stock lines which are reordered (see purchase requisitions 10429 and 10433). Appropriate details (such as reorder number) are therefore included on the materials requisitions.

(b) (i) **Tutorial note.** As per the cost accountant's note, the reorder quantity is roughly one month's stock (to the nearest five) based on last year's figures.

PURCHASE REQUISITION   Req. No.   10427

Department ___Costing___   Date   6.9.X3
Suggested Supplier:
        28043112

                    Requested by: AAT

Quantity	Code	Description	Estimated Cost	
			Unit	£
60	A2060	Brass washer 15mm	0.40	24.00

Authorised signature:

PURCHASE REQUISITION   Req. No.   10428

Department ___Costing___   Date   6.9.X3
Suggested Supplier:
        27561247

                    Requested by: AAT

Quantity	Code	Description	Estimated Cost	
			Unit	£
50	A2070	Brass washer 20mm	0.45	22.50

Authorised signature:

PURCHASE REQUISITION   Req. No.   10429

Department ___Costing___   Date   6.9.X3
Suggested Supplier:
            28043112
                                    Requested by: AAT

Quantity	Code	Description	Estimated Cost	
			Unit	£
60	A4040	Roundhead screws 30mm	0.28	16.80

Authorised signature:

PURCHASE REQUISITION   Req. No.   10430

Department ___Costing___   Date   6.9.X3
Suggested Supplier:
            23344248
                                    Requested by: AAT

Quantity	Code	Description	Estimated Cost	
			Unit	£
65	A4080	Roundhead screws 50mm	0.28	18.20

Authorised signature:

PURCHASE REQUISITION   Req. No.   10431

Department ___Costing___

Suggested Supplier:
      21840027

Date   6.9.X3

Requested by: AAT

Quantity	Code	Description	Estimated Cost	
			Unit	£
15	D2030	Lift-off Butt hinge 65mm	4.58	68.70

Authorised signature:

PURCHASE REQUISITION   Req. No.   10432

Department ___Costing___

Suggested Supplier:
      28043112

Date   6.9.X3

Requested by: AAT

Quantity	Code	Description	Estimated Cost	
			Unit	£
1	F1070	Steel tube 25mm	7.07	7.07

Authorised signature:

```
                    PURCHASE  REQUISITION   Req.  No.    10433

Department ___Costing___                        Date    6.9.X3
Suggested  Supplier:
            23344248
                                        Requested  by:   AAT
```

Quantity	Code	Description	Estimated Cost	
			Unit	£
10	DO060	Chromium Butt hinges 40mm	3.14	31.40

Authorised signature:

Tutorial note. Requisition number 10433 relates to a stock line which was not highlighted as an exception on the stock report but the raising of materials requisition no 0916 means that there is only one item left in stock. Further hinges therefore need to be ordered.

(ii)   A copy of the purchase requisition (or better, the actual order) could be attached to the stock card until the order is received.

(c)

QUERY SCHEDULE

Stock item	Query	Action
D0020	Nil stock but very slow-moving Not re-ordered	
D0030	As above	
D1020	As above	
D1030	As above	
F3080	As above	
F3090	As above	
F1020	As above, but appears to be identical to item F1030. Is this an error? (Current balance of F1030- 14 units, which is adequate on basis of previous period.)	
B0010		
B0020		
B1010	These items are all very slow moving	
B1020		
B1080		
B1090		
D0010	Very slow moving stock but 15 units delivered on 3 September. Is this OK?	
-	Invoice from Chippies Veneers- not a screw or fixing. Pass to whoever is dealing with panels stock.	
-	Invoice 671493 from Higgins (27314295) includes 60 'Screw Eyes' at £0.90. Stock list shows that 60 × 19mm screw eyes were on order at £0.76. 25mm screw eyes standard cost is £0.89. Has Higgins sent the wrong type? Have they been properly posted?	
-	Are first few items in A section missing?	
-	What are stock items C and E?	
-	GRNs 24640 - 24669 missing, or 24670 and following used out of sequence.	

Tutorial note. Your query schedule may have contained many more points, especially if you had difficulty in finding any of the stock items or knowing how to post the entries. Our solutions to other parts of the assignment should clear up such queries: the important thing in practice is that you note down any matters that you are not sure about so that somebody can help you to resolve the problems later.

(d)

Journal No. _ _ _ _ _ _ _

Date	Customer/ supplier code	Invoice	Order No.	Stock code	Quantity	Net £	VAT (17.5%) £
03.09.X3	25567840	1187	2072	F0040	50	84 00	14 70
03.09.X3	25567840	1187	2072	F6080	4	8 28	1 45
03.09.X3	23344248	87/61743	2178	A3020	15	3 60	0 63
03.09.X3	23344248	87/61743	2178	A4070	75	18 00	3 15
03.09.X3	23344248	87/61743	2178	A4090	40	14 00	2 45
03.09.X3	23344248	87/61743	2178	A3050	80	28 00	4 90
03.09.X3	23344248	87/61743	2178	B0030	10	27 20	4 76
03.09.X3	23344248	87/61743	2178	F5050	40	198 00	34 65
03.09.X3	23344248	87/61743	2178	D2070	10	62 00	10 85
03.09.X3	27314295	671493	2694	B2070	20	43 00	7 53
03.09.X3	27314295	671493	2694	B2050	30	59 70	10 45
03.09.X3	27314295	671493	2694	F3040	125	187 50	32 81
03.09.X3	27314295	671493	2694	F4080	60	54 00	9 45
03.09.X3	27314295	671493	2694	D3030	35	34 65	6 06
03.09.X3	27314295	671493	2694	B1070	60	179 40	31 40
03.09.X3	27314295	671493	2694	F1030	10	24 70	4 32

(e)

Stock code	Quantity	Actual price £	Standard price £	Difference £	Variance £
F0040	50	1.68	1.59	0.09	4.50
F6080	4	2.07	1.99	0.08	0.32
A3020	15	0.24	0.24	-	-
A4070	75	0.24	0.24	-	-
A4090	40	0.35	0.32	0.03	1.20
A3050	80	0.35	0.33	0.02	1.60
B0030	10	2.72	2.69	0.03	0.30
F5050	40	4.95	4.79	0.16	6.40
D2070	10	6.20	6.07	0.13	1.30
B2070	20	2.15	2.15	-	-
B2050	30	1.99	1.99	-	-
F3040	125	1.50	1.50	-	-
F4080	60	0.90	0.76	0.14	8.40
D3030	35	0.99	0.99	-	-
B1070	60	2.99	2.99	-	-
F1030	10	2.47	2.47	-	-
					24.02

(**Tutorial note**. Item F4080 is queried in (c) above. In practice the total variance could be calculated by comparing the total of materials purchases with the total value of receipts into stock, but this information is not available for this assignment.)

(f)　See (c)

(g)

MRN	Job K309/93	Job K312/93	Job K313/93
0914	5.55		
0915	2.80		
0916		31.40	
0917			19.92
0918			79.80
0919	3.98		
	12.33	31.40	99.72

Answers to Practice Devolved Assessment 2: Stancourt Motors

ANSWERS TO PRACTICE DEVOLVED ASSESSMENT 2: STANCOURT MOTORS

JOB COST CARD												Job No.		B638	
Customer Mr Robert				Customer's Order No.								Vehicle make		TR7	
Job Description Replace damaged vent												Vehicle reg. no.		RGY 367W	
Estimate Ref. 2574				Invoice No.											
Quoted price £159.56				Invoice price £159.56								Date to collect		14.6.X3	

Material						Labour								Overheads			
Date	Req. No.	Qty.	Price	Cost		Date	Emp-loyee	Cost Ctre	Hrs.	Rate	Bonus	Cost		Hrs	OAR	Cost	
				£	p							£	p			£	p
13.6	36867	1	72.56	72	56	13.6	016	B	3.75	6.00	1.50	24	00	3.75	2.50	9	38
13.6	36868	1	3.03	3	03												
13.6	36894	3	3.99	11	97												
Total C/F				87	56	Total C/F						24	00	Total C/F		9	38

Expenses						Job Cost Summary		Actual		Estimate	
			Cost					£	p	£	p
Date	Ref.	Description	£	p							
						Direct Materials B/F		87	56	87	56
						Direct Expenses B/F		-	-		
						Direct Labour B/F		24	00	72	00
						Direct Cost		111	56		
						Overheads B/F		9	38		
								120	94		
						Admin overhead (add 10%)		12	09		
						= Total Cost		133	03	159	56
						Invoice Price		159	56		
Total C/F						Job Profit/Loss		26	53		

Comments

Job Cost Card Completed by ....

JOB COST CARD

		Job No.	A926

Customer	Mrs Crankley	Customer's Order No.		Vehicle make	Metro
Job Description	Distributor/Commutator			Vehicle reg. no.	A987 0PB
Estimate Ref. 2583/2589		Invoice No.			
Quoted price	£249.96	Invoice price	£255.41	Date to collect	14.6.X3

Material

Date	Req. No.	Qty.	Price	Cost £	Cost p
12.6	36807	1	7.18	7	18
12.6	36808	2	1.24	2	48
12.6	36821	1	88.40	88	40
12.6	36830	1	61.90	61	90

Total C/F				159	96

Labour

Date	Employee	Cost Ctre	Hrs.	Rate	Bonus	Cost £	Cost p
11.6	012	A	2	7.00		14	00
12.6	007	A	3.17	6.00		19	02

Total C/F						33	02

Overheads

Hrs	OAR	Cost £	Cost p
5.17	3.50	18	10

Total C/F		18	10

Expenses

Date	Ref.	Description	Cost £	Cost p

Total C/F				

Job Cost Summary

	Actual £	Actual p	Estimate £	Estimate p
Direct Materials B/F	159	96	159	96
Direct Expenses B/F Direct Labour B/F	33	02	90	00
Direct Cost Overheads B/F	192 18	98 10		
Admin overhead (add 10%)	211 21	08 11		
= Total Cost	232	19	249	96
Invoice Price	255	41		
Job Profit/Loss	23	22		

Comments

Job Cost Card Completed by ....

BPP PUBLISHING

JOB COST CARD

	Job No.	A930

Customer	Mr F Jenkins	Customer's Order No.		Vehicle make	Sierra
Job Description	Overhaul clutch & readjust brakes			Vehicle reg. no.	F109 HEV
Estimate Ref. 2594		Invoice No.			
Quoted price	£186.50	Invoice price	£194.32	Date to collect	14.6.X3

Material / Labour / Overheads

Date	Req. No.	Qty.	Price	Cost £	Cost p	Date	Emp-loyee	Cost Ctre	Hrs.	Rate	Bonus	Cost £	Cost p	Hrs	OAR	Cost £	Cost p
13.6	36861	1	45.20	45	20	13.6	009	A	2.45	6.50	3.58	19	51	2.45	3.50	8	58
13.6	36874	1	6.95	6	95												
13.6	36885	1	8.75	8	75												
13.6	36902	2	35.80	71	60												
		Total C/F		132	50				Total C/F			19	51	Total C/F		8	58

Expenses

Date	Ref.	Description	Cost £	Cost p
		Total C/F		

Job Cost Summary

	Actual £	Actual p	Estimate £	Estimate p
Direct Materials B/F	132	50	132	50
Direct Expenses B/F				
Direct Labour B/F	19	51	54	00
Direct Cost	152	01		
Overheads B/F	8	58		
Admin overhead (add 10%)	160	59		
	16	06		
= Total Cost	176	65	186	50
Invoice Price	194	32		
Job Profit/Loss	17	67		

Comments

Job Cost Card Completed by ....

JOB COST CARD

		Job No.	B641

Customer Mr J White   Customer's Order No.
Vehicle make Peugeot 205 GTE

Job Description Repair damage to offside front door

Estimate Ref. 2599   Invoice No.
Vehicle reg. no. G 614 SOX

Quoted price £338.68   Invoice price £355.05
Date to collect 14.6.X3

Material						Labour								Overheads			
				Cost								Cost				Cost	
Date	Req. No.	Qty.	Price	£	p	Date	Emp-loyee	Cost Ctre	Hrs.	Rate	Bonus	£	p	Hrs	OAR	£	p
12.6	36815	1	75.49	75	49	12.6	018	B	1.98	6.50	-	12	87	7.9	2.50	19	75
12.6	36816	1	33.19	33	19	13.6	018	B	5.92	6.50	-	38	48				
12.6	36842	5	6.01	30	05						13.65	13	65				
13.6	36881	5	3.99	19	95												
Total C/F				158	68	Total C/F						65	00	Total C/F		19	75

Expenses						Job Cost Summary	Actual		Estimate	
			Cost				£	p	£	p
Date	Ref.	Description	£	p		Direct Materials B/F	158	68	158	68
						Direct Expenses B/F	50	00		
						Direct Labour B/F	65	00	180	00
12.6	/	N. Jolley Panel-beating	50	-		Direct Cost	273	68		
						Overheads B/F	19	75		
							293	43		
						Admin overhead (add 10%)	29	34		
						= Total Cost	322	77	338	68
						Invoice Price	355	05		
Total C/F			50	-		Job Profit/Loss	32	28		

Comments

Job Cost Card Completed by ....

Answers to Practice Devolved Assessment 3: Strange (Properties) Ltd

ANSWERS TO PRACTICE DEVOLVED ASSESSMENT 3: STRANGE (PROPERTIES) LTD

Tutorial note. Your approach to this assignment is more important than arriving at an answer that agrees with ours to the penny, so don't be disheartened if your figures are a bit different.

Answer

Task 1

(a)

No.	Date	Description	Code	Total
	November			
1	1	Caretaker - Clerk Court	800/999	76.50
2	1	Sankey Builders, Sheen - Ketley	800/556	600.00
3	1	Post Office	400/001	3.61
4	1	Sundries - Gibbs Ho	800/105	52.80
5	1	Perivale Glass Co.	800/101	317.00
6	3	Motor Mower - Burgess Ct	800/555	263.00
7	4	Electricity - Ketley cl. (to 28.10)	800/556	355.84
8	4	Water rates - Q.C.	800/225	92.00
9	4	Inst. Ch. Surveyors	500/003	515.00
10	5	Hanwell DIY	800/501	69.10
11	8	Law Society (subs)	500/003	742.00
12	8	Inland Revenue	100/003	8,437.50
13	8	Gas - Mallow Cl. (to 5.11)	800/605	81.50
14	9	Cleaners - Seymour M.	800/189	390.01
15	10	Power drill - Laine Ho.	800/501	48.90
16	13	Perivale Roofing	800/101	4,720.00
17	17	Dentons (sols) - re Ashby M.	800/301	723.37
18	17	Coomer PL - Caretaker	800/450	226.00
19	17	Kew Electrics	800/250	590.72
20	17	Southern Electricity (to 15.11)	300/001	1,110.43
21	17	Wyrde St Computer Supplies	400/004	33.00
22	18	Brentford Advertiser	700/001	66.50
23	19	Rentokil - Jones Co.	800/274	856.06
24	21	Neville Ho - Skip Hire (17.10-19.11)	800/376	32.40
25	21	Hanwell Timber	800/501	236.00
26	21	Sankeys - Ketley Clo.	800/556	1,800.00
27	24	Heston Service Station	200/001	8.81
28	24	Bldgs Ins - Oakwood B	800/750	408.00
29	24	Plumbing Supplies (Petersham) Ltd - Kings	800/325	426.80
30	24	Wages - Grasmere Caretaker	800/110	279.19
31	25	BACS - Salaries	100/002	12,187.89
32	25	British Gas - Tilbury	800/890	35.60

No.	Date	Description	Code	Total
	November			
1	26	Hall hire - Wyndham AGM	800/430	32.50
2	26	Sainsbury's	100/010	19.50
3	28	Caretaker - Rodway Ho.	800/001	438.00
4	28	Property Management News	700/001	18.40
5	28	British Telecom	400/002	475.70
6	28	Co. House - Wyndham	800/430	32.00
7	28	Concrete repairs - Tilbury T	800/890	2,250.00
8	28	Acton Skip Hire - 1.11-30.11 - Davison	800/801	32.40
9	28	Brentford Cleaning	300/005	183.00
10	28	Wages - Davison Clo. C/T	800/801	66.10
11	28	Wages - Endymion Pl. C/T	800/675	64.50
12	28	Middlesex Gazette	700/001	22.22
13	28	Ben Smith Stationery Supplies	400/003	178.57
14	28	Electricity - Hennigan Ho. (to 25.11)	800/429	568.35
15	28	Guardian Royal Exchange - Pub. Liab	500/002	970.00
16	28	Guardian Royal Exchange - Richm. Bldgs	800/525	1,630.00
17	28	E Strange Exps	900/001	88.90
18	28	Non-Dom Rates DD	300/003	271.25
19	28	GRE - Jaguar	200/002	1,315.50
20	28	Bank - charges	600/002	70.90
21	28	Bank - interest	600/001	949.93
22				
23				
24				
25				
26				
27				
28				
29				
30				
31				
32				

(b)   *Client charges - November 20X2*

		Direct expenses £	*Fixed fee* £	*Share of overheads* £	*Total* £
301	Ashby Mansions	723.37	1,500.00	922.29	3,145.66
555	Burgess Court	263.00	1,500.00	922.29	2,685.29
999	Clerk Court	76.50	1,500.00	922.29	2,498.79
350	Clift Flats	-	1,500.00	922.29	2,422.29
620	Clifton Gardens	-	1,500.00	922.29	2,422.29
450	Coomer Place	226.00	1,500.00	922.29	2,648.29
801	Davison Close	98.50	1,500.00	922.29	2,520.79
261	De Beauvoir Buildings	-	1,500.00	922.29	2,422.29
675	Endymion Place	64.50	1,500.00	922.29	2,486.79
401	Frampton Court	-	1,500.00	922.29	2,422.29
105	Gibbs House	52.80	1,500.00	922.29	2,475.09
101	Glebe Gardens	5,037.00	1,500.00	922.29	7,459.29
110	Grasmere Mansion	279.19	1,500.00	922.29	2,701.48
429	Hennigan House	568.35	1,500.00	922.29	2,990.64
274	Jones Court	856.06	1,500.00	922.29	3,278.35
556	Ketley Close	2,755.84	1,500.00	922.29	5,178.13
325	Kings Buildings	426.80	1,500.00	922.29	2,849.09
501	Laine House	354.00	1,500.00	922.29	2,776.29
250	Loudwater Place	590.72	1,500.00	922.29	3,013.01
100	Matkins Gardens	-	1,500.00	922.29	2,422.29
605	Mallow Close	81.50	1,500.00	922.29	2,503.79
376	Neville House	32.40	1,500.00	922.29	2,454.69
750	Oakwood Buildings	408.00	1,500.00	922.29	2,830.29
225	Queen's Court	92.00	1,500.00	922.29	2,514.29
914	Rhodes Close	-	1,500.00	922.29	2,422.29
001	Rodway House	438.00	1,500.00	922.29	2,860.29
189	Seymour Manor	390.01	1,500.00	922.29	2,812.30
890	Tilbury Tower	2,285.60	1,500.00	922.29	4,707.89
525	Undercliff Gardens	1,630.00	1,500.00	922.29	4,052.29
430	Wyndham Rise	64.50	1,500.00	922.29	2,486.79
		17,794.64	45,000.00	27,668.70	90,463.34

(**Tutorial note.** You should calculate to the penny because clients are invoiced in pounds and pence.)

Task 2

Basis	*Legal* £	*Surveying* £	*Accounts* £	*Total* £
Employees (W1)	91,264	127,770	54,759	273,793
Floor area (W2)	5,367	10,735	5,367	21,469
Directors (W3)	4,316	4,315	-	8,631
Equal split (W4)	10,313	10,313	10,313	30,939
	111,260	153,133	70,439	334,832

Workings

1   The following expenses should be split on the basis of number of employees.

	£
Wages and salaries	272,255
Staff welfare	1,538
	273,793

	Legal	*Surveying*	*Accounts*
Split 5:7:3	£91,264	£127,770	£54,759

(**Tutorial note**. The split should really be done on the basis of the actual payroll analysis. The above is likely to be a reasonable approximation however.)

2   The following expenses can be split on the basis of floor area, which can be seen (by simply looking at the floor plan) to be 1:2:1.

		£
Business rates		3,524
Heat and light		4,775
Buildings depreciation		4,000
Office equipment depreciation		1,752
Repairs and maintenance		834
Cleaning		6,584
		21,469

	Legal	Surveying	Accounts
1:2:1	£5,367	£10,735	£5,367

3   Some of the expenses are incurred solely by the two Strange brothers.

	£
Motor vehicle depreciation	7,500
Subscriptions	1,131
	8,631

These are split 50:50 between the legal and surveying departments.

4   The remaining expenses do not have any obvious basis and it is therefore most appropriate to split these equally between the three departments.

	£
Insurance (see note)	7,600
Telecommunications	1,908
Printing, postage and stationery	3,975
Audit and accountancy	4,500
Bank charges	862
Advertising	1,973
Interest	10,121
	30,939

(**Tutorial note**. It would be better to split the insurance figure between buildings, motor vehicles, public liability, employer's liability and so on, and then apportion it on more appropriate bases, but you have not been given enough information to do this.)

You can now calculate a rate per labour hour, as it were, for the absorption of overheads.

Legal department

$$\frac{£111,260}{1,709} = £65.10 \text{ per hour (say £65)}$$

(Note that the overhead is split over hours spent on existing clients only.)

Surveying department

$$\frac{£153,133}{1,749} = £87.55 \text{ per hour (say £88)}$$

Accounts department

Evenly split over 30 clients:

$$\frac{£70,439}{30} = £2,347.97 \text{ per client per annum (say £2,348)}$$

This allows a schedule to be drawn up as follows.

	Legal		Surveying		Accounts	Total
	Hours	£	Hours	£	£	£
Ashby Mansions	43	2,795	20	1,760	2,348	6,903
Burgess Court	71	4,615	82	7,216	2,348	14,179
Clerk Court	62	4,030	34	2,992	2,348	9,370
Clift Flats	15	975	113	9,944	2,348	13,267
Clifton Gardens	25	1,625	64	5,632	2,348	9,605
Coomer Place	60	3,900	80	7,040	2,348	13,288
Davison Close	49	3,185	52	4,576	2,348	10,109
De Beauvoir Buildings	74	4,810	38	3,344	2,348	10,502
Endymion Place	33	2,145	51	4,488	2,348	8,981
Frampton Court	16	1,040	73	6,424	2,348	9,812
Gibbs House	51	3,315	21	1,848	2,348	7,511
Glebe Gardens	81	5,265	60	5,280	2,348	12,893
Grasmere Mansion	84	5,460	30	2,640	2,348	10,448
Hennigan House	76	4,940	94	8,272	2,348	15,560
Jones Court	61	3,965	66	5,808	2,348	12,121
Ketley Close	49	3,185	36	3,168	2,348	8,701
Kings Buildings	63	4,095	57	5,016	2,348	11,459
Laine House	45	2,925	77	6,776	2,348	12,049
Loudwater Place	73	4,745	48	4,224	2,348	11,317
Matkins Gardens	76	4,940	35	3,080	2,348	10,368
Mallow Close	57	3,705	61	5,368	2,348	11,421
Neville House	24	1,560	92	8,096	2,348	12,004
Oakwood Buildings	117	7,605	40	3,520	2,348	13,473
Queen's Court	51	3,315	18	1,584	2,348	7,247
Rhodes Close	82	5,330	97	8,536	2,348	16,214
Rodway House	64	4,160	88	7,744	2,348	14,252
Seymour Manor	23	1,495	64	5,632	2,348	9,475
Tilbury Tower	29	1,885	59	5,192	2,348	9,425
Undercliff Gardens	80	5,200	71	6,248	2,348	13,796
Wyndham Rise	75	4,875	28	2,464	2,348	9,687
	1,709	111,085	1,749	153,912	70,440	335,437
Total overhead		111,260		153,133	70,439	334,832
(Under-)/over-absorbed		(175)		779	1	605

Notes

1   The (under)/over absorption is due to rounding, for ease of calculation.

2   The amount *actually* charged to each client for the year to 30 September can be estimated as follows, allowing for ex-clients.

$$= \frac{(\text{Administrative expenses} + \text{interest})}{\text{Number of clients}}$$

$$= \frac{£(324,711+10,121)}{32.5(\text{say})}$$

$$= £10,303$$

Task 3

MEMO

To: Edward Strange
From: John Vernon
Subject: Charges to clients and related matters
Date: 2 December 20X2

CHARGES TO CLIENTS

I refer to your memo of 1 December about charges to clients. I have given this matter some thought and done some calculations. The results are attached. Below I set out my observations and recommendations.

(a)   Part of the problem is due to the way in which we invoice clients. At present our invoices show only a lump sum charge, whereas in fact the charge is made up of three elements, as follows.

    (i)   Expenditure incurred on behalf of the property in question on things like building work, bills for communal electricity, caretaker's wages and so on. The property would have to pay these amounts whether or not we were involved, and they are bound to fluctuate from month to month, just as ordinary household expenses do. For example, for the month just past such expenses range from nil for six clients to £5,037 for Glebe Gardens.

    (ii)   Our fixed fee of £1,500 per month charged to all clients.

    (iii)   A proportion of our own expenses, divided up equally between clients (see below).

(b)   Point (iii) above is problematic because our own actual expenditure varies from month to month and so, therefore, does the amount charged to clients. For example in November 20X2 we paid a number of bills that we receive on a quarterly basis (like telephone and electricity bills) and some that only occur annually (like your motor insurance premium). However, all of this expenditure will be charged to our clients in one month.

(c)   You may remember that I mentioned to you that I had had some less than complimentary letters from some clients and ex-clients about the fairness of our charges. At present clients for whom we do relatively little work pay the same level of charges as clients for whom we do a great deal of work, and some of them seem to be aware of this and to resent it.

My recommendations are as follows.

(a)   We should show the following separately on our invoices.

    (i)   Amounts paid out on behalf of clients
    (ii)   The charge made for our services (the amount on which VAT is calculated)

(b)   Developing (ii), we should charge our clients a standard monthly amount that incorporates the following.

    (i)   Our fixed fee
    (ii)   An administration charge based on the amount of work that we expect to do for each client

The calculation of the administration charge will require us to estimate in advance both how much our total administrative expenses will be for the coming year and how much work we expect to do for each client. Pending further discussion, however, I have calculated some figures based on the accounts for the year to 30 September 20X2 and upon your own timesheets for that period and those of your brother.

From the 20X1/X2 accounts we can work out that the amount actually charged to each client to recover administrative expenses and interest paid was about £10,303 for the year. Using the fairer basis that I propose this figure would have ranged from £6,903 for Ashby Mansions to £16,214 for Rhodes Close (neither of these figures includes the fixed fee).

I propose that we adopt the fairer basis, assuming that our costs and expenditure in terms of time can be reasonably accurately forecast. Obviously we need to consider how this change would be presented to clients.

OTHER MATTERS

Since you raised the question I might add that what I am proposing is a form of absorption costing: our costs are being 'absorbed' into the amounts charged to clients on the basis of time spent. A feature of absorption costing is 'under- or over-absorbed overhead', which arises because we use estimates to calculate our absorption rates and an adjustment has to be made once the actual figures are known. For example on the schedules attached you can see the effects of rounding some of the figures to make the calculations easier to do and to understand.

Incidentally, I think you may have been misled about the nature of *process costing*. This is a method of costing that is used mainly in manufacturing businesses where products are made by means of a 'continuous process'. In other words there are always some products that have just been started, some that are completely finished and others that are only partly finished. An organisation like this has to use process costing methods to determine what the cost of their products is at a particular point in time. This is not really appropriate for Strange (Properties) Ltd's business.

Answers to Practice Devolved Assessment 4: Stately Hotels plc

ANSWERS TO PRACTICE DEVOLVED ASSESSMENT 4: STATELY HOTELS PLC

SECTION 1

Task 1

			£
(a)	8,580 soap packs should have cost (× £1.20)		10,296
	but did cost (W1)		10,614
	Soap pack price variance		318(A)

(b)	8,400 rooms should have used	8,400 packs
	but did use	8,580 packs
	Usage variance in packs	180 packs (A)
	× standard cost per pack	× £1.20
	Soap pack usage variance in £	£216 (A)

		£
(c)	2,550 hours should have cost (× £3.60)	9,180
	but did cost (W2)	8,700
	Cleaning labour rate variance	480 (F)

(d)	8,400 rooms should have taken (× ¼ hr)	2,100 hrs
	but did take	2,550 hrs
	Efficiency variance in hours	450 hrs (A)
	× standard rate per hour	× £3.60
	Cleaning labour efficiency variance	£1,620 (A)

Workings

1		£
	6,530 × £1.20	7,836
	920 × £1.30	1,196
	1,130 × £1.40	1,582
		10,614

2	1,850 × £3.00	5,550
	700 × £4.50	3,150
		8,700

Task 2

The **adverse price variance** could be due to an increase in soap pack prices above the price used in the standard or careless purchasing by the purchasing department.

The **adverse usage variance** may be due to a delivery of low quality soap packs (perhaps packs have items missing or the packaging is ripped) or there may be theft or pilferage of the packs from stores.

The **favourable rate variance** has probably arisen because the proportion of weekday hours worked was greater than anticipated.

The **adverse efficiency variance** may be due to a level of idle time greater than that allowed for in the standard, perhaps because guests had not vacated rooms and cleaners were unable to enter bedrooms.

SECTION 2

Task 1

(a)

		£	
26,500 kg should have cost (× £23)		609,500	
but did cost		662,500	
Material price variance		53,000	(A)

(b)

	£		
9,000 units should have used (×3kg)	27,000	kg	
but did use	26,500	kg	
Material usage variance in kg	500	kg	(F)
× standard cost per kg	£23		
Material usage variance in £	£11,500		(F)

(c)

	£	
18,400 hours should have cost (× £20)	368,000	
but did cost	349,600	
Labour rate variance	18,400	(F)

(d)

	£		
9,000 units should have taken (× 2 hrs)	18,000	hrs	
but did take	18,400	hrs	
Efficiency variance in hours	400	hrs	(A)
× standard rate per hour	£20		
Labour efficiency variance in £	£8,000		(A)

Task 2

STATEMENT OF COST VARIANCES (WEEK 8, QUARTER 4, 20X0)

	(F) £	(A) £	£
Material price		53,000	
Material usage	11,500		
Labour rate	18,400		
Labour efficiency		8,000	
Fixed overhead expenditure		300,000	
Fixed overhead capacity		96,000	
Fixed overhead efficiency		24,000	
	29,900	481,000	451,100 (A)

SECTION 3

Task 1

(a)

	£
Budgeted fixed overhead expenditure (12,000 × £67)	804,000
Actual fixed overhead expenditure	824,000
Fixed overhead expenditure variance	20,000 (A)

(b)

	£
Budgeted production at standard rate (12,000 × £67)	804,000
Actual production at standard rate (11,200 × £67)	750,400
Fixed overhead volume variance	53,600 (A)

(c)

Budgeted hours (12,000 × 10)	120,000 hrs
Actual hours	110,000 hrs
Fixed overhead capacity variance in hours	10,000 hrs (A)
× standard rate per hour	× £6.70
Fixed overhead capacity variance	£67,000 (A)

(d)

11,200 units should have taken (× 10 hrs)	112,000 hrs
Actual time taken	110,000 hrs
Fixed overhead efficiency variance in hours	2,000 hrs (F)
× standard rate per hour	× £6.70
Fixed overhead efficiency variance	£13,400 (F)

Task 2

REPORT

To:	Production Director
From:	Assistant Management Accountant
Date:	14 December 20X0
Subject:	Performance of Division X - 4 weeks ended 1 December 20X0

Set out below is an analysis of the cost variances in Division X for the four-week period ended 1 December 20X0.

Variances	(F) £	(A) £	£
Material price		94,000	
Material usage		88,000	
Labour rate		11,000	
Labour efficiency	16,800		
Fixed overhead expenditure		20,000	
Fixed overhead capacity		67,000	
Fixed overhead efficiency	13,400		
	30,200	280,000	249,800 (A)

Task 3

MEMORANDUM

To: Production Director
From: Assistant Management Accountant
Date: 14 December 20X0
Subject: Fixed overhead variances

This memorandum provides information on fixed overhead variances. In particular it covers the meaning of the various fixed overhead variances and the ways in which such variances might arise.

The meaning of fixed overhead variances

Whereas labour and material total variances show the effect on costs and hence profit of the difference between what the actual production volume should have cost and what it did cost (in terms of labour or material), if an organisation uses standard absorption costing (as we do), the fixed overhead total variance is the difference between actual fixed overhead expenditure and the fixed overhead absorbed (the under- or over-absorbed overhead).

The total under- or over- absorption is made up of the fixed overhead expenditure variance and the fixed overhead volume variance. The volume variance shows that part of the under- or over-absorbed overhead which is due to any difference between budgeted production volume and actual production volume.

The volume variance can be further broken down into an efficiency variance and a capacity variance. The capacity variance shows how much of the under- or over-absorbed overhead is due to working the labour force or plant more or less than planned whereas the efficiency variance shows the effect of the efficiency of the labour force or plant.

The volume variance and its two subdivisions, the efficiency variance and the capacity variance, measure the extent of under or over absorption due to production volume being different to that planned. Material usage and labour efficiency variances, on the other hand, measure the effect of usage being different from that expected for the actual volume achieved.

Reasons why fixed overhead variances might arise

Under- or over-absorbed fixed overhead is inevitable because the predetermined overhead absorption rates are based on forecasts about expenditure and the level of activity. These forecasts are always likely to be at least a bit inaccurate - the business may forecast both the budgeted expenditure and the volume of activity wrongly.

- Fixed overhead expenditure variance arises when the actual fixed production overhead is different to the budgeted figure. In our case the actual fixed overhead expenditure was £20,000 more than was forecast for the four weeks ended 1 December. This could have arisen, for example, if rent had been increased and this had not been taken account of when making the forecast.

- The fixed overhead volume variance is broken down into efficiency and capacity variances, which have arisen as follows:

    The staff worked at a more efficient rate than standard to produce the 11,200 Alphas that were made in the period. They took 2,000 hours less than would have been expected for that level of production, possibly because of increased speed as newer workers became more accustomed to the processes, or less idle time as a result of fewer mechanical breakdowns. This has led to a favourable efficiency variance.

Regardless of the level of efficiency and the number of Alphas produced, the overall total number of hours worked was 10,000 less than budgeted. This could arise through a strike, early closing, or some other incident that led to actual hours worked being less than expected. This created an adverse capacity variance, as fixed overhead was under-absorbed.

ANSWERS TO TRIAL RUN
DEVOLVED ASSESSMENT 1

DO NOT TURN THIS PAGE UNTIL YOU HAVE
COMPLETED TRIAL RUN DEVOLVED ASSESSMENT 1

STANDARD COST CARD

PRODUCT Vegetarian Chilli

DESCRIPTION	QUANTITY	COST PER KG/HOUR/ETC	EXTENSION	TOTAL
Materials		£	£	£
Rice	0.125 kg	1.37	0.17	
Lentils	0.0625 kg	0.88	0.06	
Tomatoes	0.167 kg	0.74	0.12	
Mushrooms etc	0.167 kg	1.22	0.20	
Kidney beans	0.167 kg	0.92	0.15	
Chillis	0.025 kg	1.82	0.05	
Cartons	1	0.05	0.05	
SUB-TOTAL				0.80
Labour				
Production	0.025 hr	4.00	0.10	
SUB-TOTAL				0.10
Direct cost				0.90
Variable o/h	0.01 litre	1.75		0.02
Standard variable cost				0.92
Fixed o/h	0.025 hr	10.11		0.25
Standard cost of sale				1.17

STANDARD COST CARD

PRODUCT ...Vegetarian Curry...

DESCRIPTION	QUANTITY	COST PER KG/HOUR/ETC	EXTENSION	TOTAL
Materials		£	£	£
Rice	0.125 kg	1.37	0.17	
Coconut oil	0.167 litre	1.21	0.20	
Spices	0.005 kg	9.66	0.05	
Vegetables	0.167 kg	1.12	0.19	
Cartons	1	0.05	0.05	
SUB-TOTAL				0.66
Labour				
Production	0.033 hr	4.00	0.13	
SUB-TOTAL				0.13
Direct cost				0.79
Variable o/h	0.01 litre	1.75		0.02
Standard variable cost				0.81
Fixed o/h	0.033 hr	8.45		0.28
Standard cost of sale				1.09

(a) (i)   Standard quantities are taken from Delia Craddock's letter.

(ii) The standard price per kilogram, hour and so on are calculated as follows, using the price list and compliment slip from Exotic Foods Emporium.

Item	Quantity	Price at 1.3.X3 £	5% £	Mid-year value £	Cost per unit £
Rice	100 kg	130.00	6.50	136.50	1.37
Lentils	100 kg	84.00	4.20	88.20	0.88
Tomatoes	50 kg	35.00	1.75	36.75	0.74
Mushrooms etc	50 kg	58.00	2.90	60.90	1.22
Kidney beans	50 kg	44.00	2.20	46.20	0.92
Chillis	50 kg	86.50	4.33	90.83	1.82
Coconut oil	100 ltrs	115.00	5.75	120.75	1.21
Spices	10 kg	92.00	4.60	96.60	9.66
Vegetables	50 kg	53.50	2.68	56.18	1.12

BPP
PUBLISHING

   (iii) Carton price from quotation.

(b) (i) Standard times are taken from the business plan.

  (ii) The standard rates per hour are taken from the offers of employment. The business plan recommended that overtime should not be a regular occurrence. Overtime premium should therefore not be included in the direct cost of the two products.

(c) Details of the oil are taken from the telephone message. The current price is used as the standard since the message indicates that the price is unlikely to change in the future.

(d) (i) We need to concern ourselves with the following overheads.

	Annual overhead budget £	
Salary of supervisor	16,000	(from offer of employment)
Salary of storekeeper	12,000	(from offer of employment)
Cleaners (2 hrs × £10 × 5 days × 52 weeks)	5,200	(from contract)
Heat and light	5,000	(from Business Plan)
Overtime (100 hrs × £2.00)	200	(from Business Plan)
	38,400	

Although, in reality, there would be many more overheads such as those associated with the accounting function and so on, we calculate an overhead absorption rate based on the limited information we are given.

		Overhead	Basis of apportionment	Production dept Chilli £	Production dept Curry £	Stores £
(ii)	Directly allocate	Storekeeper's salary				12,000
(iii)	Apportion	Supervisor's salary	Direct labour hours (W1)	7,500	8,500	-
		Cleaners	Area (W2)	2,600	1,560	1,040
		Heat and light	Area (W2)	2,500	1,500	1,000
		Overtime	Hours (W3)	100	100	-
				12,700	11,660	14,040
(iv)	Apportion service dept o'hds		Number of material requisitions (W4)	7,020	7,020	(14,040)
				19,720	18,680	-

Workings

		Chilli	Curry
1	Budgeted production	78,000	66,300
	Time per portion	1.5 mins	2 mins
	Budgeted total time	117,000 mins	132,600 mins
		= 1,950 hrs	= 2,210 hrs
	Proportion of salary	1,950/(1,950 + 2,210)	2,210/(1,950 + 2,210)

2 Chilli department covers $25 \times 50 = 1,250 \text{ m}^2$

   Curry department covers $25 \times 30 = 750 \text{ m}^2$

   Stores covers $25 \times 20 = 500 \text{ m}^2$

   Cleaning costs and heat and light should therefore be shared in the ratio 5:3:2.

3   We are given no indication as to the amount of overtime each product will require. The overhead should therefore be split equally between the two production departments.

4   Ingredients for both products were taken on each of the five occasions items were taken from stores. One simple method of splitting the stores cost is therefore equally between the two production departments. If Ali and Fred had taken ingredients for just one of the products on one or more occasions then a different apportionment of the overhead would be necessary.

(v)   The overhead absorption rate is to be based on direct labour hours according to the business plan. We calculated the budgeted labour hours in each production department in Working 1.

$$\text{Overhead absorption rate - chilli} = \frac{£19,720}{1,950 \text{ hrs}} = £10.11 \text{ per direct labour hour}$$

$$\text{Overhead absorption rate - curry} = \frac{£18,680}{2,210 \text{ hrs}} = £8.45 \text{ per direct labour hour}$$

(e)
5,000 portions should take (× 2 mins)	166.67 hrs
But did take (from clock cards)	170.50 hrs
Efficiency variance, (in hours)	3.83 hrs (A)
× standard rate per hour	× £4
Efficiency variance, (in £)	£15.32 (A)

(f)

STORES LEDGER ACCOUNT

Material: Lentils   Maximum Quantity:

Code: Minimum Quantity:

Date	Receipts				Issues				Stock		
	G.R.N. No.	Quantity	Unit Price £	Amount £	Stores Req. No.	Quantity	Unit Price £	Amount £	Quantity	Unit Price £	Amount £
1/3		4	84.00	336.00					4	84.00	336.00
1/3						1	84.00	84.00	3	84.00	252.00
8/3						1	84.00	84.00	2	84.00	168.00
15/3						1	84.00	84.00	1	84.00	84.00
22/3						1	84.00	84.00	-		

STORES LEDGER ACCOUNT

Material: ...Vegetables...   Maximum Quantity: ....

Code: ....   Minimum Quantity: ....

Date	Receipts				Issues				Stock		
	G.R.N. No.	Quantity	Unit Price £	Amount £	Stores Req. No.	Quantity	Unit Price £	Amount £	Quantity	Unit Price £	Amount £
1/3		10	53.50	535.00					10	53.50	535.00
1/3					1		53.50	53.50	9	53.50	481.50
3/3					2		53.50	160.50	6	53.50	321.00
8/3					5		53.50	267.50	1	53.50	53.50
12/3		11	53.75	591.25					12	53.73	644.75
15/3					4		53.73	214.92	8	53.73	429.84
22/3					5		53.73	268.65	3	53.73	161.19

(g)   Vegetables

These are used in the curry, of which 5,000 portions were made.

5,000 portions should have used ($\times$ 0.167 kg)	835 kgs
but did use (drums from stores ledger account $\times$ 50 kgs)	900 kgs
Usage variance (in kgs)	65 kgs (A)
$\times$ standard cost per kg (from standard cost card)	$\times$ £1.12
Usage variance (in £)	£72.80 (A)

(h)   During the four-week period the following overheads were absorbed (production volume $\times$ OAR per hour $\times$ time to produce one portion).

		£
Chilli department:	$5,300 \times £10.11 \times {}^{1.5}/_{60} =$	1,339.58
Curry department:	$5,000 \times £8.45 \times {}^{2}/_{60} =$	1,408.33
		2,747.91

Overheads incurred are as follows.

		£
Supervisor:	£16,000 $\times$ ${}^{1}/_{13}$	1,230.77
Storekeeper:	£12,000 $\times$ ${}^{1}/_{13}$	923.08
Cleaners:	$2 \times £10 \times 5 \times 4$	400.00
Heat and light:	per invoice	629.62
Overtime:	see working	43.50
		3,226.97

Overheads have been under absorbed by £(3,226.97 – 2,747.91) = £479.06

Working

Hours that should have been worked (normal hours) (2 men $\times$ 4 weeks $\times$ 40 hours)	320.00 hrs
Hours worked (see (b) (171.25 + 170.50))	341.75 hrs
Overtime, in hours	21.75 hrs
$\times$ overtime premium per hour	$\times$ £2
Overtime, in £	£43.50

Schedule of queries

	Query	*Action*
(a)	Why was the post-lunch entry on Wednesday 17 March handwritten on Fred's clock card?	Speak to supervisor and request he checks that Fred and Ali are adhering to time-keeping procedures.
(b)	How do I allocate the cost of the factory supervisor?	Speak to supervisor
(c)	Labour hours are highly erratic. How does this tie in with stores and supervisor?	Speak to managing director
(d)	Why does the second invoice from Exotic Foods not agree with what was delivered?	Telephone supplier
(e)	Why was the heat and light invoice much greater than anticipated?	Speak to supervisor
(f)	Why did Ali take so much longer than expected to produce the 5,300 portions of chilli?	Speak to supervisor
(g)	Some stocks need reordering	Check that they have been reordered

ANSWERS TO TRIAL RUN
DEVOLVED ASSESSMENT 2

Task 1

Tutorial note. Your standard cost card may look different to this but it should incorporate the same basic information.

```
                        STANDARD COST CARD

                    Shape         ....................
                    Taste/smell   ....................
                    Colour        ....................
                    Department    ....................

                                    Cost per
                        Quantity    input unit    Extension      Total
                         Kg/hr          £             £            £
Materials
White jenjam
Strawberry essence

Labour
Direct labour

Overheads
Total
```

Task 2

See task 6.

Task 3

Overhead	Department 1 £	Department 2 £	Maintenance and repairs £	Total £
Rent (W1)	4,666.667	6,000.000	1,333.333	12,000.000
Electricity (W2)	1,642.667	2,112.000	469.333	4,224.000
Salary			13,000.000	13,000.000
Depreciation (W3)	1,500.000	1,500.000	-	3,000.000
c/f to task 4	7,809.334	9,612.000	14,802.666	32,224.000

BPP PUBLISHING

Task 4

	Department 1 £	Department 2 £	Maintenance and repairs £	Total £
b/f from task 3	7,809.334	9,612.000	14,802.666	32,224.000
Apportion service department o/hds (W4)	6,167.777	8,634.889	(14,802.666)	-
Total	13,977.111	18,246.889	-	32,224.000

Workings

1. Total rent for the year is £12,000 (per invoice).
    Basis of apportionment is floor area (see plan).

		M²
Floor area of department 1 = $(30 \times 15) - (10 \times 10)$	=	350
Floor area of department 2 = 15×30	=	450
Floor area of maintenance and repairs = 10×10	=	100
		900

		Share of overheads £
Department 1	$350/900 \times £12,000$	4,666.667
Department 2	$450/900 \times £12,000$	6,000.000
Maintenance and repairs	$100/900 \times £12,000$	1,333.333
Total		12,000.000

2. Total electricity for the year (per invoice) = $£352 \times 12 = £4,224$.
    Basis of apportionment is floor area.

		Share of overheads £
Department 1	$350/900 \times £4,224$	1,642.667
Department 2	$450/900 \times £4,224$	2,112.000
Maintenance and repairs	$100/900 \times £4,224$	469.333
Total		4,224.000

3. Depreciation per machine = cost (per invoice)/5 years (per telephone message)
    = £7,500/5 = £1,500 per machine per annum

4. | Hours worked by service department for department 1 | = | 17.5 hours (per log book) |
    |---|---|---|
    | Hours worked by service department for department 2 | = | 24.5 hours (per log book) |
    | Total hours | = | 42.0 hours |

	£
Department 1's share of overhead = $17.5/42 \times £14,802.666$ =	6,167.777
Department 2's share of overhead = $24.5/42 \times £14,802.666$ =	8,634.889
Total	14,802.666

Task 5

Overhead absorption rates

Department 1 = £13,977.111/(15,000 × 0.1 hr*) = £9.318 per direct labour hour

Department 2 = £18,246.889/(18,000 × 0.12 hr**) = £8.448 per direct labour hour

*   6/60 from summary product specification

**   7.2/60 from summary production specification

Task 6

Quantities of materials and labour are detailed in the report by the product design engineer. Costs of materials come from the compliment slips, price list and first invoice. Labour cost per hour is detailed in the personnel record card.

		STANDARD COST CARD		
	Shape	....Teddy.bear		
	Taste/smell	....Strawberry		
	Colour	....White....		
	Department	........1.........		
	Quantity Kg/hr	*Cost per input unit* £	*Extension* £	*Total* £
Materials				
Soft white jenjam	0.25	1.500	0.375	
Fruity strawberry essence	0.10	8.000	0.800	
				1.175
Labour				
Direct labour	0.10	6.500		0.650
Overheads	0.10	9.318		0.932
Total				2.757

Task 7

Overheads absorbed during May

	£	£
Department 1 (167.5* × £9.318)	1,560.765	
Department 2 (161* × £8.448)	1,360.128	
		2,920.893

*From scribbled note of hours

Overheads incurred during May

	£	£
Rent	1,000.000	
Electricity	352.000	
Salary (£13,000 ÷ 12)	1,083.333	
Depreciation (£3,000 ÷ 12)	250.000	
		2,685.333
Over-absorbed overhead		235.560

Overheads incurred during the period were the same as those upon which the absorption rate is based. The over-absorbed overhead is therefore due to hours worked being greater than anticipated. (Details of budgeted labour hours are contained in the product design engineer's report.)

		Hours
Department 1	Budgeted labour hours ((15,000 × 0.1)/12) =	125.0
	Actual labour hours =	167.5
		42.5
	Over-absorbed overhead = 42.5 × £9.318 =	£396.015

		Hours
Department 2	Budgeted labour hours ((18,000 × 0.12)/12) =	180
	Actual labour hours =	161
		19
	Under-absorbed overhead = 19 × £8.448 =	£160.512

Over-absorbed overhead = £(396.015 − 160.512) = £235.503

Due to rounding to three decimal places a difference of £0.057 has occurred.

Task 8

MEMORANDUM

To: Aunt Leanne
From: Louise Chandler
Date: 20.06.X8
Subject: *Control over labour and material*

Whilst preparing the monthly cost accounts for Leanne's Orthodontic Soothers Ltd, I noticed a lack of control over materials and labour. Although the company is still very small, you do intend to expand and therefore, in order to ensure that controls are in place both now (when staff are inexperienced and production methods untried) and in the future (when you have a much larger product range and hence more complex systems, more stock lines and more staff), the immediate introduction of a system of control is vital.

To assist you in this, I have set out in this memorandum the steps which you should consider taking to establish the necessary procedures.

(i)   *Recording of labour hours*

The manual recording of the hours worked by John and Julie on a scrappy piece of paper is inappropriate. I assume that you are either asking the two production workers how many hours they have worked or are watching their movements to ascertain the time they arrive at and leave the premises, neither of which can be guaranteed to produce accurate and complete information. Employees may not tell the truth about their hours of work or you may miss their arrival/departure time. Moreover, you may lose the piece of paper on which you are recording the hours.

   (1) *Attendance time*

The bare minimum record of employees' time is a simple attendance record showing days absent because of holiday, sickness or other reason. Such a system is suitable if John and Julie's time is taken up doing just one job and no further analysis is required. At the moment this is so but as the product range expands a more detailed recording system may be necessary. The next step up is to have some record of time of arrival, time of breaks and time of departure. The simplest form is a signing-in book but unless someone is watching constantly, this system is open to abuse. Many employers therefore use a time recording clock which stamps the time on a clock card inserted by an employee. More modern systems involve the use of a plastic card like a credit card which is swiped through a device which makes a computer record of the time of arrival and departure.

As John and Julie are paid on an hourly basis, one of the methods outlined above should ensure that they are paid for the hours they actually work.

   (2) *Job time*

The next step is to analyse the hours spent at work according to what was done during those hours. The method adopted depends upon the size of the organisation and the nature of the work. As Leanne's Orthodontic Soothers Ltd involves routine, repetitive work (especially at the moment when only two variants of the soother are being produced as two separate processes by two workers) it is sufficient to measure work by keeping a note of the number of units that pass through each department. This type of information can be obtained from the monthly production report and should be sufficient to provide you with labour utilisation information.

(ii) *Control over ordering and delivering stock*

At present there is no control over the ordering and subsequent delivery of stock. No record appears to be kept of what has been ordered, what has been delivered (and whether this matches what was ordered) and what is invoiced (and whether this matches what was delivered). To rectify this you should set up a system involving the use of purchase order forms and goods received notes.

(1) *Purchase order forms*

When stocks need reordering a purchase order form should be completed. It should contain the following details.

- Your company's name and address

- The date of the order

- The order reference

- The address and date(s) for delivery/collection

- Details of goods (quantity, code (if any), specification, unit costs and so on)

An order form should be sent even if goods are initially ordered by telephone, to confirm that the order is a legitimate one and to make sure that the supplier does not overlook it.

The purchase order is important because it provides a means by which you can later check that the goods received are the same as those ordered.

(2) *Goods received note (GRN)*

Once goods have been delivered they should be inspected as soon as possible and a GRN completed on the basis of a physical check of the goods, which involves counting the items received and seeing that they are not damaged. A copy of the GRN should be matched with the purchase order to make sure that the correct number and specification of items have been received. Any discrepancies should be taken up with the supplier. A copy of the GRN should also be matched to the invoice when it is received to ensure that you are paying for the goods you actually received.

(iii) *Control over stock movements*

At present you have no proper stock records to show stock movements (materials received, materials issued to production, materials transferred between the production departments and so on). There is therefore no control over these movements (stock may disappear from stores without trace, stock may arrive at the factory but never find its way into the store) and hence information about materials usage may not be accurate. The introduction of the following documents would greatly assist the control over materials.

Bin cards. These are kept with the actual stock and are updated whenever items are removed or added to provide an accurate record of the quantity in stock for each stores item.

Stores ledger accounts. Details from GRNs and materials requisition notes (see below) are used to update stores ledger accounts, which then provide a record of the quantity and value of each line of stock in the stores.

Materials requisition note. When a production department requires raw materials they will complete a materials requisition note.

Materials returned note. If the amount of materials required is overestimated the excess should be put back into stores accompanied by a materials returned note.

Materials transfer note. There may be occasions when materials already issued but not required for one job can be used for another job in progress. In this case there is no point returning the materials to stores. Instead a materials transfer note can be raised.

(iv) *Monthly stock report*

By introducing the aforementioned stock control documents, a monthly stock control report can be produced which will summarise the stock movements during the month and show unit cost and month-end stock values for each line of stock. A suggested format for the report, with data for May included for illustration purposes, is shown below.

By introducing the aforementioned stock control documents, a monthly stock control report can be produced which will summarise the stock movements during the month and show unit cost and month-end stock values for each line of stock. A suggested format for the report, with data for May included for illustration purposes, is shown below.

MONTHLY STOCK REPORT - MAY 20X8

Code	Description	Unit	Std Cost per unit £	Balance Beg month	In	Out	Balance Month end	Value £
J001	Jenjam - spring yellow	Kg	1.00	0	450	420	30	30
J002	Jenjam - pale blue	Kg	1.65	0	300	0	300	495
J003	Jenjam - mint green	Kg	2.10	0	300	50	250	525
J004	Jenjam - blush pink	Kg	1.40	0	250	0	250	350
J005	Jenjam - soft white	Kg	1.50	0	350	350	0	0
E001	Essence - warm milk chocolate	Kg	9.30	0	100	0	100	930
E002	Essence -fruity strawberry	Kg	8.00	0	100	100	0	0
E003	Essence - smooth vanilla	Kg	8.00	0	100	99	1	8
E004	Essence - tropical banana	Kg	10.50	0	100	0	100	1,050

I hope this information has been useful to your Aunt Leanne. If you want to know anything else give me a quick ring.

Task 9

Material usage variance - white jenjam

950 units should have used (× 0.25 kgs)	237.5 kgs
but did use (none left at month end)	350.0 kgs
Variance in kgs	112.5 kgs (A)
× standard cost per kg	× £1.50
	£168.75 (A)

Material usage variance - strawberry essence

950 units should have used (× 0.1 kgs)	95 kgs
but did use (none left at month end)	100 kgs
Variance in kgs	5 kgs (A)
× standard cost per kg	× £8.00
	£40.00 (A)

Labour efficiency variance

950 units should have taken (× 0.1 hrs)	95.0 hrs
but did take	167.5 hrs
Variance in hours	72.5 hrs (A)
× standard rate per hour	× £6.50
	£471.25 (A)

Overhead volume efficiency variance

Variance in hours	72.5 hrs (A)
× standard OAR per hour	× £9.318
	£675.555 (A)

Task 10

MEMORANDUM

To: Aunt Leanne
From: Louise
Date: 26 June 20X8
Subject: Variance analysis - May 20X8

I have been looking at how efficiently materials are being used in department 1 and how efficiently Julie is working using a technique called variance analysis. Basically, this involves comparing actual efficiency levels with expected or standard efficiency levels. The comparisons throw up differences known as variances.

All of the variances I calculated are adverse (which means that actual efficiency levels are worse than expected efficiency levels). This is probably due to the fact that the company has been operational for just a very short time.

Julie has been doing her job for just one month and so is unlikely to be able to meet pre-set efficiency standards (which should reflect average efficiency levels). Once she has built up the necessary experience, however, she is likely to become more efficient and the size of both the adverse labour efficiency variance and the adverse overhead volume efficiency variance should reduce and, hopefully, the variances will eventually become favourable (ie actual efficiency levels will be better than standard efficiency levels).

Material wastage is also likely to be problem at the beginning of production: the machine may have been set incorrectly, leading to wasted material or rejected units of finished product; the machine may have wasted materials when it broke down; Julie's inexperience may have led to material being used inefficiently; the raw material used may not have been up to the quality expected when the standard was set. All of these factors would result in an adverse materials usage variance.

There could, of course, be an interdependency between the labour efficiency and materials usage variances. Poor quality materials would produce an adverse material usage variance *and* would lead to an adverse labour efficiency variance as Julie struggles to produce acceptable output with unacceptable materials.

The overhead volume efficiency variance is dependent on the labour efficiency variance since overheads are absorbed on the basis of direct labour hours. Reasons for its occurrence are therefore the same as those for the occurrence of the labour efficiency variance.

You should review these usage and efficiency variances frequently so as to ensure that the variance trend moves from the adverse variances of May to smaller adverse variances and eventually to favourable variances once initial teething problems connected with the introduction of the process are resolved. If the variance trend fails to improve, management action will be necessary. Julie may need additional training if the labour efficiency variance does not improve. Another supplier of raw materials may have to be found if the material usage variance is due to poor quality materials. The machines may need to be adjusted so that standard units are produced and material is not wasted. An investigation of the variances should reveal their cause and allow you to initiate action to correct them.

If you need any further help or information, please let me know.

Schedule of queries

Query: Only 250 kgs of pink jenjam delivered on 1.5.X8

Action: Speak to Julie to check whether the additional 50 kgs have been delivered. Phone Perfect Plastic Ltd if they still haven't arrived. Ensure that 300 kgs are not paid for if only 250 kgs have been received.

Query: 50 kgs of green jenjam appears to have gone missing between the time 300 kgs were delivered and the time John wrote the memo.

Action: Speak to John and Julie to see whether they can throw any light on the situation. Reinforce the necessity of a stock control system with Aunt Leanne.

Query: Julie's hours fluctuate between six and eight hours a day. John's remain constant at seven hours a day. On the last day of the month Julie worked 14 hours.

Action: Check with John and Julie to ensure that Leanne has been recording their hours correctly. If so, establish why Julie's hours vary so much.

Query: Electricity is assumed to remain constant each month.

Action: Consider the reasonableness of this. Check plans to see whether production levels are likely to change dramatically and hence cause changes to the electricity cost.

Query: Darryl's work patterns in May are assumed to reflect future work patterns.

Action: Speak to Darryl to ascertain the reasonableness of this. Consider another method of apportioning the service department overheads if necessary.

Query: The machines appear to be breaking down on a regular basis.

Action: Ascertain whether it is possible to claim compensation from the manufacturers of the machines.

Query: Stock has been ordered which is not likely to be used for at least twelve months when additional varieties are finally produced.

Action: Speak to Leanne about setting up a suitable stock ordering system.

Query: Darryl appears to be idle for a large proportion of the time.

Action: Discuss with Leanne the possibility of either using contractors for repairs and maintenance or involving Darryl in new product development .

Task 1

STORES LEDGER ACCOUNT

Material description: *Plastic poppers, boxes of 100*

Code no: *PP29*

		Maximum quantity:	*180*
		Minimum quantity:	*62*
		Reorder level:	*95*
		Reorder quantity:	*100*

Date	Receipts			Issues			Stock balance		
	Quantity	Price per box £	Total £	Quantity	Price per box £	Total £	Quantity	Price per box £	Total £
1 March							*75*	*62.50*	*4,687.50*
2 March	*100*	*63.70*	*6,370.00*				*75*	*62.50*	*4,687.50*
							100	*63.70*	*6,370.00*
							175		*11,057.50*
6 March				*75*	*62.50*	*4,687.50*			
				15	*63.70*	*955.50*			
				90		*5,643.00*	*85*	*63.70*	*5,414.50*
9 March	*100*	*64.40*	*6,440.00*				*85*	*63.70*	*5,414.50*
							100	*64.40*	*6,440.00*
							185		*11,854.50*
12 March	*100*	*66.50*	*6,650.00*				*85*	*63.70*	*5,414.50*
							100	*64.40*	*6,440.00*
							100	*66.50*	*6,650.00*
							285		*18,504.50*
20 March				*85*	*63.70*	*5,414.50*	*75*	*64.40*	*4,830.00*
				25	*64.40*	*1,610.00*	*100*	*66.50*	*6,650.00*
				110		*7,024.50*	*175*		*11,480.00*

STORES LEDGER ACCOUNT

Material description: *Cotton, 50m rolls*

Code no: *C733*

Maximum quantity: 175
Minimum quantity: 55
Reorder level: 75
Reorder quantity: 90

Date	Receipts			Issues			Stock balance		
	Quantity	Price per roll £	Total £	Quantity	Price per roll £	Total £	Quantity	Price per roll £	Total £
1 March							65	85.50	5,557.50
6 March	90	86.80	7,812.00				65	85.50	5,557.50
							90	86.80	7,812.00
							155		13,369.50
10 March				50	85.50	4,275.00	15	85.50	1,282.50
							90	86.80	7,812.00
							105		9,094.50
12 March	90	88.20	7,938.00				15	85.50	1,282.50
							90	86.80	7,812.00
							90	88.20	7,938.00
							195		17,032.50
18 March				15	85.50	1,282.50	65	86.80	5,642.00
				25	86.80	2,170.00	90	88.20	7,938.00
				40		3,452.50	155		13,580.00
30 March				30	86.80	2,604.00	35	86.80	3,038.00
							90	88.20	7,938.00
							125		10,976.00

Task 2

MEMO

To: Patrick McGrath
From: Lesley Hunt
Date: 3 April 1998
Subject: Stock levels during March

During March the stock levels of both plastic poppers (PP29) and 50 metre cotton rolls exceeded their maximum levels.

In the case of the cotton, stock of 195 rolls was held between 12 March and 18 March (maximum level: 175 rolls).

In the case of the plastic poppers, the maximum level is 180 boxes but this was exceeded on 9 March when a new delivery brought stocks up to 185. The situation became worse on 12 March when a delivery of a further 100 boxes was received. Clearly we should never have placed this additional order: the usual reorder level is 95 boxes.

I recommend that in future we should institute more thorough checks before orders are placed with suppliers and in particular a check to ensure that the reorder level has been reached.

BPP PUBLISHING

Task 3

TIMESHEET

Week ending   *6 March 1998*

Employee name   *Amy Harding*   **Employee number**   *2173*

Department   *Finishing*   **Employee grade**   *2*

Activity	Monday Hours	Tuesday Hours	Wednes-day Hours	Thursday Hours	Friday Hours	Total Hours
Machining	7	10	4		4	25
Holiday			4	8		12
Waiting for work	1					1
Training					4	4
Total hours payable for day	8	10	8	8	8	42
Number of covers produced	65	72	30	0	32	
Bonus payable @ £0.15 per cover above 60 per day	£0.75	£1.80	-	-	-	£2.55

Signed   *Amy Harding*   Manager   *Jim Stubbs*

- -

Analysis for week	Hours	Rate per hour £	Wages cost £
Direct wages	25	3.00	75.00
Indirect wages			
Basic hours	17	3.00	51.00
Overtime premium	1	3.00	3.00
Bonus	-	-	2.55
	43		131.55

TIMESHEET

Week ending   *6 March 1998*

Employee name *Jane Amber*   **Employee number**   *2487*

Department   *Cutting*   **Employee grade**   *1*

Activity	Monday Hours	Tuesday Hours	Wednes-day Hours	Thursday Hours	Friday Hours	Total Hours
Cutting	*10*	*6*	*6*		*8*	*30*
Waiting for work		*3*	*2*			*5*
Sick				*8*		*8*
Training					*2*	*2*
Discrepancy		*(1)*				*(1)*
Total hours payable for day	*10*	*8*	*8*	*8*	*10*	*44*
Number of covers produced	*70*	*51*	*62*	*0*	*62*	
Bonus payable @ £0.15 per cover above 60 per day	*£1.50*	*-*	*£0.30*	*-*	*£0.30*	*£2.10*

Signed   *Jane Amber*   Manager   *Jim Stubbs*

Analysis for week	Hours	Rate per hour £	Wages cost £
Direct wages	*29*	*4.00*	*116.00*
Indirect wages			
Basic hours	*15*	*4.00*	*60.00*
Overtime premium	*2*	*4.00*	*8.00*
Bonus	*-*	*-*	*2.10*
	46		*186.10*

COST LEDGER DATA ENTRY SHEET

Week ending   *6 March 1998*

Debit accounts

Cost centre code	Expenditure code	Amount to be debited £
C100	E300	116.00
C200	E300	75.00
C300	E300	-
C400	E300	-
C100	E310	70.10
C200	E310	56.55
C300	E310	-
C400	E310	-
Check total: total wages for the two employees		317.65

Task 4

MEMO

To: Jim Stubbs
From: Lesley Hunt
Date: 10 March 1998
Subject: Discrepancy on timesheet

I have a query on an employee's timesheet for the week ending 6 March 1998. The employee in question is Jane Amber, in the cutting department. A copy of the timesheet is enclosed.

You will see that I have had to adjust for a discrepancy of one hour. The total number of hours shown for Tuesday is eight, but the analysis totals to nine hours.

Could you please look into this for me? I have made the usual adjustments, pending the outcome of your enquires. Thanks for your help.

Task 5

MEMO

To: Jim Stubbs, production manager
From: Lesley Hunt, accounts assistant
Date: 10 March 1998
Subject: Standard rates for overhead absorption, 1998/99

Why the present absorption rate might not be the most appropriate for the company

The present system of absorbing production overheads using a percentage of direct labour cost may distort the overhead costs absorbed by individual products because of differential wage rates.

Our employees are paid different hourly rates. If a cost unit happens to be worked on by a highly paid employee its labour cost would be higher and the overhead absorbed would therefore also be higher. However the overhead actually incurred by this product would not necessarily be high, particularly if the higher paid employees work more quickly.

Many overhead costs tend to increase with time, for example rent, rates, salaries and so on. Therefore it makes sense to absorb overheads according to the time taken on a cost unit. Although a labour cost percentage is to an extent time based, it can lead to distortions when there are differential wage rates.

The hourly rates suggested would be preferable because the overhead absorbed would be directly related to the time taken to produce the cost unit.

Why separate hourly rates would be more suitable

The activity in the finishing and packing departments is labour intensive. Therefore a direct labour hour rate is most appropriate in these two departments. Using a separate rate for each department would more accurately reflect the load placed by a cost unit on the facilities of each department.

The cutting department is machine intensive. Therefore many of the overhead costs are likely to be machine related (for example depreciation and maintenance) and would be linked to the amount of time spent by a cost unit on the machines. Therefore a machine hour is more suitable in this department.

Task 6

OVERHEAD ANALYSIS SHEET: 1998/99

Overhead expense: primary apportionments and allocations	Basis of allocation/ apportionment	Total £	Cutting dept £	Finishing dept £	Packing dept £	Stores £
Rent and rates	Floor area	79,500	19,941	27,812	19,941	11,806
Catering	Number of employees	1,200	183	623	366	28
Machine maintenance	Quotation	45,850	25,250	5,600	11,000	4,000
Depreciation on machines	Cost of machines	13,490	7,412	1,663	3,230	1,185
Production manager's salary	Time spent	21,000	7,000	7,000	7,000	
Storekeeper's salary	Allocation	14,000				14,000
Other overheads	Even appor- tionment	40,000	10,000	10,000	10,000	10,000
Total of primary allocations		215,040	69,786	52,698	51,537	41,019
Re-apportion stores			16,404	13,692	10,923	(41,019)
Total production cost centre overhead		215,040	86,190	66,390	62,460	
Machine hours			30,750			
Direct labour hours				129,750	67,500	
Overhead absorption rate for 1998/99			£2.80	£0.51	£0.93	

Task 7a

MEMO

To: Jim Stubbs
From: Lesley Hunt
Date: 6 July 1998
Subject: Wages paid to temporary employee during the quarter ending 30 June 1998

I have been informed that £1,920 was paid to a temporary employee for 320 hours worked during the quarter ending 30 June 1998. To enable me to analyse and classify the hours worked by the employee and the wages paid, could you please provide me with the following information.

- How many of the 320 hours were worked on direct tasks, and how many were worked on indirect tasks? This will help me to determine the correct expenditure code for the wages payment.

- How many hours were worked in each of the three departments? This will help me to determine the correct cost centre code, and to complete the analysis of labour hours for the period.

Thank you for your help.

Working sheet for calculation of overhead under/over absorbed

Packing department, quarter ending 30 June 1998

7(b) Production overhead absorbed (using direct labour hour rate)	$18,300 \times £0.93$	£17,019
7(c) Actual production overhead incurred	$£855 + £4,045 +$ $£10,800 + £800$	£16,500
7(d) Production overhead under or over absorbed, to be transferred to profit and loss account		£519 over absorbed

BPP PUBLISHING

Task 8

STANDARD COST CARD 1998/99

Product: Box of 6 double duvet covers
Product code no: 00214

Description	Material code no/direct labour grade	Quantity	Std price £ per metre/ hour etc	Total £
Direct materials				
Cotton fabric	CT33	38.2 metres	1.85	70.67
Plastic poppers	PP29	60	0.67	40.20
Polyester thread	TP72	22 metres	0.00142	0.03
Packing - cardboard box	PB03	1 box	0.25	0.25
Other materials	Various	-	-	0.81
Subtotal, direct materials			(A)	111.96
Direct labour				
Cutting	Grade 1	0.35 hours	4.20	1.47
Finishing	Grade 1	4.10 hours	4.20	17.22
Packing	Grade 3	0.50 hours	2.63	1.31
Subtotal, direct labour			(B)	20.00
Production overhead				
Cutting department		1.80 machine hours	2.80	5.04
Finishing department		4.10 labour hours	0.51	2.09
Packing department		0.50 labour hours	0.93	0.46
Subtotal, production overhead			(C)	7.59
Total standard production cost			(A + B + C)	139.55

Task 9

MEMO

To: Patrick McGrath
From: Lesley Hunt
Date: 13 July 1998
Subject: Standard cost report - double duvet covers in Cutting department

As you requested, here is my interim report on the cost variances for week ended 8 July 1998.

Favourable		*Adverse*	
	£		£
Cotton price variance			568
Cotton usage variance			268
Direct labour rate variance			24
Direct labour efficiency variance	55		
Fixed overhead expenditure variance			54
Fixed overhead capacity variance			28
Fixed overhead efficiency variance			90
	£55		£1,032

Clearly the two variances that require investigation are those for usage and price of cotton. I will look into these as soon as possible, but likely explanations are as follows:

- We may have been unrealistic in setting our standards for price and usage.

- There may have been a recent price increase.

- We may have switched to a higher grade of cotton.

- Wastage levels may have increased.

BPP PUBLISHING

Workings - variances for week ended 8/7/98 (cutting department)

	£	
Cotton price variance		
11,350 metres should cost (@ £1.85)	20,997	
did cost	21,565	
Variance	568	(A)
Cotton usage variance	*Metres*	
1,760 covers should require (@ 38.2/6)	11,205	
did require	11,350	
Difference	145	
@ standard rate (£1.85)	£268	(A)
Direct labour rate variance	£	
90 hours should cost (@ £4.20)	378	
did cost	402	
Variance	24	(A)
Direct labour efficiency variance	*Hours*	
1,760 covers should require (@ 0.35/6)	103	
did require	90	
Difference	13	
@ standard rate (£4.20)	£55	(F)
Fixed overhead expenditure variance	£	
Budgeted overheads (1,900 × (1.8/6) × £2.80)	1,596	
Actual overheads	1,650	
Variance	54	(A)
Fixed overhead capacity variance	*Hours*	
Budgeted hours worked (1,900 × 1.8/6)	570	
Actual hours worked	560	
Difference	10	
@ standard rate (£2.80)	£28	(A)
Fixed overhead efficiency variance	*Hours*	
Standard hours (1,760 × 1.8/6)	528	
Actual hours	560	
Difference	32	
@ standard rate (£2.80)	£90	(A)

PART C

CENTRAL ASSESSMENTS

Practice Central Assessments

PRACTICE CENTRAL ASSESSMENT 1: DOWRA LTD (JUNE 1995)

SECTION 1

The suggested time allocation for this exercise is 75 minutes.

Data

Dowra Ltd manufactures high quality wooden toys. Production varies from long runs of popular models to short runs of specially designed expensive toys.

The factory is divided into five cost centres for analysis purposes.

Production

The **cutting department** cuts the timber to shape.

The **assembly department** assembles the parts of the toy which have been pre-cut by the cutting department.

The **finishing department** paints, varnishes and packs the completed wooden toys.

Service

The **design department** prepares drawings and product specifications for the individual wooden toys.

The **stores department** stores and handles the following.

(a)   The materials used in production, including timber, paint, glue, screws, nails and packing materials

(b)   The work-in-progress

(c)   The finished goods

The company's system for dealing with budgeted factory overheads is as follows.

(a)   Where possible, budgeted overheads are allocated to the five cost centres as shown in the data below. Any overheads which cannot be directly allocated to cost centres are allocated to an overall factory cost centre and apportioned to the five cost centres according to floor area.

(b)   Budgeted stores overheads are apportioned to the other four cost centres according to the value of materials requisitions

(c)   Budgeted design overheads are apportioned to the production cost centres in equal proportions.

(d)   Production overheads are charged to production runs on the basis of machine hours in each of the three production cost centres.

Budgeted data for the year ending 30 June 20X1 is as follows.

Allocated overheads	Cutting	Assembly	Finishing	Design	Stores
Indirect labour (£)	72,400	83,900	108,600	126,100	18,500
Indirect materials (£)	1,850	780	12,640	4,650	600
Machine costs (£)	64,000	56,400	48,900	63,400	2,900
Total allocated overhead(£)	138,250	141,080	170,140	194,150	22,000

Unallocated budgeted factory overheads amount to £184,000.

Other data:

Floor area (sq metres)	770	1,310	1,080	480	360	4000
Material requisitions (£)	97,760	109,400	45,000	4,640	-	256800
Material requisitions (No.)	800	750	1,200	550	-	
Machine hours	180,000	85,000	240,000	-	-	

Task 1

Using the overhead analysis sheet below, calculate a machine hour overhead absorption rate for each of the three production cost centres.

DOWRA LTD					
Overhead analysis sheet					
Department	*Cutting* £	*Assembly* £	*Finishing* £	*Design* £	*Stores* £
Allocated overheads	138250	141080	170140	194150	22000
Factory overheads	35420	60260	49680	22080	16560
Stores	14679	16427	6757	697	(38560)
Design	72309	72309	72309	(216,927)	—
Total	260658	290,076	298,886	—	—
Machine hours	180,000	85,000	240,000		
Absorption rate per machine hour	1.45	3.41	1.25		

Data

One of the products manufactured by Dowra Ltd is a small wooden duck on wheels, pulled by a string.

The product materials specification is as follows.

Materials Specification Wooden Duck on Wheels		
Materials	*Quantity*	*Treatment*
5 mm board	0.2 sq metres	Direct
4 cm diameter wheels	4	Direct
String	30cm	Indirect
Wire	20cm	Indirect
White paint		Indirect
Brown paint		Indirect
Red paint		Indirect
Varnish		Indirect
Glue		Indirect
Box	1	Direct

The standard time for manufacture is as follows.

Wooden Duck on Wheels	
Process	*Time*
Cutting head	20 seconds
Cutting body	40 seconds
Cutting base	30 seconds
Assembly	3 minutes
Painting	4 minutes
Packing	30 seconds

Note: All the above times are both direct labour hours and machine hours.

Additional information is as follows.

Materials Price List (extract)	
Board: 5 mm	£4.60 per sq. metre
Wheels: 4cm diameter	£18.20 per 100
Boxes: Wooden duck	£16.00 per 100

Current Wage Rates	
Grade	*Rate per hour*
Cutter	£7.50
Assembler	£6.80
Painter	£8.20
Packer	£5.00

Task 2

Complete the Standard Cost Card below for the wooden duck on wheels. Use the overhead absorption rates you calculated in task 1.

Standard Cost Card Wooden Duck on Wheels			
Materials	*Quantity*	*Price* £	*Value* £
5 mm board	0.2 M.	14.60 M²	0.92
4 cm diameter wheels	4	18.20/100	0.73
Box	1	16.00/100	0.16
Subtotal:			1.81
Labour	*Time*	*Rate* £/HR	*Value* £
Cutter	1½ mins	7.50	0.19
Assembler	3 mins	6.80	0.34
Painter	4 mins	8.20	0.55
Packer	½ min	5.00	0.04
Subtotal:			1.12
Production overheads	*Time*	*Rate* £/HR	*Value* £
Cutting	1½ mins	1.45	0.04
Assembly	3 mins	3.41	0.17
Finishing	4 mins	1.25	0.08
Subtotal:			0.29
GRAND TOTAL			3.22

Data

The sales manager was concerned that demand for many of the popular products was falling. Quotations were being sent out to potential customers, but were being rejected in favour of lower quotations from other suppliers. On the other hand, quotations for one-off expensive items were being accepted.

The production manager was certain that materials being used were similar to those used by other manufacturers and that wage rates were no higher than elsewhere in the industry. He thought that the answer might lie in the way the production overheads were apportioned to the different products.

Task 3

Write a short memorandum to the sales manager and production manager suggesting ways in which the apportionment of the production overheads might be improved to give more accurate product costs.

The memorandum should consider the apportionment of each of the following production overheads in separate paragraphs.

(a)   Unallocated factory costs

(b)   Stores overheads

(c)   Design overheads

In each case the present method of apportionment should be criticised and a fairer alternative suggested.

Data

The standard costs of wooden ducks on wheels, for the **CURRENT** year, for 5 mm board and for cutting are as follows.

5 mm board: 0.2 sq metres at £4.50 per sq metre

Cutters: 1.5 minutes at £7.20 per hour.

In the most recent period, 120 wooden ducks on wheels were produced.

25 sq metres of 5 mm board were requisitioned from Stores at a total cost of £110.

2.75 hours were recorded for cutters at a total cost of £22.

Task 4

(a)   (i)   Calculate the material price variance and material usage variance for 5 mm board.

       (ii)   Calculate the wage rate variance and labour efficiency variance for cutters.

(b)   Suggest possible reasons for the variances calculated.

SECTION 2

All the questions in this exercise relate to the data concerning Dowra Ltd provided in Section 1.

The suggested time allocation for this exercise is 45 minutes.

1   Give TWO examples of work in progress that would apply to Dowra Ltd.

2   Give TWO examples of indirect materials used by the design department.

3   Suggest why string and wire are treated as indirect materials.

4   How would the standard labour times for manufacture in Section 1, Task 2 have been calculated?

5   Which method of stock valuation should be used in the preparation of quotations in order to cost at the most realistic valuation? Give reasons for your answer.

6   Explain why it has been possible to allocate some production overheads directly to cost centres. Give an example of such an allocation.

7   The management accountant is considering introducing an idle time variance in the labour variance calculations.

     What is the purpose of an idle time variance?

8   The factory manager has been considering the possibility of introducing a system of bonus payments.

     What should a good bonus payments system achieve for both the company and the employees?

9   In the company's stock control system, explain the terms 'reorder level' and 'minimum level'.

10 The formula to calculate the economic ordering quantity depends upon stockholding costs and ordering costs.

    (a) Give TWO examples of stockholding costs.

    (b) Give TWO examples of ordering costs.

11 The warehouse is concerned with the time taken up with stocktaking. The warehouse manager has heard that computerised stock control systems hold records on stock levels at all times and that, therefore, stocktaking will not be necessary.

    Is the warehouse manager correct? Give reasons for your answer.

12 The company is planning to produce a wooden model based on a cartoon character. To do this, it will have to pay the copyright holder a copyright fee of £1 per model produced. The company is not sure how to treat the £1 copyright fee: it might be a production overhead, a direct expense or a selling and distribution overhead.

    Explain which classification of cost it should be, giving reasons for your answer.

A SUGGESTED ANSWER TO THIS PRACTICE CENTRAL ASSESSMENT IS GIVEN ON PAGE 365.

A SUGGESTED ANSWER TO THIS PRACTICE CENTRAL ASSESSMENT IS GIVEN ON PAGE 365.

PRACTICE CENTRAL ASSESSMENT 2: SOUTHWOOD COLLEGE (DECEMBER 1995)

SECTION 1

The suggested time allocation for this exercise is 80 minutes.

Data

Southwood College is a small private college in the south of England. It runs courses in accountancy and banking, largely for groups of employees from large and medium-sized companies.

The college consists of three classrooms, one of which is a computer room, an administrative office, a dining room and a kitchen.

You are employed by the college and you have been given a number of tasks by the chief accountant to help introduce more rigorous cost controls and develop a new pricing system.

There is some uncertainty about how to value the stock of paper used to photocopy teaching materials.

At present a system of standard costing is in operation.

The following data applies to October 20X5:

Standard cost of photocopy paper: £24 per ream*

| 2 October | Opening stock | 84 reams (all bought at £23 per ream) |

Purchases were as follows.

| 5 October | 100 reams | £2,400 less 10% quantity discount |
| 12 October | 80 reams | £2,100 |

Issues:

2 October	Acdo Ltd AAT course	70 reams
9 October	Barco Ltd Introductory Banking	80 reams
26 October	Casco Ltd Introductory Costing	70 reams

*NB. A ream is a unit used to express quantities of paper.

Task 1

Complete the stores ledger record card below for October, assuming that issues are priced on a FIFO basis.

STORES LEDGER RECORD									
PHOTOCOPY PAPER									
Date	*Receipts*			*Issues*			*Balance*		
	Qty	Price £	Value £	Qty	Price £	Value £	Qty	Price £	Value £
Oct 2							84	23.00	1,932
– 2				70		1610	14	23.00	322
– 5	100	21.60	2160				14	23.00	322
							100	21.60	2160
							114		2482
– 9				14	23.00	322			
				66	21.60	1425.60	34	21.60	734.40
12	80	26.25	2100				34	21.60	734.40
							80	26.25	2100 –
									2834.40
26				34	21.60	734.40			
				36	26.25	945.00	44	26.25	1155.00

Task 2

Calculate the value of closing stock using the following methods.

(i)   FIFO;
(ii)   LIFO;
(iii)   standard cost.

Give your answer in the table below.

Method	*Closing stock valuation*		
	Quantity	*Price £*	*Value £*
FIFO	44	26.25	1155.00
LIFO	14 20 10	23.00 21.60 26.25	1016.50
Standard cost	44	24.00	1056.00

Task 3

Write a short memorandum to the chief accountant which explains the difference between the FIFO, LIFO and standard cost methods of stock valuation. Recommend which method should be used when charging for photocopies on courses, giving your reasons.

Task 4

Write a short memorandum to the administration manager which includes a calculation of the total material price variance for all purchases of photocopy paper for October. Explain the variance.

Task 5

10% discount is available on purchases of photocopy paper when 100 or more reams are purchased and 15% when 200 or more reams are purchased. The administration manager is keen to take advantage of this discount. Write a short report to the administration manager outlining the advantages and disadvantages of buying in bulk and outlining the information you would require in order to calculate the optimum purchase quantity.

Data

You have been given the following budget data for the five cost centres within Southwood college for the forthcoming year.

	Classroom A	Classroom B	Classroom C	Admin	Catering
Wages (£)	-	-	-	76,000	48,000
Student days	3,800	2,600	1,600	-	- 8000
Book value of equipment (£)	4,000	6,000	60,000	20,000	10,000 109000
Areas (m²)	250	200	150	200	200 1000

The following costs are common to all cost centres in the college:

Heating and lighting	£40,000
Depreciation of equipment	£60,000

The following is an example of a costing document used to calculate the cost of a course:

Course:	AAT Recording Cost Information	
Duration:	10 days @ 7 hours per day	
Estimated students	20	
		£
Direct costs:		
Teaching time 10×7×£30.		2100.00
Photocopy costs 0.1Rnx £30 P/Rian=x20		66.00
Food and drink 20×10DAYS×£3		600.00
Indirect costs		
Catering 200DAYS× £7.75 DAR		1550.00
Administration		800.00
Other overhead costs 200× 4.46		892.00
Total cost		6002

NB. All figures to the nearest £

Task 6

Complete the costing document above, according to the following instructions.

1   Teaching time is costed at the current standard hourly rate, which is £30 per hour.

2 ✓ Standard photocopy costs are £30 per ream. Each student will use 0.1 reams.

3 ✓ The cost of food and drink has been estimated at £3 per student day.

4 ✓ Heating and lighting is apportioned between the five cost centres according to area and depreciation of equipment is apportioned between the five cost centres according to the book value of equipment.

5 ✓ Catering costs

The three elements of catering (wages, heating and lighting and depreciation of equipment) are totalled and divided by the budgeted total student days to give an absorption rate per student day.

6 ✓ Administration costs

The three elements of administration cost (wages, heating and lighting and depreciation of equipment) are totalled and divided by the estimated number of courses to give an absorption rate per course. The estimated number of courses for the forthcoming year is 120.

7 Other overhead costs

These relate to classroom overheads and consist of the heating and lighting and depreciation of equipment apportioned to each classroom. The total of these overheads for each classroom is divided by the estimated student days, to arrive at an absorption rate per student day. The AAT Recording Cost Information course will take place in Classroom B.

8 The three absorption rates calculated in 5, 6 and 7 above, are used to calculate the indirect costs for the course.

Notes

(1) All absorption rates are calculated to two decimal places.

(2) Use the table below to help calculate the absorption rates.

	Classroom A £	Classroom B £	Classroom C £	Admin £	Catering £	Total £
Wages	-	-	-	76,000	48,000	124,000
Heating and lighting	10,000	8000	6000	8000	8000	40,000
Depreciation of equipment	2400	3600	36000	12000	6000	60,000
Total	12400	11,600	42,000	96,000	62,000	224,000
		2600		120	18000	
		4.46		£800	£7.75	
				P/c	s/DAY.	

SECTION 2

The suggested time allocation for this exercise is 40 minutes.

The first five questions are based on the following information.

J Thompson Ltd is a small engineering company making specialist components for use in the oil industry. Shown below is a job card for the manufacture of a batch of machine tool components for R Patel & Co.

Note: The company uses a labour hour rate for absorbing production overheads.

JOB CARD					
Customer: R Patel & Co				**Job No:** 172467	
	Materials	*Labour*		*Other direct costs*	*Overheads*
20X5	£	hours	£	£	£
13 October MR 648	642				
16 October MR 652	192				
17 October Consultant's fee				700	
20 October Wages analysis (w/e 20.10.X5)		80	960		880
23 October MRN 214	(68)				

1   Describe what the entry for 13 October means.

2   Explain why the consultant's fee of £700, charged on 17 October, was judged to be a direct cost.

3   Where would the information about the 80 labour hours worked on the job on w/e 20.10.X5 have come from?

4   Calculate the overhead absorption rate.

5   Explain the entry for 23 October.

The following questions do not refer to the job card above and are general questions

6   Should overtime premium paid to a direct labour force be classified as a direct or an indirect cost? Give reasons for your answer.

7   If a member of the direct labour force of a building company spends one week building a new extension to the company premises, how should the pay for that week be dealt with in the accounts? Give reasons for your answer.

8   A company's wages control account for last week had two credit entries:

(a) Work-in-progress control account   £8,200
(b) Production overhead control account   £3,800

Explain the purpose of the two entries.

9   Explain what is meant by 'lead time' and why it is important in the calculation of stock re-order levels.

10   For one of its materials for last month, a company has a favourable material price variance and an adverse material usage variance. Explain how these two variances might be connected.

11   A company's management should take action on reported variances that are both significant and controllable. Explain the terms 'significant' and 'controllable', giving examples.

12   The workers in a factory which makes jeans are paid a piecework rate of £1.19 per pair produced. Would this be a fixed cost or a variable cost?

A SUGGESTED ANSWER TO THIS PRACTICE CENTRAL ASSESSMENT IS GIVEN ON PAGE 370.

PRACTICE CENTRAL ASSESSMENT 3: WHITEWALL LIMITED (JUNE 1996)

SECTION 1

The suggested time allocation for this exercise is 80 minutes.

Data

You are employed as an Accounting Technician in the cost office of Whitewall Limited, an engineering company. You report to the Cost Accountant and have been given a number of tasks concerned with the cost data on a job for a client. The job is coded 'Wheelbase' and was undertaken during the month of May.

Job Wheelbase used two materials during May, Exon and Delton. Company policy is to issue material Exon on a FIFO basis and material Delton on a LIFO basis. You are given the following movements for May for both materials by a cost clerk within the costing office. The issues on May 18 and May 19 were to Job Wheelbase and there were no issues of Exon or Delton for any other job during May.

MATERIAL EXON - FIFO BASIS

		Kilos	£ price
May 1	Opening balance	30,000	2.00
May 7	Receipts	10,000	2.25
May 14	Receipts	12,000	2.50
May 18	Issue	35,000	

MATERIAL DELTON - LIFO BASIS

		Kilos	£ price
May 1	Opening balance	25,000	3.00
May 8	Receipts	9,000	3.20
May 15	Receipts	8,000	3.40
May 19	Issue	20,000	

Task 1

(a) Complete the stores ledger for May for Exon and Delton below.

STORES LEDGER RECORD
MATERIAL: EXON

Date	Receipts			Issues			Balance		
	Kilos	*Price* £	*Value* £	*Kilos*	*Price* £	*Value* £	*Kilos*	*Price* £	*Balance* £
May 1							30,000	2.00	60,000
May 7	10,000	2.25	22,500				40,000	2.25	22500
May 14	12,000	2.50	30,000				52000	2.50	30,000
May 18				30,000 / 5000	2.00 / 225	69000 / 11,250	35000 / 12000	2.25 / 2.50	11250 / 30,000
							17,000		41,250

STORES LEDGER RECORD
MATERIAL: DELTON

Date	Receipts			Issues			Balance		
	Kilos	*Price* £	*Value* £	*Kilos*	*Price* £	*Value* £	*Kilos*	*Price* £	*Balance* £
May 1							25,000	3.00	75,000
May 8	9,000	3.20	28,800				34000		103,800
May 15	8,000	3.40	27,200				42000		131,000
May 19				8000	3.40	27,200			
				9000	3.20	28,800			
				3.000	3.00	9,000	22,000	3.00	66,000

(b) One of your assistants in the Cost Office has had a telephone conversation with the stores supervisor who acknowledge that FIFO stands for 'first in first out' and LIFO stands for 'last in first out' but understands this to relate to the physical movement of stock.

Set out for your assistant notes for a telephone call in reply to the stores supervisor.

The reply should cover:

(i) why FIFO and LIFO are used as methods of pricing issues;

(ii) whether the stores supervisor is correct in his understanding of FIFO and LIFO.

Data

Job Wheelbase used labour from the assembly, moulding and finishing departments. Data relating to labour is given on the labour cost card below.

The Company has negotiated with the workforce a bonus scheme whereby the workers receive 50% of standard hours saved in each department paid at the *actual* labour rate paid per hour. This is not included in the actual wage cost given below, which shows actual hours paid at the basic actual wage rate per hour. There have been no overtime payments.

Task 2

Cost the labour requirements for Job Wheelbase using the labour cost card below.

LABOUR COST CARD			
JOB: WHEELBASE Date: May 20X6			
	Assembly	*Moulding*	*Finishing*
Actual wage cost £	26,970	34,020	36,540
Standard hours produced	6,000	7,500	7,600
Actual hours worked	6,200	7,000	7,000
Standard hours saved		500	600
Actual wage rate per hour £	4.35	4.86	5.22
Bonus £		1,215	1566
Total labour cost £	26,970	35,235	38,106

Data

Whitewall Ltd charges overheads on the basis of machine hours. Budgeted data for the company available to you within the cost office is shown on the overhead analysis sheet below. The totalled amounts are after service departments' overheads have been apportioned to the production departments.

OVERHEAD ANALYSIS SHEET

	Assembly	*Moulding*	*Finishing*
Budgeted total overheads	£3,249,000	£3,950,400	£3,419,900
Budgeted machine hours	90,000	120,000	110,000
Budgeted overhead absorption rate	36.10	32.92	31.09

The details relevant to Job Wheelbase are given in the job overhead analysis card below.

JOB OVERHEAD ANALYSIS CARD

		Assembly	*Moulding*	*Finishing*
Job machine hours		6,000	6,800	6,600
Budgeted overhead absorption rate	£	36.10	32.92	31.09
Overhead absorbed by job	£	216,600	223,856	205,194

Task 3

(a)   Calculate the overhead absorption rates for each department and insert them in the overhead analysis sheet above.

(b)   Calculate the overhead absorbed by the job and insert it in the job overhead analysis card above.

BPP PUBLISHING

(c)   The supervisor for Job Wheelbase is questioning the use of budgeted machine hours as a basis to absorb overheads. He feels that a simpler approach would be to divide the budgeted total overheads for the company by the number of jobs for that year.

Reply to the Job Wheelbase supervisor in a memorandum. Your reply should:

(i)   outline the purpose of overhead absorption;

(ii)   give reasons why machine hours have been used as a basis of absorption;

(iii) state whether you agree or disagree with the supervisor's suggested approach.

Data

Below is the job cost card for Job Wheelbase. Whitewall's pricing policy is to charge a profit of 25% of the job price.

Task 4

Using the data you have prepared in tasks 1, 2 and 3, complete the job card for Job Wheelbase to the nearest pound.

JOB COST CARD

Job: Wheelbase   Date: May 20X6

Material	*Total*
Exon	71250
Delton	65,000
	136,250
Labour	
Assembly	26,970
Moulding	35,235
Finishing	38,106
	100,311
Overhead	
Assembly	216,600
Moulding	223,856
Finishing	205,194
	645,650
Total cost	882,211
Profit	294070
Job price	1,176,281

Data

You have been asked by the Production Manager to review the labour cost associated with the assembly department on Job Wheelbase, a summary of which is given below.

SUMMARY OF ASSEMBLY WAGE COSTS ON JOB WHEELBASE

Budgeted wage rate	£4.50
Standard hours produced	6,000
Actual hours worked	6,200
Actual wage costs	£26,970

Task 5

(a) Calculate the following for the assembly department labour costs only:

  (i)   total labour cost variance;
  (ii) labour efficiency variance;
  (iii) labour wage rate variance.

(b) Write a short memo to the Production Manager explaining the variances for the assembly department and offering explanations.

Data

You have been asked to review the overhead expenditure for the finishing department for the period under review. You are given the following data for the period.

Finishing department		Data
Budgeted total overheads		£3,419,900
Budgeted machine hours		110,000
Budgeted overhead absorption rate	£	31·09
Actual machine hours		108,000
Overhead absorbed	£	3357720
Actual overheads		£3,572,000
Over/(under) absorption of overheads	£	214,280 u.

Task 6

Complete the above table and write a short report to the Cost Accountant explaining:

(i)   the consequences of these results;
(ii) the possible causes;
(iii) the effect on costing such jobs as Wheelbase;
(iv) possible remedial action for the future.

SECTION 2

All the questions in this exercise relate to the data concerning Whitewall Limited provided in Section 1.

The suggested time allocation for this exercise is 40 minutes.

1   Materials Exon and Delton were costed on a FIFO and LIFO basis respectively. Briefly explain the difference between these two methods.

2   Give *two* examples of:

  (i)   stock holding costs and
  (ii) stock ordering costs

  that Whitewall Limited is likely to incur.

3 Explain the nature and purpose of a stocktake.

4 Give *two* different methods of a stocktake that Whitewall Limited might use.

5 Whitewall Limited uses standard hours produced to measure its labour output. Explain what a standard hour produced is.

6 State *two* ways in which information on actual labour hours worked on Job Wheelbase could have been collected.

7 Give a ratio that would measure the efficiency of the direct workers on Job Wheelbase and explain how it would be calculated.

8 Provide the double entry for the under/over absorbed overheads in the finishing department that will appear in the cost accounts for Whitewall Limited.

9 Task 3 in Section 1 gives the budgeted overheads for each production department after service department overheads (eg catering, stores etc) have been apportioned. *Briefly* explain the purpose for apportioning overheads of service cost centres to production cost centres, giving *one* example of a basis of apportionment for a service cost centre.

10 Job Wheelbase has incurred overheads but not direct expenses. *Briefly* explain the difference between these two costs.

11 Give *two* examples of overhead costs that might have been incurred on Job Wheelbase.

12 Whitewall Limited is considering an activity-based costing system to replace its current system of overhead absorption. Such a system uses cost drivers.

   (a) Explain what a cost driver is.
   (b) Give an example of a possible cost driver on Job Wheelbase.

A SUGGESTED ANSWER TO THIS PRACTICE CENTRAL ASSESSMENT IS GIVEN ON PAGE 374.

PRACTICE CENTRAL ASSESSMENT 4: TAMWORTH LTD (DECEMBER 1996)

SECTION 1

The suggested time allocation for this exercise is 75 minutes.

Data

You are employed as an accounting technician by Tamworth Limited and you report to the management accountant. Tamworth is a medium-sized company employing 760 people at a factory in northern England and it is primarily engaged in the manufacture of a bathroom accessory. You have been given a number of tasks concerned with the performance of the cutting, moulding, finishing and packaging departments for the year ended 30 November 20X6.

Tamworth Ltd has a budgetary control system and uses standard costing. You have been given the following budget and actual performance data.

Year ended 30 November 20X6

Department	Cutting	Moulding	Finishing	Packaging
Budgeted production (units)	379,000	356,000	362,100	375,000
Standard time per unit	6 mins	7.5 mins	8 mins	4 mins
Budgeted wage rate per hour	£5.25	£4.60	£5.10	£5.05
Actual production (units)	376,400	353,200	364,125	372,825
Actual wages	£200,956	£197,823	£247,720	£124,000
Actual labour hours worked	37,214	41,213	45,874	24,315
Average number of workers	164	173	162	195
Workers leaving during the year	35	14	11	13

Task 1

The production manager, who has responsibility for all four departments, is concerned about staff retention rates.

(a) Complete the following table using data from the table above.

(*Note.* Round off your workings to one decimal place.)

Department	Cutting	Moulding	Finishing	Packaging
Average number of workers	164	173	162	195
Workers leaving during the year	35	14	11	13
% of staff leaving 20X6	21.3	8.1	6.8	6.7
% of staff leaving 20X5	12.1%	7.8%	7.3%	7.4%

(b) Write a memo to the production manager

    (i) analysing your results from Task 1 (a);
    (ii) highlighting areas of concern and possible causes;
    (iii) explaining the potential costs and consequences for the company.

Task 2

The management accountant is keen to inform the packaging department of its efficiency and capacity performance in relation to other departments.

(a) Using the data above you have been asked by the management accountant to complete the following table for the packaging department.

    (*Note.* Round off your ratio workings to one decimal place.)

Department	Cutting	Moulding	Finishing	Packaging
Budgeted production (hours)	37,900	44,500	48,280	25000
Actual labour hours worked	37,214	41,213	45,874	24315
Standard hours produced	37,640	44,150	48,550	24855
Capacity ratio	98.2%	92.6%	95.0%	97·3
Efficiency ratio	101.1%	107.1%	105.8%	102.2

Note: Capacity ratio $= \dfrac{\text{Actual labour hours worked}}{\text{Budgeted hours}}$

Efficiency ratio $= \dfrac{\text{Standard hours produced}}{\text{Actual labour hours worked}}$

(b) Write a note to the packaging department supervisor explaining the results of his department and giving possible reasons.

Task 3

The production manager is considering purchasing a new cutting machine for the cutting department. The cost of the machine is likely to be £180,000 and it will have a life of approximately five years and scrap value of between £10,000 and £15,000. Past experience has shown that such machinery will lose value and have most usage in the early part of its life.

Write a report to the production manager detailing:

(i) the method of depreciation that should be used;

(ii) an approximate rate that could be applied, showing any workings that allow you to arrive at that rate;

(iii) reasons for the choice of depreciation method.

Task 4

Tamworth Limited uses a budgeted overhead absorption rate based on labour hours. Data relating to the year ended 30 November 20X6 is given in the table below and on the following page.

Complete the table below for the four production departments in the factory.

Note. Round off your figures to the nearest £.

Department	Cutting	Moulding	Finishing	Packaging
Actual overheads incurred	£1,234,736	£1,156,347	£938,463	£834,674
Budgeted absorption rate per labour hour	£33.82	£26.80	£20.25	£29.62
Actual labour hours worked	37214	41213	45874	24,315
Overheads absorbed	1,258,577	1,104,508	928,949	720,210
(Under) / over absorbed overheads	23841 o	51839 u	9,514 u	114,464 u

Task 5

Your assistant has taken a telephone call from the production manager, who has asked about effectiveness of standard cost as a method of pricing material issues and valuing stock.

List some points that will form the basis of a reply to the production manager. You should explain:

(i) what a standard material price represents;

(ii) how standard prices for materials will be ascertained;

(iii) the benefits and weaknesses of such a system.

SECTION 2

The suggested time allocation for this exercise is 45 minutes.

1 Where would the information about workers leaving the company in Task 1 of Section 1 have come from?

2 The budgeted wage rate per hour for the finishing department is £5.10. Explain how this might have been arrived at.

3 List *three* indirect wage costs that might have been incurred in the packaging department.

4 The material used by the production departments of Tamworth Ltd would have come from the stores department, a service cost centre. Suggest how the costs for the stores department would be incorporated into product cost.

5 Activity-based costing has been put forward as a realistic alternative to more traditional methods of overhead absorption. Explain one way in which an activity-based costing (ABC) system differs from the more traditional methods of overhead absorption.

6 An order has been placed for a particular material that is used in the cutting department. The order delivery time could take from 2 to 4 weeks and the usage of the material fluctuates from a minimum of 3,000 units to a maximum of 5,000 units per week. Calculate the re-order level.

7 The output of a process cost system will usually be reduced by normal loss and abnormal loss. Briefly explain the difference between the two and state how they will be treated in the accounts.

8 Give an example of a cost centre from the data provided in Section 1 for Tamworth Ltd.

9 Overhead costs will either be allocated to a cost centre or apportioned to a cost centre.

   (a) Briefly explain the difference between the processes of allocation and apportionment.

   (b) Give *one* example of:

      (i) an allocated overhead for the packaging department;
      (ii) an apportioned overhead for the moulding department.

10 The overheads for four production departments were under-absorbed by £151,977.

   (a) Does this mean actual overheads are less than absorbed overheads?

   (b) What effect will this under-absorption have on budgeted profit?

11 Explain the purpose of coding costs.

12 A company has the following details for the movement of an item of stock for November.

		Units	Cost per unit £	Cost £
1 Nov	Opening balance	1,000	3	3,000
10 Nov	Receipts	1,200	3.5	4,200
25 Nov	Issues	1,800		

Complete the following table for FIFO and LIFO.

Date	Description	FIFO £	LIFO £
25 Nov	Total issue value	5800	6000
30 Nov	Total closing stock value	1400	1200

A SUGGESTED ANSWER TO THIS PRACTICE CENTRAL ASSESSMENT IS GIVEN ON PAGE 379.

Trial Run Central Assessments

TRIAL RUN CENTRAL ASSESSMENT 1

INTERMEDIATE STAGE - NVQ/SVQ3

Unit 6

Recording cost information
December 1998

TRIAL RUN CENTRAL ASSESSMENT 1 (DECEMBER 1998)

This central assessment is in THREE sections. You are reminded that competence must be achieved in each section. You should therefore attempt and aim to complete EVERY task in EACH section.

Essential calculations should be included in your answers where appropriate.

SECTION 1

You are advised to spend approximately 1 hour on this section.

Please note that the tasks should be attempted in numerical order.

The tasks are detailed on pages 309 to 313.

Data

Crunchy-Bites Ltd is a small manufacturing company that makes biscuits which are sold to supermarkets.

Production is carried out within a single factory. The factory is organised into the following three production departments.

- Mixing
- Baking
- Packing

Materials are issued to production from a central stores department.

You are an accounting technician working in the administration department that is responsible for providing cost information to the general manager.

The general manager has given you a number of tasks concerned with factory operations and performance for 1998 and the plans for 1999.

Task 1.1

The administration department is responsible for the purchase of sugar that is used in the production of biscuits. The price of sugar is volatile and company policy is to issue it from the stores department to the mixing department on a First-In-First-Out (FIFO) basis.

(a) **Complete the stores ledger card using the First-In-First-Out basis to cost issues and value stocks of sugar for the month of November 1998.**

Note. Entries in the cost columns should be to three decimal places. Workings for the value column should be shown.

Material:	STORES LEDGER CARD							Month:		
	Receipts			Issues			Stock			
Date	Quantity (kilos)	Cost (per kilo)	Value	Quantity (kilos)	Cost (per kilo)	Value	Quantity (kilos)	Cost (per kilo)	Value	
	'000	£	£	'000	£	£	'000	£	£	
Balance b/f Nov 1							50	0.175	8,750	
Nov 4	34	0.180	6,120				84	50,000×0.175 / 34,000×0.180	14,870	
Nov 10				46	0.175	8050	38	4000×0.175 / 34000×0.180	6820	
Nov 15	29	0.200	5,800				67	4,000×0.175 / 34000×0.180 / 29,000×0.200	12620	
Nov 19	16	0.240	3,840				83	4000×0.175 / 34000×0.180 / 29000×0.200	16460	
Nov 22				52	4000×0.175 / 34000×0.180 / 14000×0.200	700 / 6120 / 2800	31	16000×0.240 / 15000×0.200 / 16000×0.240	6840	
Nov 26	32	0.220	7,040				63	15000×0.200 / 16000×0.240 / 32000×0.220	13880	
Nov 28				39	15000×0.200 / 16000×0.240 / 8000×0.220	3000 / 3840 / 1760	24	24000×0.220	5280	

Data on file shows that on average the factory uses 35,000 kilos of sugar per week. There is a lead-time of one week and the company policy is to hold a buffer stock of one week's average usage.

(b)   **Complete the following table**

	Quantity (kilos)
Buffer stock	35,000
Re-Order level	70,000

Task 1.2

You are reviewing the performance of the packing department for November 1998 against standard. Each packer is budgeted to pack 25 boxes of biscuits per hour and is budgeted to be paid a rate of £5.25 per hour.

Actual performance data for November 1998 shows.

Boxes packed	412,000
Actual wages	£84,800
Actual hours worked	16,000

Complete the labour variance schedule below.

Note. Do not complete the shaded boxes.

LABOUR VARIANCE SCHEDULE

Department:		Month:		
Variance	Standard cost	Actual cost	Variance	
Labour wage rate			£	800 A
Labour efficiency			£	2520 F
Total	£ 86,520	£ 84,800	£	1720 F

Task 1.3

The general manager has given you the task of supplying cost data for the manufacture of a specific brand of chocolate biscuit for 1999 on the basis of projected costs. A cost clerk has given you data on variable and fixed costs, which are relevant over the range of production.

(a) **Complete the budgeted cost schedule for the different levels of production.**

BUDGETED COST SCHEDULE				YEAR 1999
		ACTIVITY (packets)		
		175,000	200,000	225,000
Description	Cost	£	£	£
Direct material	8p per packet	14000	16,000	18,000
Direct labour	6p per packet	10,500	12,000	13,500
Packing costs	1p per packet	1,750	2,000	2,250
Depreciation costs	£12,000	12000	12000	12000
Rent and rates	£26,000	26000	26000	26000
Supervisory costs	£12,000	12000	12000	12000
Administration costs	£8,000	8000	8000	8000

(b) **Using your data from part (a) complete the table below for costs at the three levels of production.**

Costs per packet should be rounded to three decimal places.

	ACTIVITY (packets)		
	175,000	200,000	225,000
COST	£	£	£
Total variable cost	26250	30,000	33,750
Total fixed cost	58,000	58,000	58000
Total cost	84,250	88,000	91,750
Cost per packet	0.481	0.440	0.408

Task 1.4

The general manager has asked you to monitor the absorption of overheads for the production departments for November 1998.

Company policy is to absorb overheads on the following basis.

Department	Basis
Mixing	Per £ of labour cost
Baking	Machine hours
Packing	Labour hours

Budgeted and actual data for November 1998 is:

	Mixing	Baking	Packing
Budgeted overheads	£164,000	£228,900	£215,000
Actual labour hours worked			16,000
Budgeted labour hours			17,200
Actual machine hours		16,100	
Budgeted machine hours		16,350	
Actual labour costs	£63,700		
Budgeted labour costs	£65,600		

(a) Calculate the budgeted overhead absorption rate for each department.

	Mixing £	Baking £	Packing £
Budgeted overhead absorption rate	2.50	14.00	12.50

(b) Complete the production overhead schedule below.

Note. Overheads should be absorbed on the basis of actual performance.

PRODUCTION OVERHEAD SCHEDULE			
Month:	Mixing £	Baking £	Packing £
Budgeted overheads	164,000	228,900	215,000
Actual overheads	171,500	224,000	229,000
Overhead absorbed	159,250	225,400	200,000

(c)   Complete the table below.

	Mixing £	Baking £	Packing £
Over absorbed overheads		1,400	
Under absorbed overheads	12,250		29,000

SECTION 2

You are advised to spend approximately 1 hour on this section. The questions are detailed on pages 313 to 316.

Task 2.1

In Task 1.1(a) you costed issues of sugar to the mixing department on a First-In-First-Out (FIFO) basis. The general manager wants a costing method for issues that charges the mixing department with the most recent prices. Does FIFO meet this objective? Give a reason for your answer.

....

....

....

....

Task 2.2

(a)   The material usage variance for November 1998 is £3,010 favourable. Explain what this means.

....

....

....

(b)   Explain how the material usage standard may have been established.

....

....

....

Task 2.3

In Task 1.1(b) you calculated the re-order level and buffer stock. Explain the difference between these two terms.

....

....

....

....

....

Task 2.4

In Task 1.2 you calculated the labour cost variances for the packing department for November 1998. Show the labour efficiency variance as an efficiency ratio.

$$\frac{16480}{16,000} = 103\%. \qquad \left(\frac{412,000)}{25}\right) = 16,480$$

Task 2.5

Complete the variance account for the labour cost variances that you have calculated in task 1.2.

Variance account

LABOUR WAGE RATE PER A/C	800	LABOUR EFFICIENCY	2,520
	1,720		
	2,520		2,520

Task 2.6

In future Crunchy-Bites Ltd would like to pay a bonus to its workers. The bonus would be paid at actual wage rates for 50% of standard hours saved. On the basis of your figures in task 1.2 calculate the bonus that would be paid to workers in the packing department.

BUDGETED HOURS   16,480

ACTUAL HOURS 16,000

480 SAVING × 50% = 240 Hrs SAVD

240 × £5.30 = £1,272.00

Task 2.7

Using your results from task 1.3(b)

(a) identify the trend in cost per packet of biscuits for production between 175,000 and 225,000 packets;

(b) give reasons for this trend.

Task 2.8

Task 1.3 deals with fixed and variable costs. Two other classifications of cost behaviour are semi-variable costs and stepped fixed costs.

Sketch graphs below and give an example of each.

Semi-variable

Cost
£

Activity

Example

....

Stepped fixed

Cost
£

Activity

Example

....

Task 2.9

Justify your choice of examples in task 2.8.

....

....

....

....

....

Task 2.10

Crunchy-Bites Ltd plans to buy a machine which will be used most in its initial years.

Suggest a suitable method of depreciation giving a reason for your choice.

• **Method**

....

• **Reason**

....

....

....

Task 2.11

In task 1.4 you were given the budgeted production overheads for the mixing, baking and packing departments to arrive at overhead absorption rates for each department.

(a) **Explain why you do not have to calculate a budgeted overhead absorption rate for the stores department.**

....

....

(b)   **Explain what will have happened to the budgeted overheads for the stores department.**

....

....

....

....

Task 2.12

In task 1.4 the budgeted overhead absorption rates for the baking and packing departments were based upon time, whilst the rate for the mixing department was based upon value.

State which approach to overhead absorption is more appropriate, giving a reason for your answer.

....

....

....

....

SECTION 3

You are advised to spend approximately 1 hour on this section. The task is detailed on page 317.

Data

The production manager has asked you to provide cost information on the performance of the packing department for November 1998.

Some of the work has already been done;

*   the material variances have been calculated and inserted;
*   you have calculated the labour variances in task 1.2.

The fixed overhead variances have not been calculated. However, you have been provided with the following information for November 1998 for the packing department.

Budgeted overhead	£215,000
Budgeted labour hours	17,200
Actual labour hours	16,000
Standard labour hours produced	16,480
Actual overheads	£229,000

There have been several complaints about the quality of the packing material that has been used and the resultant high wastage. As a consequence a new supplier was used in November 1998 whose price was higher than standard. The company had also used a more experienced packing team. It was originally planned that trainee packers would be used.

Task 3.1

Using the information given above complete the table of variances shown below and prepare a report.

Your report should:

- identify the total variances;

- identify any significant sub-variances in excess of £5,000;

- explain the possible causes of the material and labour variances;

- explain what the overhead sub-variances mean and note any overhead variance that should be brought to the attention of the production manager.

Note. Do not complete the shaded boxes.

STANDARD COST REPORT		
To:		Period:
Description	Sub-variance	Total variance
	£	£
Material		
Material price	5,390 (A)	
Material usage	3,010 (F)	
Total material cost		2,380 (A)
Labour		
Labour wage rate	800(A)	
Labour efficiency	2,520(F)	
Total labour cost		1,720(F)
Overheads		
Overhead expenditure	14,000 A	
Overhead capacity	15,000(A)	
Overhead efficiency	6,000(F)	
Overhead volume	19,000(A)	
Total overhead cost		23,000 (A).

TRIAL RUN CENTRAL ASSESSMENT 2

INTERMEDIATE STAGE - NVQ/SVQ3

Unit 6

Recording cost information
June 1999

TRIAL RUN CENTRAL ASSESSMENT 2 (JUNE 1999)

This central assessment is in THREE sections. You are reminded that competence must be achieved in each section. You should therefore attempt and aim to complete EVERY task in EACH section.

Essential calculations should be included within your answers where appropriate.

SECTION 1

You are advised to spend approximately 1 hour 15 minutes on this section.

Please note that the tasks should be attempted in numerical order.

The tasks are detailed on pages 321 to 324.

Data

Golden Plum Limited is a small company that bottles and packages specialist jams.

The jam is bought in after the glucose, sugar syrup and fruit extract have been blended and set and passes through the following production departments:

- Inspection
- Bottling
- Packing

The following service departments support these production departments:

- Stores
- Maintenance
- General office

You work as an accounting technician in the general office reporting to the accountant. You have been given a number of tasks concerned with the company's activities for 1999 and 2000.

Task 1.1

There have been several increases recently in the cost of glass jars that are used to bottle jam. The accountant says that she wants these rises reflected in the value of issues from store.

Complete the stores ledger card using the First-In-First-Out (LIFO) method to cost the issues of glass and value stock for May 1999.

Note. Totals for the value columns for Issues and Balance **must** be shown for each date. Also workings to arrive at values for Issues and Balance should be shown.

	STORES LEDGER CARD						Month:		
Material:									
	Receipts			Issues			Balance		
Date	Quantity	Cost (per jar) £	Value £	Quantity	Cost (per jar) £	Value £	Quantity	Cost (per jar) £	Value £
Balance b/f May 1							48,000	35,600 × 0.12 / 12,400 × 0.13	5,884
May 6	31,000	0.15	4,650				79,000	35,600 × 0.12 / 12,400 × 0.13 / 31,000 × 0.15	10,534
May 9				28,000	0.15	4200	51,000	35,600 × 0.12 / 12,400 × 0.13 / 3,000 × 0.15	6334
May 14				37,000	3,000×0.15 / 12,400×0.13 / 21,600×0.12	450 / 1,612 / 2592	14,000	14,000×0.12	1,680
May 20	22,500	0.16	3,600				36,500	14,000×0.12 / 22,500×0.16	5280
May 26				24,000	22,500×.16 / 1,500×0.12	3600 / 180	12,500	12,500×0.12	1500

Task 1.2

Golden Plum Limited operates a system of standard costing and variance analysis.

One of your monthly tasks is to assess labour performance in each production department. A cost clerk in the general office has collated the following labour performance statistics for the packing department for May 1999.

Standard time to pack a case	45 seconds
Actual cases packed	102,000
Standard labour hour rate	£6.75 per hour
Actual wages paid	£8,418
Actual hours worked	1,220

Complete the labour variance schedule below to TWO decimal places.

Note the shaded areas should not be filled in but all other boxes should be completed.

LABOUR VARIANCE SCHEDULE			
Department:		Month:	
Variance	Actual cost	Standard cost	Variance
	£	£	£
Labour efficiency			£ 371.25 (F)
Labour wage rate			£ 183.00 (A)
Total labour cost	£ 8,418	£ 8606.25	£ 188.25 F

Task 1.3

The accountant wants you to complete cost projections for the year ended 31 May 2000 for a special 'Millennium Marmalade' presentation package for which Golden Plum Limited has identified a market.

Investigations have revealed the following.

- Costs are either fixed or variable
- All material costs are variable
- Some labour and overhead costs are fixed and some variable

Complete the table below and calculate the cost per jar for each level of production to TWO decimal places.

	BUDGETED PRODUCTION SCHEDULE			
Product:				Year:
	PRODUCTION (JARS)			
	150,000	175,000	190,000	220,000
COST	£	£	£	£
Material	34,500	40,250	43,700	50,600
Labour	42,000	44,000	45,200	47,600
Overhead	60,000	65,000	68,000	74,000
Total cost	136,500	149,250	156,900	172,200
Cost per jar (£)	0.91	0.85	0.83	0.78

Task 1.4

The accountant has asked you to do some work on overhead absorption in the production departments for 1999.

From company budgets it has been established that:

- budgeted stores overheads for 1999 are £125,000

- budgeted maintenance overheads for 1999 are £85,600

- the bottling department is to be reapportioned with 45% of the budgeted stores overheads and 40% of the budgeted maintenance overheads

- the packing department is to be reapportioned with 35% of the budgeted stores overheads and 40% of the budgeted maintenance overheads

- the bottling department absorbs overheads on the basis of machine hours

- the packing department absorbs overheads on the basis of labour hours

(a) **Complete the table below to arrive at the budgeted production overhead absorption rates of the bottling and packing departments to TWO decimal places.**

BUDGETED PRODUCTION OVERHEAD SCHEDULE (EXTRACT) YEAR: 1999	Bottling department	Packing department
Allocated overheads (£)	85,000	96,000
Apportioned overheads (£)	246,000	194,000
Reapportioned stores overheads (£)	56,250	43,750
Reapportioned maintenance overheads (£)	34,240	34,240
Total production overheads (£)	421,490	367,990
Budgeted machine hours	17,381	11,807
Budgeted labour hours	14,605	16,919
Budgeted production overhead Absorption rate (£)	24.25 M/H	21.75 L/H.

The accountant wants you to review the absorption of production overheads in the bottling department, for the three months ended May 1999.

The standard time to bottle one jar is 30 seconds and overheads are absorbed on the basis of standard hours produced.

(b)   **Complete the schedule below for the bottling department.**

Note: production overheads absorbed should be rounded to the nearest £.

BOTTLNG DEPARTMENT OVERHEAD ABSORPTION SCHEDULE	March 1999	April 1999	May 1999
Actual production overheads (£)	31,650	32,398	32,880
Jars bottled	157,392	159,804	163,500
Standard machine hours produced (to one decimal place)	1,311.60	1,331.7	1,362.5
Budgeted production overheads absorption rate (£)	24.25	24.25	24.25
Overheads absorbed (£)	31,806	32,294	33,041
Over/(under) absorbed production overheads (£)	156 (o)	104(u)	161(o)

SECTION 2

You are advised to spend approximately 45 minutes on this section. The task is detailed on pages 325 and 328.

Task 2.1

In task 1.1. you calculated the value of the closing stock on May 26 using the Last-In-First-Out method.

(a) Would the value of the closing stock be higher or lower if the First-In-First-Out (FIFO) method of valuation was used?

....

(b) Explain the reason for the difference in the closing stock value between using the First-In-First-Out method and the Last-In-First-Out method of valuation.

....
....
....
....
....
....

Task 2.2

The accountant is worried because the number of glass jars has gone below the reorder level and a new order has not been placed.

Explain how the reorder level is arrived at.

....
....
....
....

Task 2.3

The materials that come into store are coded for costing purposes.

List two benefits to the company from coding materials

(i) ....
....

(ii) ....
....

BPP PUBLISHING

Task 2.4

In task 1.2 you calculated the labour sub-variances. Explain how the standard for the labour wage rate might have been arrived at.

....

....

....

....

Task 2.5

Explain what a standard labour hour produced is.

....

....

....

....

....

Task 2.6

The company wishes to calculate labour turnover in the packing department.

(a)   Give a ratio that would express labour turnover.

....

....

(b)   Give one source of information for labour turnover.

....

Task 2.7

In task 1.3 costs were classified as being either fixed or variable. Another classification of cost is stepped-fixed.

Sketch in the graph below to show how stepped-fixed costs behave with changes in the level of production and give an example of a stepped-fixed cost.

Costs (£)

Level of production

Example of a stepped-fixed cost:

....

Task 2.8

In task 1.3 labour and overhead costs were identified as being either fixed or variable. Give one example of a fixed cost for:

Labour...

Overheads...

Task 2.9

Identify the trend in the cost per jar as production moves from 150,000 to 220,000 jars from your answer to task 1.3 and explain the reason for this trend.

Trend:..

....

....

Explanation for trend: ....

....

....

....

....

....

Task 2.10

In task 1.4 the service cost centres were reapportioned to the production cost centres. Explain why this is done.

....

....

....

....

....

Task 2.11

Below are four types of costs that have been included in task 1.4(a) in either allocated overheads or apportioned overheads for the bottling department.

Identify whether they are an apportioned cost or an allocated cost for the bottling department by circling the appropriate classification.

(i)	Rent of factory	Apportioned cost	Allocated cost
(ii)	Wages of bottling department supervisor	Apportioned cost	Allocated cost
(iii)	Maintenance costs of machinery in bottling department	Apportioned cost	Allocated cost
(iv)	Insurance of factory buildings	Apportioned cost	Allocated cost

Task 2.12

Complete the production overhead control account for the bottling department for April 1999 using your answer from task 1.4(b).

PRODUCTION OVERHEAD CONTROL A/C

	£		£
ACTUAL OVERHEADS (BANK)	32,398	OVERHEADS ABSORBED (WIP)	32,294
		PEL.	104
	32,398		32,398

SECTION 3

You are advised to spend approximately 1 hour on this section. The task is detailed on pages 329 and 331.

DATA

The accountant has asked you to review the performance of the bottling department against the budget for January to May 1999.

A cost clerk has calculated the material and labour variances and these have been inserted in the standard cost report on page 330.

The fixed overhead variances have not been calculated. In order to calculate the variances you have collected the following information for the year-to-date in the bottling department.

Budgeted production overheads	£178,359
Budgeted machine hours	7,355
Actual machine hours	6,925
Standard machine hours produced (to nearest hour)	6,659
Actual production overheads	£164,379

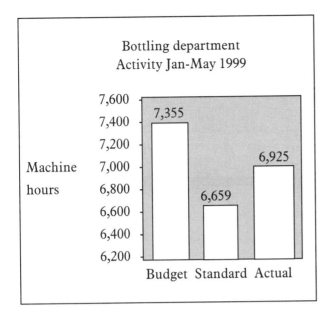

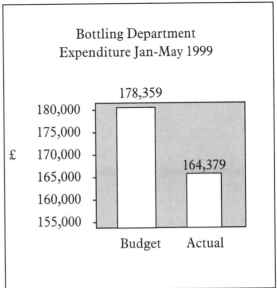

The budgeted production overhead absorption rate should be to TWO decimal places and be calculated on the basis of budgeted machine hours.

The company has be under pressure recently to reduce costs. A proposed pay increase has not been implemented and training of new operatives in the production departments has been reduced. The price of the glass that is provided by the company's only supplier has increased unexpectedly.

Task 3.1

Complete the standard cost report on page 330 by:

- calculating the overhead variances
- summarising the total variances
- listing any sub-variance in excess of £2,500
- commenting on the possible causes of all the material and labour variances and sub-variances from **the information given**
- explaining what the variances for fixed overheads mean and noting any overhead variance that should be brought to the attention of the accountant.

Note. The stationery available on pages 330 and 331 is indicative of the length of report required. However, if you require additional stationery a continuation sheet is available on page 332.

Task 3.1

Notes. Entries should be to the nearest £. Do not complete the shaded boxes.

STANDARD COST REPORT		
To:	Period:	
Description	Sub-variance	Total variance
	£	£
MATERIAL		
Material price	2,840 (A)	
Material usage	390 (A)	
Total material cost		3,230 (A)
LABOUR		
Labour wage rate	890 (F)	
Labour efficiency	2,875 (A)	
Total labour cost		1,985 (A)
OVERHEADS		
Overhead expenditure	13,980 (F)	
Overhead capacity	3552 (F)	
Overhead efficiency	10,428 (F)	
Overhead volume	6451 (F)	13,980 (F)
Total overhead cost		

COMMENTS

Task 3.1 (continued)

COMMENTS

CONTINUATION SHEET (This sheet is provided for the continuation of the report. It will not need to be used by all candidates.)

COMMENTS

TRIAL RUN CENTRAL ASSESSMENT 3

INTERMEDIATE STAGE - NVQ/SVQ3

Unit 6

Recording cost information
December 1999

TRIAL RUN CENTRAL ASSESSMENT 3 (DECEMBER 1999)

This central assessment is in TWO sections. Section 1 is divided into two parts; Parts A and B. Part A consists of longer questions, whilst Part B comprises short answer questions.

You are reminded that competence must be achieved in each section. You should therefore attempt and aim to complete EVERY task in EACH section.

Essential calculations should be included in your answers where appropriate.

You are advised to spend approximately 1hour 15 minutes on Section 1: Part A, 45 minutes on Section 1: Part B and 1 hour on Section 2.

SECTION 1

You are advised to spend approximately 2 hours on this section.

Please note that the tasks should be attempted in numerical order.

This section is in two parts.

PART A

Data

You are an accounting technician working in the cost office of a firm of builders and reporting to the cost accountant. The firm builds two-bedroom and three-bedroom houses to a standard specification.

The houses are built on three sites: Northsite, Southsite and Westsite. Each site has a team of workers, which consists of bricklayers, plumbers, an electrician and painters. On each site a site manager oversees the team of workers. There is a central stores that distributes materials to each site and the administration for the three sites is done centrally at the head office.

The cost accountant has given you a number of tasks.

Task 1.1

Data

The Cotswold brick is a specific brick used on Northsite. A cost clerk has completed the ledger card below on a First-In-First-Out basis for issues from stores during November 1999.

BPP PUBLISHING

STORES LEDGER CARD

Material: Cotswold Brick　　　　　　　　　　　　　　　　　Month: November 1999

Date	Receipts			Issues			Balance		
	Quantity	Cost per 1,000 £	Value £	Quantity	Cost per 1,000 £	Value £	Quantity	Cost per 1,000 £	Value £
Balance b/f November 1							19,500	1,100	21,450
November 6	10,500	1,150	12,075				30,000	(19.5 × 1,100) + (10.50 × 1,150)	33,525
November 8				14,000	1,100	15,400	16,000	(5.5 × 1,100) + (10.5 × 1,150)	18,125
November 13	16,000	1,175	18,800				32,000	(5.5 × 1,100) + (10.5 × 1,150) + (16 × 1,175)	36,925
November 15				19,000	(5.5 × 1,100) + (10.5 × 1,150) + (3 × 1,175)	21,650	13,000	1,175	15,275
November 22				10,000	1,175	11,750	3,000	1,175	3,525

Task 1.1

However, company policy is to use the Last-In-First-Out basis of valuation.

Complete the stores ledger card below using the Last-In-First-Out (LIFO) basis to cost the issues and value stock for November 1999.

Notes. Totals for the value columns for Issues and Balance for each date must be shown. Workings to arrive at values for Issues and Balance should be shown.

	STORES LEDGER CARD								
Material: Cotswold Brick						Month: November 1999			
	Receipts			Issues			Balance		
Date	Quantity	Cost per 1,000 £	Value £	Quantity	Cost per 1,000 £	Value £	Quantity	Cost per 1,000 £	Value £
Balance b/f November 1							19,500	1,100	21,450
November 6	10,500	1,150	12,075				30,000	19.5 × 1,100 10.5 × 1,150	21,450 33,525
November 8				14,000	10.5 × 1,150 3.5 × 1,100	12,075 3,850	16,000	16.0 × 1,100	17,600
November 13	16,000	1,175	18,800				32,000	16.0 × 1,100 16.0 × 1,175	36,400
November 15				19,000	16.0 × 1.175 3.0 × 1,100	18,800 3300	13,000	13.0 × 1,100	14,300
November 22				10,000	10.0 × 1,100	11,000	3,000	3.0 × 1,100	3,300

Task 1.2

Data

The cost accountant has asked you to do some pay and efficiency calculations for the electricians on the three sites for November 1999. You are told that:

- there is one electrician on each site
- each electrician works a 35-hour week
- there are four operating weeks in November
- each electrician is allowed the following standard times for their work

2-bedroom house	9 hours
3-bedroom house	15 hours

- the company has a bonus scheme in operation that pays 75% of any standard hours saved at the basic wage rate.

BPP PUBLISHING

A cost clerk provides you with the following operating statistics for the electricians.

	Northsite	Southsite	Westsite
Houses completed			
2-bedroom	8	8	6
3-bedroom	6	4	7
Wage rate per hour (£)	7.70	7.60	7.20

Task 1.2

Complete the schedule below for November 1999.

Notes:

• bonus calculations should be rounded to the nearest £

• the labour efficiency calculation should be a ratio expressed as a percentage, rounded to the nearest whole number

ELECTRICIAN BONUS AND EFFICIENCY SCHEDULE

Description	Northsite	Southsite	Westsite	Total
Actual hours worked	140	140	140	420
Standard hours produced	162	132	159	453
Standard hours saved	22		19	41
Basic wages (£)	1,078	1,064	1,008	3,150
Bonus (£)	127		108	235
Total labour cost (£)	1,205	1,064	1,116	3,385
Labour efficiency (%)	116	94	114	108

Task 1.3

Data

The cost accountant has asked you to prepare budgeted overhead absorption rates on the basis of labour hours for the year ending 31 December 2000. A cost clerk presents you with the following information.

- Allocated overheads are budgeted as follows:

Northsite	£230,000
Southsite	£195,000
Westsite	£176,000

- Head office and stores expenses of £1,920,000 are to be apportioned to each site in proportion to the number of direct workers on each site.

- Depreciation of £319,000 is to be apportioned to each site on the basis of machine usage which is as follows:

Northsite	13,200 hours
Southsite	9,900 hours
Westsite	8,800 hours

The following budgeted data is available to determine the total budgeted labour hours for each site.

- Direct workers on each site are:

Northsite	9
Southsite	8
Westsite	7

- Each worker is budgeted to work 35 hours per week for 50 weeks a year.

Task 1.3

Complete the budgeted overhead schedule below for the year ending 31 December 2000 to arrive at a budgeted overhead absorption rate for each site based upon labour hours.

Notes. The budgeted overhead absorption rate should be rounded to two decimal places. Do not complete the shaded boxes.

BUDGETED OVERHEAD SCHEDULE YEAR ENDING 31 DECEMBER 2000				
	Northsite	**Southsite**	**Westsite**	**Total**
	£	£	£	£
Allocated overheads	230,000	195,000	176,000	601,000
Apportioned overheads				
Head office and stores expenses	720,000	640,000	560,000	1,920,000
Depreciation	132,000	99,000	88,000	319,000
Total budgeted overheads	1,082,000	934,000	824,000	2,840,000
Total budgeted labour hours	15,750	14,000	12250	
Budgeted overhead absorption rate per labour hour	68.70	66.71	67.27	

Task 1.4

Data

The managing director has asked for costings for a standard two-bedroom house and a standard three-bedroom house that are going to be built at Westsite during the year ended 31 December 2000.

The cost office has provided the following incomplete budgeted data.

	2-bedroom house	3-bedroom house
Materials		
Floor area (square metres)	160	200
Bricks	£4,800	★
Timber	£1,200	★
Consumables	£600	★
Furnishings	£7,200	★
★ To be calculated		

	Rate	2-bedroom house	3-bedroom house
Labour	£	Hours	Hours
Type			
Bricklayer	8.20	50	60
Plumber	7.00	8	10
Electrician	7.50	9	15
Painter	6.50	16	20

Upon investigation you are told that:

- all the cost of the bricks and timber varies with floor area
- £300 of the consumables' cost and £2,880 of the furnishings' cost is fixed
- the remainder of consumables' and furnishings' costs vary with floor area
- it is company policy to take a profit of one-third of selling price

Task 1.4

Complete the job cost card below for the two houses using the information on page 342 and the relevant overhead absorption rate that you calculated in task 1.3

Note. All workings should be to the nearest £.

BUDGETED JOB COST CARD WESTSITE YEAR ENDING 31 DECEMBER 2000		
	2-bedroom house £	3-bedroom house £
MATERIALS: Bricks	4,800	6,000
Wood	1,200	1,500
Consumables	600	675
Furnishings	7,200	8,280
TOTAL MATERIALS	13,800	16,455
LABOUR: Bricklayer	410	492
Plumber	56	70
Electrician	68	113
Painter	104	130
TOTAL LABOUR	638	805
OVERHEADS	5,583	7,063.
TOTAL COST	20,021	24,323
PROFIT	10,011	12,162
PRICE	30,032	36,485

PART B

Task 1.5

The task consists of parts (a)-(1) and is detailed on pages 343 to 345.

(a) In task 1.1 it was stated that company policy is to use the Last-In-First-Out method to cost issues and value stock.

Does this mean that the last receipt of bricks must be used first? Give a reason for your answer.

....

....

....

....

....

(b) Explain how the Last-In-First-Out method differs from the First-In-First-Out method for costing issues of stock.

....

....

....

....

(c) It is company policy to keep a buffer stock of bricks equivalent to one week's usage. Give a reason why the company would want to keep a buffer stock.

....

....

....

....

(d) In task 1.2 the electricians were paid a guaranteed hourly rate. Another method of labour payment is the piecework basis.

(i) Explain how piecework payments are calculated

....

....

....

....

....

(ii) List one weakness of this method

....

....

....

(e)   Overtime is not normal policy for the company and is only worked at the customer's request. Circle the type of cost that this will be classified as.

Direct labour/Direct expense/Overhead

(f)   In task 1.2 the electricians were allowed a standard time of 9 hours to work on the 2-bedroom house.

Explain how this standard time allowance could have been set.

....

....

....

....

....

....

(g)   Office machinery bought for £10,000 with a life of 5 years and a residual value of £1,000 is depreciated on a straight line basis.

Calculate the annual depreciation charge.

....

....

....

....

....

(h)   On review it was found that the office machinery has most of its usage in the earlier years. Do you think that the straight line method is the appropriate method. If not, state an alternative, giving your reasons.

....

....

....

....

(i)   Two of the costs budgeted for the year ended 31 December 2000 at head office are:

- telephone charges
- premises rental

The same premises are to be used throughout the year.

Sketch the behaviour and classify these costs below.

Telephone	Premises rental
Cost £	Cost £
Activity	Activity
Type of cost...................	Type of cost.....................

(j) The company's overheads are absorbed on the basis of labour hours.

    (i) List one other basis for overhead absorption.

....

....

....

    (ii) Explain when this basis should be used.

....

....

....

(k) Task 1.3 included allocated and apportioned overheads.

    (i) Give an example of an allocated overhead for one of the building sites.

....

    (ii) Explain the difference between allocated overheads and apportioned overheads.

....

....

....

....

....

(l) Cost data for the company for the year to 30 November 1999 for overheads shows:

	£
Budgeted overheads	2,135,000
Actual overheads	2,240,000
Absorbed overheads	2,170,000

Calculate the under/over recovery of overheads for the period.

....

....

....

SECTION 2

You are advised to spend approximately 1 hour on this section.

Data

One of your monthly tasks is to prepare a standard cost report for the performance of the three sites. Some work has already been done on the November 1999 report for Southsite.

The following variances have been calculated:

- All of the material variances with the exception of bricks for which information has only just become available

- All of the labour variances; and

- The fixed overhead expenditure and fixed overhead volume variances.

In order to finish the calculation of the variances a cost clerk provides you with the following data for November 1999.

Materials (bricks)		Overheads	
Actual usage	230,000	Budgeted overheads	£96,000
Standard usage	235,000	Budgeted labour hours	1,600
Standard cost per 1,000 bricks	£1,200	Actual labour hours	1,350
Actual cost	£280,750	Standard labour hours produced	1,480
		Actual overheads	£101,200

BAR-CHART
ACTIVITY IN LABOUR HOURS

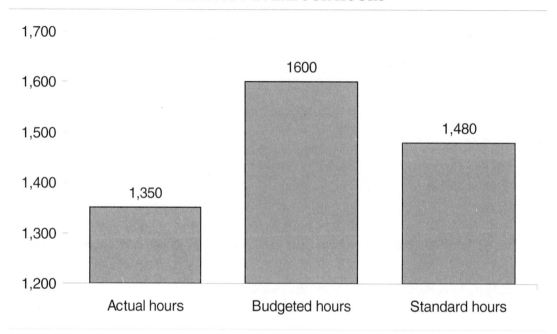

It is company policy to absorb overheads on the basis of labour hours.

The company has recently reviewed the quality of the materials that it has used and has chosen better quality materials than those budgeted for. The company has also increased wage rates above the budgeted level in order to retain existing staff and attract new staff.

Task 2.1

Complete the standard cost report by:

(a) • calculating the material variances for bricks

- using these variances and the material variances given below to calculate the total material variances for all materials for inclusion in the standard cost report

- calculating the remaining fixed overhead variances

Note: The material variances for other materials exclusive of bricks are:

- Material Price = £1,390 (A)
- Material usage = £2,840 (F)
- Total material cost = £1,450 (F)

All workings should be to the nearest £.

<table>
<tr><td colspan="3" align="center">STANDARD COST REPORT</td></tr>
<tr><td>Site: Southsite</td><td></td><td align="right">Period: November 1999</td></tr>
<tr><td>Description</td><td align="center">Sub-variance</td><td align="center">Total variance</td></tr>
<tr><td></td><td align="center">£</td><td align="center">£</td></tr>
<tr><td>MATERIAL</td><td></td><td></td></tr>
<tr><td>Material price</td><td align="center">4,750 (A)</td><td></td></tr>
<tr><td>Material usage</td><td align="center">6,000 (F)</td><td></td></tr>
<tr><td>Total material cost</td><td align="center">1,250 (F)</td><td align="center">1,250 (F)</td></tr>
<tr><td>LABOUR</td><td></td><td></td></tr>
<tr><td>Labour wage rate</td><td align="center">1,890 (A)</td><td></td></tr>
<tr><td>Labour efficiency</td><td align="center">3,875 (F)</td><td></td></tr>
<tr><td>Total labour cost</td><td></td><td align="center">1,985 (F)</td></tr>
<tr><td>OVERHEADS</td><td></td><td></td></tr>
<tr><td>Overhead expenditure</td><td align="center">5,200 (A)</td><td></td></tr>
<tr><td></td><td></td><td></td></tr>
<tr><td>Overhead capacity</td><td align="center">15,000 (A)</td><td></td></tr>
<tr><td>Overhead efficiency</td><td align="center">7,800 (F)</td><td></td></tr>
<tr><td>Overhead volume</td><td align="center">7,200 (A)</td><td></td></tr>
<tr><td>Total overhead cost</td><td></td><td align="center">12,400 (A)</td></tr>
</table>

(b) • **summarising the total variances**

• **commenting on the possible causes of all the material and labour variances and sub-variances from the information given**

• **explaining what the variances for fixed overheads mean and noting any overhead variance that should be brought to the attention of the cost accountant**

COMMENTARY

CONTINUATION SHEET (This sheet is provided for the continuation of the report. it will not need to be used by all candidates.)

COMMENTS

BPP PUBLISHING

SAMPLE CENTRAL ASSESSMENT

INTERMEDIATE STAGE - NVQ/SVQ3

Unit 6

Recording cost information
(AAT Specimen)

This Sample Central Assessment is the AAT's Specimen Central Assessment for Unit 6. Its purpose is to give you an idea of what an AAT central assessment looks like. It is not intended as a definitive guide to the tasks you may be required to perform.

The suggested time allowance for this Assessment is three hours. You are advised to spend approximately 75 minutes on Section 1, 45 minutes on Section 2 and 60 minutes on Section 3.

Calculators may be used but no reference material is permitted.

DO NOT OPEN THIS PAPER UNTIL YOU ARE READY TO START
UNDER TIMED CONDITIONS

INSTRUCTIONS

This Central Assessment is designed to test your ability to record cost information.

The Central Assessment is in **three** sections.

You are provided with data which you must use to complete the tasks, and space to set out your answers.

You are allowed **three hours** to complete your work. You are reminded that competence must be achieved in each section. You should therefore attempt and aim to complete **every** task in **each** section. All essential workings should be included in your answer where appropriate.

A high level of accuracy is required. Check your work carefully.

Correcting fluid may be used in moderation. Errors should be crossed out neatly and clearly. You should write in black ink, not pencil.

A suggested answer to this Assessment is given on page 419.

WICKFORD LIMITED

SECTION 1

You are advised to spend approximately 75 minutes on this section.

Please note that the tasks should be attempted in numerical order.

Data

Wickford Limited is a company that specialises in the manufacture of crystal glass. It makes a number of standard products, for which there is a buoyant demand, and also makes one-off products. One such one-off product is a commemorative vase to celebrate one hundred and fifty years of glass-making within the factory.

The manufacturing process within the factory is organised into three production cost centres, which are:

- Blowing
- Cutting
- Engraving

These production cost centres are serviced by three service cost centres, which are:

- Quality control
- Stores
- Maintenance

You are an accounting technician working in the cost department and you report to the cost accountant. You have been given a number of tasks concerned with the factory's activities for 1997 and its plans for 1998.

Task 1

Your office has been given the responsibility of compiling the budgeted costs for the commemorative vase. Initially, production was forecast at 750,000 units; however, overseas interest now means that demand could be as high as 1,000,000 or 1,250,000 units.

Complete the budgeted cost schedule below for 1,000,000 and 1,250,000 units.

	1998 BUDGETED PRODUCTION COSTS		
Costs Units	750,000	1,000,000	1,250,000
Variable costs	£	£	£
Material	2,250,000	3,000,000	3,750,000
Labour	2,437,500	3,250,000	4,062,500
Overhead	2,062,500	2,750,000	3,437,500
Total	**6,750,000**	9,000,000	11,250,000
Fixed costs			
Labour	1,100,000	1,100,000	1,100,000
Overhead	1,750,000	1,750,000	1,750,000
Total	**2,850,000**	2,850,000	2,850,000
Total production cost	9,600,000	11,850,000	14,100,000
Cost per unit	12.80	11.85	11.28

Task 2

Labour in the blowing department is organised into teams of three. For the manufacturing of the commemorative vase there will be a master blower, blower and a general assistant in each team.

You are told that the following rates of pay apply in the blowing department:

Master blower   £8.60 per hour
Blower   £6.40 per hour
General assistant   £4.20 per hour

Standards set for the production of the commemorative vase are that each team should produce 30 vases per hour. In order to encourage production, it has been agreed that each member of the team should receive a bonus of 50% of any time saved, paid at the standard rate.

During January 1998, Team Alpha in the blowing department produced 5,370 vases. Team Alpha worked four five-day weeks in January 1998 and each working day was seven and three-quarters hours.

Complete the wage schedule below to determine the total pay for each member of Team Alpha for January 1998.

WAGE SCHEDULE				
Blowing dept: Team Alpha			Month: January 1998	
	Team	*Master Blower*	*Blower*	*Gen Assistant*
Wage rate (£)		8.60	6.40	4.20
Hrs worked		155	155	155
Total wage (£)		1333	992	651
Standard hours produced	179			
Standard hours saved	24			
Bonus (£)		103.20	76.80	50.40
Total wage + bonus (£)		1,436.20	1,068.80	700.40

Task 3

The raw materials that are used in the manufacture of the commemorative crystal vase are silica sand, potash and lead monoxide. The company has noted that the cost of silica sand from suppliers fluctuates and it needs to ensure that it issues the sand to production at a cost that reflects the most recent price.

Complete the store card below using the last-in-first-out costing method to cost issues of silica sand and value stock for the month of November 1997.

STORE CARD

Material: Silica Sand   MONTH: NOV 97

Date	Receipts			Issues			Stock		
	Qty	Cost per kg	Value	Qty	Cost per kg	Value	Qty	Cost per kg	Value
Nov	'000 kg	£	£'000	'000 kg	£	£'000	'000 kg	£	£'000
Bal 1							1,470	2.00	2,940
5	860	2.15	1849				2,330	1470×2.00 / 860×2.15	4,789
9				1,060	860×2.15 / 200×2.00	1849 / 400	1270	1270×2.00	2,540
14	1,100	2.25	2,475				2,370	1,270×2.00 / 1,100×2.25	5,015
18	1,050	2.20	2,310				3,420	1270×2.00 / 1100×2.25 / 1050×2.20	7,325
21				2,300	1,050×2.20 / 1100×2.25 / 150×2.00	2310 / 2475 / 360	1,120	1120×2.00	2,240
23	1,430	2.40	3,432				2,550	1,120×2.00 / 1,430×2.40	5,672
25				1,540	1430×2.40 / 110×2.00	3432 / 220	1,010	1,010×2.00	2,020
28				820	820×2.00	1640	190	190×2.00	380

Task 4

It has been decided that production overheads will be charged to the commemorative vases on the basis of the pre-determined production overhead rates for each of the production cost centres.

You are given the following budgeted information for 1998:

- The production departments (blowing, cutting and engraving) are serviced by the quality control, stores and maintenance departments.

- The maintenance department will provide the following service hours to the other departments for 1998:

Blowing	1,400
Cutting	725
Engraving	475
Quality control	240
Stores	240

- The stores department is budgeted to receive the following requisitions orders from the other cost centres:

Blowing	1,944
Cutting	712
Engraving	524
Quality control	172

- The quality control department is budgeted to provide the following hours of service to the production cost centres:

Blowing	6,300
Cutting	2,100
Engraving	1,800

- Production overheads will be absorbed on a labour hour basis.

(a) **Complete the budgeted production overhead schedule below to reapportion the service department overheads and calculate the total budgeted overheads for the three production departments. Ignore variable overheads.**

Year: 1998	Budgeted Production Overhead Schedule						
Cost centre Cost	Blowing £'000	Cutting £'000	Engrav- ing £'000	Quality control £'000	Stores £'000	Maint- enance £'000	Total £'000
Allocated overhead	876	534	413	278	374	292	2,767
Apportioned overhead	1,138	793	541	311	416	324	3,523
Sub-total	**2,014**	**1,327**	**954**	**589**	**790**	**616**	**6,290**
Maintenance	280	145	95	48	48	(616)	
Stores	486	178	131	43	(838)		
Quality control	420	140	120	(680)			
Total budgeted overheads	3,200	1,790	1,300				6,290

(b) **Complete the following table when you have completed part (a).**

	Blowing	*Cutting*	*Engraving*
Total budgeted overheads (£)	3,200,000	1,799,800	1,300,000
Budgeted labour hours	48,000	35,800	32,500
Budgeted overhead absorption rate £ per labour hour	66.67	50.00	40.00

Note. Show the budgeted overhead absorption rate to two decimal places.

It is envisaged that each commemorative vase will spend the following times in the production cost centres.

	Blowing	*Cutting*	*Engraving*
Labour time (mins)	9	7½	12

(c) **Complete the following table to show the production overhead to be absorbed by each vase.**

Department	*Time*	*Budgeted overhead absorption rate per labour hour*	*Overhead absorbed*
	Minutes	£	£
Blowing	9	66.67	10.00
Cutting	7½	50.00	6.25
Engraving	12	40.00	8.00
Total			24.25

SECTION 2

You are advised to spent 45 minutes on this section.

Task 1

Briefly describe and explain the trend in costs per unit for the three budgeted levels of production in Task 1, Section 1.

....

....

....

....

....

....

....

....

....

Task 2

Sketch in the graphs below to show how fixed and variable costs behave in general with changes in the level of production.

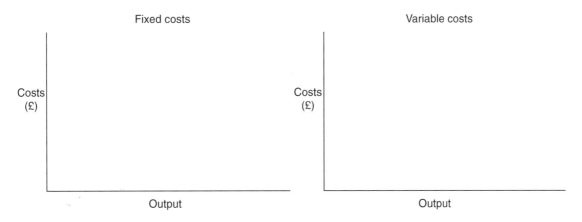

Task 3

The cost schedule in Task 1 of Section 1 defined overhead costs as being either fixed or variable with changes in the level of activity.

Give ONE other classification of behaviour of overhead cost and an example of an overhead cost that matches this classification. Then sketch a graph to show how the cost behaves with changes in the level of activity.

Classification ....

Example ....

357

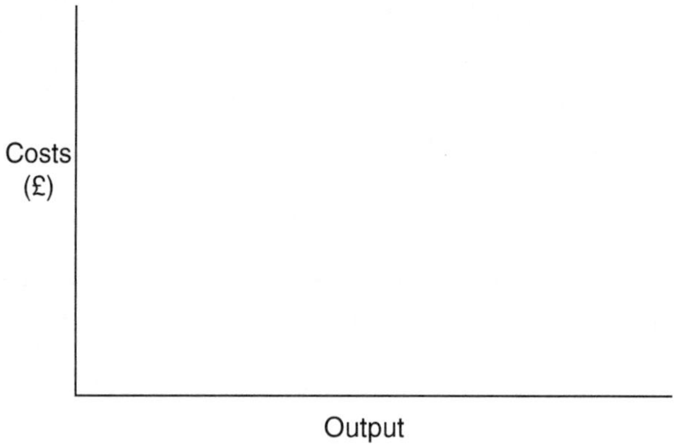

A graph with the vertical axis labelled "Costs (£)" and the horizontal axis labelled "Output".

Task 4

Briefly explain the benefits of a bonus scheme to workers and employers.

(a)   **Benefits to workers**

....

....

....

....

....

(b)   **Benefits to employers**

....

....

....

....

....

....

Task 5

In order to introduce a bonus in Task 2 of Section 1, it was necessary to establish standard times of production. Briefly explain how these standard times for the blowing team will have been established.

....

....

....

....

....

....

Task 6

Wickford Limited wants to identify periods of absence in the blowing department during 1998. Identify TWO documents that will provide this information.

(i) ....

....

....

....

....

....

(ii) ....

....

....

....

....

Task 7

Explain why LIFO was chosen as the method to cost issues of silica sand in Task 3 of Section 1.

....

....

....

....

....

....

Task 8

Briefly highlight the weaknesses of the LIFO method of costing issues and valuing stock.

....

....

....

....

....

....

BPP PUBLISHING

Task 9

The company carries a large volume of silica sand, potash and lead monoxide and is concerned about the costs of holding and ordering stock.

List TWO costs of holding stock and TWO costs of ordering stock.

Holding cost   Ordering cost

(i)   ....   (i)   ....

(ii) ....   (ii) ....

Task 10

(a)   **Identify a method that the company could use to minimise the costs listed in Task 9 above.**

....

....

....

....

....

(b)   **Briefly explain what this method sets out to achieve.**

....

....

....

....

....

Task 11

Task 4 in Section 1 shows allocated overheads and apportioned overheads for each cost centre. Give one example of each type for the blowing department.

Blowing department allocated overhead ....

Blowing department apportioned overhead ....

Task 12

Briefly explain the reasons for your choice of allocated and apportioned overheads for the blowing department in task 11 above.

....

....

....

....

SECTION 3

You are advised to spend approximately 60 minutes on this section.

Task 1

You have been given the task of reviewing the performance of the blowing department for the month of January 1998. Variances for material and labour have been calculated by a cost clerk in your office and are shown in the table on page 362.

The fixed overhead variances have not been calculated but you have ascertained the following information for the blowing department for January 1998.

Budgeted overheads (£)	217,750
Budgeted hours	3,250
Budgeted overhead absorption rate (£)	£67 per labour hour
Actual overheads (£)	234,270
Actual hours worked	3,100
Standard hour produced	3,180

You have been told that the material used in the blowing department has been acquired from new suppliers as the company is concerned to keep costs under control and the new supplier's prices were cheaper.

The company had budgeted for a small cost-of-living wage increase to be implemented in January 1998; however, this had been renegotiated to a figure that was almost double the original rise.

Complete the table of variances and prepare a report, using the proforma on page 196 that:

- Summarises the variances for material, labour and overheads and notes any significant sub-variance in excess of £4,000.

- Highlights the causes of all material and labour variances from information given.

- Derives the under/over-absorption of overheads from the variances calculated and explains how the under/over-absorption has come about.

BPP
PUBLISHING

VARIANCE SCHEDULE

Blowing dept			January 1998
		£	£
Material variance			
Material usage			4,236 (A)
Material price			1,125 (F)
Total			**3,111 (A)**
Labour variance			
Labour efficiency			1,750 (F)
Labour wage-rate			5,865 (A)
Total			**4,115 (A)**
Fixed overhead variance			
Expenditure			
	Capacity		
	Efficiency		
Volume			
Total			

REPORT

Answers to Practice Central Assessments

ANSWERS TO PRACTICE CENTRAL ASSESSMENT 1: DOWRA LTD

SECTION 1

Task 1

DOWRA LTD					
Overhead analysis sheet					
Department	Cutting	Assembly	Finishing	Design	Stores
	£	£	£	£	£
Allocated overheads	138,250	141,080	170,140	194,150	22,000
Factory overheads (W1)	35,420	60,260	49,680	22,080	16,560
Stores (W2)	14,679	16,427	6,757	697	(38,560)
Design	72,309	72,309	72,309	(216,927)	-
Total	260,658	290,076	298,886	-	-
Machine hours	180,000	85,000	240,000		
Absorption rate per machine hour	£1.45	£3.41	£1.25		

Workings

1 Overhead per square metre $= \dfrac{£184,000}{(770+1,310+1,080+480+360)}$

$= \dfrac{£184,000}{4,000} = £46$

2 Overhead per £ of requisition $= \dfrac{£38,560}{(97,760+109,400+45,000+4,640)}$

$= \dfrac{£38,560}{256,800} = £0.1501557$

Task 2

Standard Cost Card
Wooden Duck on Wheels

Materials	Quantity	Price £	Value £
5 mm board	0.2 sq m	4.60 per m^2	0.92000
4 cm diameter wheels	4	18.20 per 100	0.72800
Box	1	16.00 per 100	0.16000
Subtotal:			1.80800

Labour	Time	Rate £	Value £
Cutter	1.5 mins	7.50 per hr	0.18750
Assembler	3 mins	6.80 per hr	0.34000
Painter	4 mins	8.20 per hr	0.54667
Packer	30 secs	5.00 per hr	0.04167
Sub total:			1.11584

Production overheads	Time	Rate £	Value £
Cutting	1.5 mins	1.45 per hr	0.03625
Assembly	3 mins	3.41 per hr	0.17050
Finishing	4.5 mins	1.25 per hr	0.09375
Subtotal:			0.30050
GRAND TOTAL			3.22434

Task 3

MEMORANDUM

TO: Sales manager/production manager
FROM: A Technician
DATE: X.X.XX
SUBJECT: Overhead apportionment

As a result of falling demand for many of our popular products I have reviewed the method used by Dowra Ltd to apportion production overheads (unallocated factory costs, stores overheads and design overheads) to different products. The results of my investigation and my conclusions are set out in the following paragraphs.

(a)   *Unallocated factory overheads*

At present unallocated factory overheads are apportioned to the five cost centres on the basis of floor area. Unless the size of *all* the overheads which have been allocated to the overall factory cost centre can be related in some way to floor area, such a method of apportionment will not be fair. The costs of heating and lighting could be apportioned on the basis of floor area because the greater the floor area of a cost centre, the greater (in general) will be the consumption of heating and lighting within that cost centre. Other costs (such as canteen costs) could perhaps be apportioned on a more suitable basis, such as number of employees per cost centre.

Instead of grouping all unallocated factory overheads together they should be analysed in more detail and individual overheads apportioned to the cost centres using bases appropriate to the overhead in question.

(b) *Stores overheads*

Stores overheads are currently apportioned to the other four cost centres according to the *value* of materials requisitions. Apportionment on the basis of the *number* of materials requisition may be more appropriate. Using value, the assembly cost centres bears the largest share of the overhead. Using the number of requisitions, on the other hand, it would bear the second smallest share. The choice of method will depend on whether, in general, the value of requisitions varies because of the value of individual items requisitioned or because requisitions with a higher value are made up of more items. It is only fair to charge the stores overhead to the cost centres on the basis of the amount of work the stores cost centre does for each department. A requisition involving a great many items will involve more work than a requisition made up of just one expensive item.

(c) *Design overheads*

Using the present system, design overheads are apportioned in equal proportions to the three production departments and then applied to products using machine hours as a basis, a totally inaccurate representation of the usage of design costs by products. At present the costs are applied to products whenever one unit is produced whereas in reality the costs are incurred, just once, when the product is designed. Absorption costing is therefore unsuitable and consideration should be given to the use of activity based costing, which is particularly appropriate for support overheads.

Conclusion

The introduction of activity based costing may well improve the fairness of the apportionment of all production overheads. This should produce more accurate product costs which will, in turn, enable sensible pricing decisions to be made.

Task 4

(a) (i)

	£
25 sq m should have cost (× £4.50)	112.50
but did cost	110.00
Materials price variance	2.50 (F)

120 ducks should have used (× 0.2 sq m)	24 sq m
but did use	25 sq m
Materials usage variance in sq m	1 sq m (A)
× standard cost per sq m	× £4.50
Materials usage variance in £	£4.50
	(A)

(ii)

	£
2.75 hours should have cost (× £7.20)	19.80
but did cost	22.00
Wage rate variance	2.20 (A)

120 ducks should have taken (× 1.5 mins)	180 mins
but did take (2.75 × 60)	165 mins
Labour efficiency variance in mins	15 mins (F)
× standard rate per minute (£7.20 ÷ 60)	× £0.12
Labour efficiency variance in £	£1.80 (F)

(b) The favourable material price variance may be due to unforeseen discounts received or greater care taken in purchasing or the purchase of lower quality material.

The adverse material usage variance may be due to defective material, excessive waste, theft or stricter quality control.

There could be an interrelationship between the favourable material price variance and the adverse usage variance. Cheaper material than standard could have been purchased, which proved to be more difficult to work with than anticipated, causing greater waste than standard.

The adverse wage rate variance could have been caused by the use of workers with a rate of pay higher than standard or an unexpected wage rate increase.

The favourable labour efficiency variance means that the ducks were produced more quickly than expected which might be due to worker motivation or the use of better quality materials or machines.

There could be a link between the labour rate and efficiency variances. The use of more skilled, and hence more expensive, labour could result in production at a rate quicker than standard.

SECTION 2

1 Work in progress at Dowra Ltd could include (two of) timber that has been cut to shape (but not assembled), assembled toys (before being painted and varnished) or painted and varnished toys (before being packed).

2 Indirect materials in the design department could include pencils and paper (the cost of these being too insignificant to allocate to individual products).

3 String and wire are treated as indirect materials because their cost per toy is too insignificant to justify the administrative effort of allocating them to individual products.

4 Standard labour times would have been set by using time and motion study. Individual operations (cutting head for example) would be observed and timed with a stop watch.

5 In order to cost at the most realistic valuation (that is, a valuation which represents the current cost of the materials used), LIFO (last in, first out) could be used since stocks are issued from stocks at a price which is close to current market value. (Replacement cost *should* be used if available but this is unlikely.)

6 Some production overheads can be allocated directly to cost centres because the overhead can be associated in total with that particular cost centre. For example, the salary of the foreman in the cutting department can be charged direct to that department.

7 The idle time variance identifies the cost of idle time (that is, the time when the labour force, although being paid, were unable to work due to machine breakdowns, bottlenecks in production, or shortage of customer orders). The labour efficiency variance will then relate only to the productivity of the labour force during the time spent *actively* working.

8 Under a good bonus payments system, employees are paid more for their efficiency but, in spite of the extra labour cost, the unit cost of output is reduced and the profit earned per unit of sale is increased. The profits arising from productivity improvements are therefore shared between the company and employees.

9   *Reorder level.* When stocks reach this level action should be taken to replenish stocks.

Minimum level. This is a warning level to draw management attention to the fact that stocks are approaching a dangerously low level and that stockouts are possible. It is essentially a buffer stock.

10   (a) Stockholding costs include (two of) the following.

      (i)   Costs of storage and stores operations

      (ii) Interest charges

      (iii) Insurance

      (iv) Risk of obsolescence

      (v)   Deterioration

      (vi) Theft

    (b) Ordering costs include (two of) the following.

      (i)   Clerical and administrative costs associated with purchasing, accounting for and receiving goods

      (ii) Transport costs

      (iii) Production run costs

11   Although computerised stock control systems hold records on stock levels at all times, stocktaking will still be necessary to ensure that there are no discrepancies between the physical amount of an item in stock and the amount shown in the stock records. Just because the stock control system is computerised does not mean that the following types of discrepancies will not occur.

    (a) Suppliers deliver a different quantity of goods to that shown on the goods received note. Since this note is used to update stock records, a discrepancy will arise.

    (b) The quantity of stock issued to production is different from that shown on the materials requisition note.

    (c) Excess stock is returned from production without documentation.

    (d) Clerical errors may occur in the stock records such as an entry having been made in the wrong stock account.

    (e) Breakages in stores may go unrecorded.

    (f) Employees may steal stock.

12   The copyright fee should be classified as a direct expense because each fee of £1 will be incurred as a direct consequence of making one unit of the model.

ANSWERS TO PRACTICE CENTRAL ASSESSMENT 2: SOUTHWOOD COLLEGE

SECTION 1

Task 1

STORES LEDGER CARD								
PHOTOCOPY PAPER								
Date	*Receipts*			*Issues*			*Balance*		
	Quantity	*Price*	*Value*	*Quantity*	*Price*	*Value*	*Quantity*	*Price*	*Value*
		£	£		£	£		£	£
Oct 2							84	23.00	1,932.00
Oct 2				70	23.00	1,610.00	14	23.00	322.00
Oct 5	100	21.60	2,160.00				100	21.60	2,160.00
							114		2,482.00
Oct 9				14	23.00	322.00			
				66	21.60	1,425.60	34	21.60	734.40
Oct 12	80	26.25	2,100.00				80	26.25	2,100.00
							114		2,834.40
Oct 26				34	21.60	734.40			
				36	26.25	945.00	44	26.25	1,155.00

Task 2

Method	Closing stock valuation		
	Reams	*Price* £	*Value* £
FIFO	44	26.25	1,155.00
LIFO	14	23.00	322.00
	20	21.60	432.00
	10	26.25	262.50
	44		1,016.50
Standard cost	44	24.00	1,056.00

Task 3

MEMORANDUM

TO: Chief Accountant
FROM: A Technician
DATE: X.X.XX
SUBJECT: Stock valuation methods - photocopy paper

(a) *FIFO*

FIFO costs stock issues at the price of the earliest purchased stock. Stock is thus valued at the most recent purchase price. Stock is therefore valued realistically; however, if there is inflation, issues will be underpriced.

(b) *LIFO*

LIFO costs stock issues at the price of the most recently purchased stock. Stock is thus valued at the price of the earliest purchased stock. Stock will therefore be undervalued in a time of inflation but issues costed at a realistic price.

(c) *Standard cost*

Under standard costing, stock is costed at standard cost, the cost forecast and budgeted for by the organisation. Such a system may undercost or overcost depending on how the actual cost differs from the standard cost. Standard costs are most useful at a time of relatively stable prices.

(d) *Method to use*

Use of the LIFO method will ensure that the cost of courses is not understated. However, stocks cannot be valued at LIFO for financial accounting purposes, and therefore a different system (probably FIFO) will have to be used for the financial accounts. Standard costing is not really suitable as the price of paper appears to be rising.

Task 4

MEMORANDUM

TO: Administration Manager
FROM: A Technician
DATE: 5 December 20X5
SUBJECT: Material price variance photocopy paper - October

(a) *Material price variance*

	£
Actual cost of purchases	4,260
Standard cost of purchases (180 × £24)	4,320
Variance	60 (F)

(b) *Explanation of variance*

The reason for the favourable variance is the purchase of 100 reams of paper at a 10% quantity discount. However, this was offset by an increase in the basic price to £26.25 per ream of the other 80 units bought during the month.

BPP
PUBLISHING

Task 5

REPORT

THE POSSIBLE BULK BUYING OF PHOTOCOPY PAPER

Advantages

Bulk buying will reduce:

(a)   the basic cost of the material being purchased;

(b)   the ordering costs (since fewer orders will be required during the year).

Disadvantages

Bulk buying will increase stockholding costs since more of the material will have to be stored.

Information required

The information that will be required to calculate the optimum purchase quantity is:

(a)   ordering costs. These include stationary, postage, telephone and buying department wages;

(b)   holding costs. These include rent and rates, insurance, light and heat, wage costs and obsolescence and deterioration;

(c)   annual demand for paper.

Task 6

Course:	AAT Recording Cost Information (Classroom B)	
Duration:	10 days @ 7 hours per day	
Estimated students	20	
		£
Direct costs:		
Teaching time 70 hours at £30		2,100
Photocopy costs $20 \times 0.1 \times £30$		60
Food and drink $20 \times 10 \times £3$		600
Indirect costs:		
Catering $20 \times 10 \times £7.75$		1,550
Administration		800
Other overhead costs $20 \times 10 \times £4.46$		892
Total cost		6,002

Workings

	Classroom A	Classroom B	Classroom C	Admin	Catering	Total
	£	£	£	£	£	£
Wages	-	-	-	76,000	48,000	-
Heating and lighting (£40 per m^2)	10,000	8,000	6,000	8,000	8,000	40,000
Depreciation of equipment	2,400	3,600	36,000	12,000	6,000	60,000
Total	12,400	11,600	36,000	96,000	562,000	
Student days	3,800	2,600	1,600	-	8,000	
Courses	-	-	-	120	-	
Absorption rates						
Catering (per student day)					7.75	
Admin (per course)				800.00		
Other overheads (per student day)	3.26	4.46	22.50			

SECTION 2

1   Materials costing £642 were requisitioned for the job, by material requisition 648.

2   The consultant's fee would have been directly related to this job, and this job alone.

3   The information on the labour hours would have come from timesheets identifying the jobs worked on by different employees.

4   £880/80 hours = £11 per direct labour hour.

5   Materials costing £68 were returned by the job to the stores (recorded on materials return note 214).

6   The treatment of overtime premium will depend on the circumstances. It will be a direct cost if it occurs because of a specific request by the customer to ensure speedy completion of the job. Otherwise it will generally be indirect, as there is no reason other than chance that means a specific job will be worked on during an employee's overtime.

7   The cost should be allocated to the land and buildings fixed asset account. The reason is that the labour is being used to create a fixed asset, not to produce what is sold by the organisation. It is therefore capital expenditure, and not a cost of sale.

8   (a) This represents the amount of direct wages incurred by the company for that period on manufacturing the product.

       (b) This represents the amount of indirect production wages for the period, for example wages of supervision staff, overtime rates or bonus payments.

9   Lead time is the time between the issue of a purchase order and the receipt of goods. Re-order level must be set so that it is greater than maximum usage of stock × maximum lead time, otherwise the company may run out of stock.

10   The connection between the variances may be that the company is using cheaper material, but of poorer quality leading to higher wastage.

11   Significant variances are those whose size is worth investigating (eg ± 10% of budget).

    Variances reported to a manager should be controllable by that manager. For example the purchasing manager may be responsible for the material price variance, unless there is a universal price over which he/she can have no influence.

12   A variable cost.

ANSWERS TO PRACTICE CENTRAL ASSESSMENT 3: WHITEWALL LTD

SECTION 1

Task 1

(a)

STORES LEDGER RECORD
MATERIAL: EXON

Date	Receipts			Issues			Balance		
	Kgs	Price £	Value £	Kgs	Price £	Value £	Kgs	Price £	Value £
May 1							30,000	2.00	60,000
May 7	10,000	2.25	22,500				40,000		82,500
May 14	12,000	2.50	30,000				52,000		112,500
May 18				30,000	2.00				
				5,000	2.25	71,250	17,000		41,250

STORES LEDGER RECORD
MATERIAL: DELTON

Date	Receipts			Issues			Balance		
	Kgs	Price £	Value £	Kgs	Price £	Value £	Kgs	Price £	Value £
May 1							25,000	3.00	75,000
May 8	9,000	3.20	28,800				34,000		103,800
May 15	8,000	3.40	27,200				42,000		131,000
May 19				8,000	3.40				
				9,000	3.20				
				3,000	3.00	65,000	22,000		66,000

(b) (i) FIFO and LIFO are used as methods of pricing issues because it is not possible to identify which specific units of material such as Exon and Delton are being issued at any issue. Hence reasonable assumptions such as FIFO or LIFO need to be made about the price of the units being issued.

(ii) The stores supervisor's understanding of FIFO and LIFO is incorrect. FIFO and LIFO are methods of pricing, they are not methods of stock control. As individual stock units cannot be precisely identified, the physical movement of stock will not normally be related to the pricing of stock issues.

Task 2

LABOUR COST CARD			
JOB: WHEELBASE Date: May 20X6			
	Assembly	*Moulding*	*Finishing*
Actual wage cost £	26,970	34,020	36,540
Standard hours produced	6,000	7,500	7,600
Actual hours worked	6,200	7,000	7,000
Standard hours saved	-	500	600
Actual wage rate per hour £	-	4.86	5.22
Bonus £	-	1,215	1,566
Total labour cost £	26,970	35,235	38,106

Task 3

(a)   OVERHEAD ANALYSIS SHEET

		Assembly	*Moulding*	*Finishing*
Budgeted total overheads	£	3,249,000	3,950,400	3,419,900
Budgeted machine hours		90,000	120,000	110,000
Budgeted overhead absorption rate	£	36.10	32.92	31.09

(b)   JOB OVERHEAD ANALYSIS CARD

		Assembly	*Moulding*	*Finishing*
Job machine hours		6,000	6,800	6,600
Budgeted overhead absorption rate	£	36.10	32.92	31.09
Overhead absorbed by job	£	216,600	223,856	205,194

(c)   MEMORANDUM

To: Job Wheelbase Supervisor
From: A Technician
Date: 18 June 20X6
Subject: Overhead absorption rates

(i)   Purpose of overhead absorption

The purpose of overhead absorption is to allow overheads to be absorbed by a cost unit on a predetermined basis, so that all costs are recovered by budgeted output.

(ii) Reasons for using machine hours

The overhead absorption rate should mean that cost units are charged with a level of overheads that reflects the resources that have been used in producing them. Machine hours will probably have been used as machine usage is felt to have the most direct relationship to overheads incurred.

(iii) *Your suggested approach*

Your suggested approach is not appropriate as the overheads charged to a cost unit will not reflect the overheads incurred in making that unit. Consequently some jobs will bear too many overheads, others too few and hence pricing will be distorted.

Task 4

JOB COST CARD

JOB: WHEELBASE   Date: May 20X6

	Total *£*
Material	
Exon	71,250
Delton	65,000
	136,250
Labour	
Assembly	26,970
Moulding	35,235
Finishing	38,106
	100,311
Overhead	
Assembly	216,600
Moulding	223,856
Finishing	205,194
	645,650
Total cost	882,211
Profit	294,070
Job price	1,176,281

Task 5

(a)   (i)

Total labour cost variance assembly department	£	
6,000 hours should have cost ($\times$ £4.50)	27,000	
but did cost	26,970	
otal labour cost variance	30	(F)

(ii)

Labour efficiency variance		
Work should have taken	6,000	hrs
but did take	6,200	hrs
Labour efficiency variances in hrs	200	hrs (A)
$\times$ Standard rate per hour	$\times$ £4.50	
Labour efficiency variance in £	£900	(A)

(iii)

Labour rate variance	£	
Work should have cost 6,200 $\times$ 4.50	27,900	
but did cost	26,970	
Labour rate variance	930	(F)

(b)

MEMORANDUM

To: Production Manager
From: A Technician
Date: 18 June 20X6
Subject: Labour cost variance: Assembly Department

Actual labour costs are £30 lower than standard labour costs. The £30 favourable variance is made up of two elements:

(a)   A £930 favourable labour wage rate variance, possibly explained by cheaper than budgeted labour being used.

(b)   A £900 adverse labour efficiency variance. This may be due to cheaper labour being used. Investigation will be needed of whether use of cheaper labour has had any adverse effects on the quality of products.

Task 6

Finishing department	Data
Budgeted total overheads	£3,419,900
Budgeted machine hours	110,000
Budgeted overhead absorption rate per machine hour	£31.09
Actual machine hours	108,000
Overhead absorbed (108,000 × 31.09)	£3,357,720
Actual overheads	£3,572,000
Over/(under) absorption of overheads	£214,280

REPORT

To: Cost Accountant
From: A Technician
Date: 18 June 20X6
Subject: Finishing department overheads

(a)   *Consequence of results*

There has been an under-absorption of overheads of £214,280. In consequence the budgeted profit for Whitewall will be reduced by this sum.

(b)   *Possible causes*

One cause of the under-absorption is that the actual capacity of 108,000 hours is less than the budgeted capacity 110,000 hours. Other possible causes include:

(i)   too low a level of overheads being budgeted;

(ii)   too slack a rate of recovery being set;

(iii) a lack of control over overhead costs;

(iv)   an absorption basis being used that does not reflect how overheads are incurred within the finishing department.

(c)   *Effect on costing*

The underrecovery of overheads on costing such jobs as Wheelbase will mean that the job is underpriced. This will adversely affect Whitewall's profitability.

(d)   *Possible remedial action*

One way to reflect better the overheads incurred in the finishing department would be to base overhead recovery on the activities that drive costs in the department rather than machine hours.

SECTION 2

1   The FIFO method prices issues with the oldest material price first, whereas the LIFO method uses the most recent material price first. As a result, stock will be valued using the price of most recent receipts if FIFO is used. If LIFO is used, stock will be valued using the price of the earliest receipts.

2   (i)   Any two of the following.

Rent and rates, light and heat, insurance, wage costs, obsolescence, deterioration and security.

(ii) Any two of the following.

Stationery, postage, wages and telephone.

3   A stocktake is a count of physical stock on hand, to check against the balance shown by stock records to see if there has been any theft or deterioration.

4   (i)   Periodic.
     (ii) Continuous stocktaking.

5   A standard hour is the predetermined output from one worker for one hour as a result of detailed study of the operations involved in a task.

6   Any two from:

Timesheets, job cards, clock cards and route cards.

7    $\dfrac{\text{Standard hours produced}}{\text{Actual hours}} \times 100\%$

Standard hours produced are divided by actual hours and a % derived to measure the efficiency of actual production.

8

		Debit £	*Credit* £
DEBIT	Profit and loss account	214,280	
CREDIT	Production overheads		214,280

9   Service cost centre overheads are apportioned on the basis of the service they provide to production cost centres and other service centres (eg catering services may be apportioned on the basis of the number of workers in other departments).

10   A direct expense can be traced directly to the job concerned, whilst overheads are incurred for a number of jobs/cost centres, and shared to each job/cost centre on a predetermined basis.

11   Administration costs

Light and heat (many other examples are possible).

12   (a)   A cost driver is the factor that causes the costs associated with an activity/output.

(b)   An example of a possible cost driver is production runs.

ANSWERS TO PRACTICE CENTRAL ASSESSMENT 4: TAMWORTH LTD

SECTION 1

Task 1

(a)

Department	Cutting	Moulding	Finishing	Packaging
Average number of workers	164	173	162	195
Workers leaving during the year	35	14	11	13
% staff leaving 20X6	21.3%	8.1%	6.8%	6.7%
% staff leaving 20X5	12.1%	7.8%	7.3%	7.4%

(b)

MEMO

To: Production Manager
From: A Technician
Date: 3 December 20X6
Re: STAFF RETENTION RATES

Departmental rates

The staff turnover rates for the moulding, finishing and packaging departments in 20X6 are similar to the 20X5 rates. However, the cutting department's turnover rate has increased significantly from 12.1% to 21.3%. In 20X5, the staff turnover rate in the cutting department was one and a half times as large as the next most rapid rate. In 20X6, the staff turnover rate in the cutting department was two and a half times the size of the next most rapid rate.

Causes of high staff turnover

Causes may include:

(i)   low wages;
(ii) poor conditions;
(iii) long or uncongenial hours;
(iv) poor relationships between management and staff;
(v)   lack of opportunity for advancement;
(vi) poor recruitment procedures.

Costs and consequences for the company

These include:

(i)   costs of recruitment;

(ii) inefficiency of new labour;

(iii) costs of training;

(iv) lost output arising from staff shortages because of gaps between staff leaving and joining;

(v)   increased waste due to lack of skills of new staff.

Task 2

(a)

Department	Cutting	Moulding	Finishing	Packaging
Budgeted production (hours)	37,900	44,500	48,280	25,000 (1)
Actual labour hours worked	37,214	41,213	45,874	24,315
Standard hours produced	37,640	44,150	48,550	24,855 (2)
Capacity ratio	98.2%	92.6%	95.0%	97.3%
Efficiency ratio	101.1%	107.1%	105.8%	102.2%

Workings

(1) $\dfrac{375,000}{60 \text{ minutes}} \times 4 \text{ minutes} = 25,000 \text{ hours}$

(2) $\dfrac{372,825}{60 \text{ minutes}} \times 4 \text{ minutes} = 24,855$

(b)

NOTE

To: Packaging Department Manager
From: A Technician
Date: 3 December 20X6
Re: CAPACITY AND EFFICIENCY RATIOS

The capacity ratio shows that only 97.3% of hours budgeted were worked. The efficiency ratio demonstrates that actual production was 102.2% of production that should have been produced in the actual hours worked.

Reasons for capacity being less than budgeted might include:

(i)   production being less than planned;

(ii)   stoppages occurring which were not accounted for separately as idle time;

(iii)   actual staff numbers employed being less than budgeted staff;

(iv)   staff being more efficient than expected (this explanation would be borne out by the efficiency ratio).

Task 3

Report

To: Production Manager
From: A Technician
Date: 3 December 20X6
Re: DEPRECIATION OF CUTTING MACHINE

Method of depreciation

The method of depreciation that should be used is the reducing balance method. Using this method, a % depreciation rate is charged on the net book value of the machine at the start of the accounting year. Thus the amount charged to the profit and loss account will be higher in earlier years when the net book value is higher.

Reason for using reducing balance method

The main reason for using this method is that it approximates to what is actually happening, ie the machine is losing most value and having most usage early on in its life.

Calculation of rate

Using a rate of 40% would mean that the cutting machine was depreciated to a value within the range of possible scrap values, as demonstrated below.

Capital costs	Balance Sheet £	Profit and loss account £
Year 1 charge c/f	(72,000)	72,000
	108,000	
Year 2 charge c/f	(43,200)	43,200
	64,800	
Year 3 charge c/f	(29,920)	25,920
	38,880	
Year 4 charge c/f	(15,552)	15,552
	23,328	
Year 5 charge	(9,331)	9,331
Final value	13,997	

Tutorial note. Any rate that produces a final value between £10,000 and £15,000 would be acceptable. The range of possible rates is between 39.2% and 44%.

Task 4

Department	Cutting	Moulding	Finishing	Packaging
Actual overheads incurred	£1,234,736	£1,156,347	£938,463	£834,674
Budgeted absorption rate per labour hour	£33.82	£26.80	£20.25	£29.62
Actual labour hours worked	37,214	41,213	45,874	24,315
Overheads absorbed	£1,258,577	£1,104,508	£928,948	£720,210
(Under) / over absorbed overheads	£23,841	(£51,839)	(£9,515)	(£114,464)

Task 5

Standard material prices

Standard material price is the price at which the material issues and closing stock will be priced. It is the price expected to be paid for materials delivered.

Ascertaining standard material prices

Standard material prices will be set taking account of:

(i)   past prices;
(ii)   contracted purchase terms;
(iii)   expectations of price rises;
(iv)   availability of discounts.

Advantages of standard material prices

(i)   All issues are made at a constant price, and therefore comparisons can easily be made.

(ii)   It is easier to use and administer than FIFO and LIFO, because under FIFO and LIFO it is necessary to take into account previous stock movements when pricing materials.

Disadvantages of standard material prices

(i)   Standards may not reflect actual prices paid because of inflation or unexpected developments. Hence significant variances may occur.

(ii) Determination of standards can be difficult and time-consuming.

(iii) Altering standards frequently can cause confusion.

SECTION 2

1 Records of leavers maintained by the personnel department.

2 The wage rate may have been set, taking account of:

    (a) past pay rates, together with an allowance for increases due to inflation;

    (b) amounts other businesses are paying for this type of work;

    (c) what management consider the work 'to be worth'.

3   (a) Overtime

    (b) Holiday pay

    (c) Idle time

4   (a) The costs of the stores department would be apportioned to the production department on a fair basis, such as the value of requisitions.

    (b) The costs of each production department (including the allocated stores costs) would be absorbed by the cost units on the basis of labour or machine hours required to produce each unit.

5 Under activity-based costing, overheads are assigned to a product on the basis of consumption of activities; under more traditional methods, overheads are generally assigned using measures of production volume such as labour hours or machine hours.

6 Re-order level = maximum usage x maximum delivery time

               = 5,000 x 4

               = 20,000 units

7 A normal loss is an unavoidable loss expected during the normal course of operations, whilst an abnormal loss is an unexpected loss. The costs of a normal loss will be spread across the expected units of good output; the costs of an abnormal loss will be written off to the profit and loss account.

8 One of the four production departments (Cutting, Moulding, Finishing, Packaging).

9   (a) Allocation is the assignment of directly attributable costs to cost units or cost centres. Apportionment is the process of spreading costs jointly incurred by a number of cost centres over individual centres on the basis of benefits received.

    (b) (i) Salary of supervisor.

         (ii) Share of cleaning costs.

10 (a) No, it means actual overheads are greater than absorbed overheads by £151,977.

    (b) Under-absorption will mean actual profit is less than budgeted profit.

11 Costs are coded in order to provide a succinct reference which contains the key characteristics (cost nature, type, relevant cost centre) of the cost.

12

Date	Description	FIFO £	LIFO £
25 Nov	Total issue value	5,800	6,000
30 Nov	Total closing stock value	1,400	1,200

Answers to Trial Run Central Assessments

ANSWERS TO TRIAL RUN CENTRAL ASSESSMENT 1

SECTION 1

Task 1.1

(a)

Material: **Sugar**			STORES LEDGER CARD					Month: **November 1998**	
	Receipts			*Issues*			*Stock*		
Date	*Quantity (kilos)*	*Cost (per kilo)*	*Value*	*Quantity (kilos)*	*Cost (per kilo)*	*Value*	*Quantity (kilos)*	*Cost (per kilo)*	*Value*
	'000	£	£	'000	£	£	'000	£	£
Balance b/f Nov 1							50	0.175	8,750
Nov 4	34	0.180	6,120				84	50,000 × 0.175 34,000 × 0.180	14,870
Nov 10				46	0.175	8,050	38	4,000 × 0.175 34,000 × 0.180	6,820
Nov 15	29	0.200	5,800				67	4,000 × 0.175 34,000 × 0.180 29,000 × 0.200	12,620
Nov 19	16	0.240	3,840				83	4,000 × 0.175 34,000 × 0.180 29,000 × 0.200 16,000 × 0.240	16,460
Nov 22				52	4,000 × 0.175 34,000 × 0.180 14,000 × 0.200	9,620	31	15,000 × 0.200 16,000 × 0.240	6,840
Nov 26	32	0.220	7,040				63	15,000 × 0.200 16,000 × 0.240 32,000 × 0.220	13,880
Nov 28				39	15,000 × 0.200 16,000 × 0.240 8,000 × 0.220	8,600	24	24,000 × 0.220	5,280

(b)

	Quantity (kilos)
Buffer stock	35,000
Re-Order level	70,000

Task 1.2

LABOUR VARIANCE SCHEDULE			
Department: Packing		**Month: November 1998**	
Variance	**Standard cost**	**Actual cost**	**Variance**
Labour wage rate			£800 (A)
Labour efficiency			£2,520 (F)
Total	£86,520	£84,800	£1,720 (F)

Labour wage rate

		£
16,000 hours should have cost (× £5.25)		84,000
but did cost		84,800
		800 (A)

Labour efficiency variance

412,000 boxes packed should have taken (÷ 25)		16,480	hrs
but did take		16,000	hrs
		480	hrs (F)
standard rate per hour		× £5.25	
		2,520	(F)

Standard labour cost $\quad=\quad \dfrac{412,000}{25} \times £5.25 \quad=\quad £ \underline{\underline{86,520}}$

Task 1.3

(a)

BUDGETED COST SCHEDULE				YEAR 1999
		ACTIVITY (packets)		
		175,000	**200,000**	**225,000**
Description	**Cost**	£	£	£
Direct material	8p per packet	14,000	16,000	18,000
Direct labour	6p per packet	10,500	12,000	13,500
Packing costs	1p per packet	1,750	2,000	2,250
Depreciation costs	£12,000	12,000	12,000	12,000
Rent and rates	£26,000	26,000	26,000	26,000
Supervisory costs	£12,000	12,000	12,000	12,000
Administration costs	£8,000	8,000	8,000	8,000

(b)

	ACTIVITY (packets)		
	175,000	**200,000**	**225,000**
COST	£	£	£
Total variable cost	26,250	30,000	33,750
Total fixed cost	58,000	58,000	58,000
Total cost	84,250	88,000	91,750
Cost per packet	0.481	0.440	0.408

Task 1.4

(a)

	Mixing £	Baking £	Packing £
Budgeted overhead absorption rate	$\dfrac{£164,000}{£65,600} =$ £2.50 per £1 direct labour	$\dfrac{£228,900}{16,350 \text{ hrs}} =$ £14 per machine hour	$\dfrac{£215,000}{17,200 \text{ hrs}} =$ £12.50 per labour hour

(b)

PRODUCTION OVERHEAD SCHEDULE			
Month:	Mixing £	Baking £	Packing £
Budgeted overheads	164,000	228,900	215,000
Actual overheads	171,500	224,000	229,000
Overhead absorbed	159,250 [1]	225,400 [2]	200,000 [3]

(1) £63,700 × £2.50 = £159,250
(2) 16,100 hours × £14 = £225,400
(3) 16,000 hours × £12.50 = £200,000

(c)

	Mixing £	Baking £	Packing £
Over absorbed overheads		1,400 [5]	
Under absorbed overheads	12,250 [4]		29,000 [6]

(4) £171,500 - £159,250 = £12,250 under-absorbed overhead
(5) £224,000 - £225,400 = £1,400 over-absorbed overhead
(6) £229,000 - £200,000 = £29,000 under-absorbed overhead

SECTION 2

Task 2.1

FIFO does not meet this objective as issues from stores to production are based upon the oldest prices rather than the most recent.

Task 2.2

(a) The quantity of materials used valued at standard price was £3,010 less than the standard usage. Actual results were therefore better than expected results.

(b) Looking at past results of material usage (taking into account any wastage).

Task 2.3

The re-order level is the level at which a new order should be placed and will consist of the material consumed in the lead-time and buffer stock. The buffer stock is the reserve to avoid the risk of stock-out.

Task 2.4

Efficiency ratio = $\dfrac{\text{Expected hours to make output}}{\text{Actual hours taken}} \times 100\%$

$= \dfrac{16{,}480}{16{,}000} \times 100\% = 103\%$

Task 2.5

Variance account

	£		£
Wages control a/c	800	Work in progress a/c	2,520
P&L a/c	1,720		
	2,520		2,520

Task 2.6

Standard hours produced	16,480
Actual hours worked	16,000
Standard hours saved	480

Bonus = standard hours produced × 50% × actual labour rate = 480 × 50% × £5.30 = £1,272

Task 2.7

(a) The cost per packet moved from 48.1p per packet at 175,000 units of production to 40.8p per packet at 225,000 units of production. The cost per packet therefore demonstrates a downward trend.

(b) The reasons for this is that fixed costs of £58,000 remain constant even though the level of activity changes. As a consequence, as more units are produced fixed costs are spread over more units and the cost per unit therefore falls.

Task 2.8

Example - telephone

Stepped fixed

Example - rent

Task 2.9

A semi-variable cost is one which is part-fixed and part-variable. For telephone bills, the standing charge is fixed, whatever the usage, whilst there is a variable charge for each call that is made.

Rent would be a stepped fixed cost since accommodation requirements would increase, as output levels increase.

Task 2.10

- **Method**   Reducing balance method.

- **Reason**   This method depreciates more in the initial year which reflects the fact that most usage is made in the earlier years.

Task 2.11

(a)   Stores is not a production cost centre - it is a service cost centre. Service cost centres do not produce units of production.

(b)   Stores overheads are reapportioned to the production cost centres.

Task 2.12

A direct labour hour rate or a machine hour rate (ie a time-based rate) would be more appropriate.

If a wage-based rate is used (based upon value) a unit produced by a trainee would be charged with too little overhead.

SECTION 3

Task 3.1

STANDARD COST REPORT		
To: Production Manager		Period: November 1998
Description	Sub-variance	Total variance
	£	£
Material		
Material price	5,390 (A)	
Material usage	3,010 (F)	
Total material cost		2,380 (A)
Labour		
Labour wage rate	800 (A)	
Labour efficiency	2,520 (F)	
Total labour cost		1,720 (F)
Overheads		
Overhead expenditure	14,000 (A)	
Overhead capacity	15,000 (A)	
Overhead efficiency	6,000 (F)	
Overhead volume	9,000 (A)	
Total overhead cost		23,000 (A)

The total variances for material, labour and overheads are £2,380 (A), £1,720 (F) and £23,000 (A) respectively. Significant sub-variances are as follows.

- Materials price variance (£5,390 (A))
- Overhead expenditure variance (£14,000 (A))
- Overhead capacity variance (£15,000 (A))

(*Note*. The overhead expenditure variance and the overhead capacity variance make up the overhead volume variance.)

Possible causes of variances are detailed as follows.

Material variances

A new supplier was used in November 1998 and their price was higher than standard (variance = £5,390 (A)).

Material usage variance

- A more experienced packing team was used in November 1998 (rather than trainee packers)
- Higher quality material was supplied by the new supplier and hence there was less wastage (variance = £3,010 (F))

Labour wage rate variance

- As a more experienced packing team was used than planned, higher wages were being paid, and an adverse labour wage rate variance therefore resulted (£800 (A))

Labour efficiency variance

- The experienced packing team worked more quickly and efficiently than the trainees would have. This team therefore led to a favourable labour efficiency variance (£2,520 (F)).

Total fixed overhead variance

This is the total of the under- or over-absorbed overheads. In this case, overheads were under-absorbed by £23,000 (£229,000 actually incurred, compared with the £206,000 absorbed).

The overhead expenditure sub-variance is the difference between the budgeted and actual fixed overhead expenditure. The overhead volume variance is the total of the efficiency and capacity variances and compares the difference between the budgeted activity level of 430,000 boxes (17,200 hrs × 25) and the actual activity level of 412,000 boxes being packed. Hence the variance of packing was 18,000 (A) boxes and this total is multiplied by an overhead absorption rate of 50p per unit to arrive at the total adverse variance of £9,000.

The usage efficiency sub variance shows the difference between the number of hours actual production should have taken (ie standard hours produced of 16,480) and the number of hours actually worked (16,000). This means that there was a 480 (F) labour efficiency variance (in hours) which was multiplied by the fixed overhead absorption rate per labour hour (× £12.50) and therefore resulted in a £6,000 (F) variance.

The capacity variance compares how many hours should have been worked (budgeted) with how many hours were actually worked. Since less hours were worked (16,000) than budgeted (17,200) an adverse capacity variance of £15,000 (1,200 hrs × £12.50) resulted.

The overhead expenditure variance should be brought to the attention of the production manager because it is a large adverse variance (£14,000) which has arisen even though actual production was less than budgeted production.

Workings

Overhead expenditure variance

	£
Budgeted overhead expenditure	215,000
Actual overhead expenditure	229,000
	14,000 (A)

Overhead capacity variance

Budgeted hours of work	17,200 hrs
Actual hours of work	16,000 hrs
Overhead capacity variance (in hours)	1,200 hrs (A)
× budgeted overhead absorption rate	£12.50
	£15,000 (A)

Overhead efficiency variance

Standard labour hours	16,480 hrs
Actual labour hours	16,000 hrs
	480 hrs (F)
× budgeted overhead absorption rate	× £12.50
	£6,000 (F)

Overhead volume variance

	£
Budgeted labour hours	17,200 hrs
Standard labour hours	16,480
	720 hrs (A)
× budgeted overhead absorption rate	£12.50
	£9,000 (A)

Total overhead cost variance

	£
Overhead incurred	229,000
Overhead absorbed (16,480 hrs × £12.50)	206,000
	23,000 (A)

ANSWERS TO TRIAL RUN CENTRAL ASSESSMENT 2

SECTION 1

Task 1.1

Material: Glass jars				**STORES LEDGER CARD**			Month: May 1999		
	Receipts			*Issues*			*Balance*		
Date	*Quantity*	*Cost (per jar)*	*Value*	*Quantity*	*Cost (per jar)*	*Value*	*Quantity*	*Cost (per jar)*	*Value*
		£	£		£	£		£	£
Balance b/f May 1							48,000	(35,600 × 0.12) + (12,400 × 0.13)	5,884
May 6	31,000	0.15	4,650				79,000	(35,600 × 0.12) + (12,400 × 0.13) + (31,000 × 0.15)	10,534
May 9				28,000	0.15	4,200	51,000	(35,600 × 0.12) + (12,400 × 0.13) + (3,000 × 0.15)	6,334
May 14				37,000	(3,000 × 0.15) + (12,400 × 0.13) +(21,600 × 0.12)	4,654	14,000	0.12	1,680
May 20	22,500	0.16	3,600				36,500	14,000 × 0.12 22,500 × 0.16	5,280
May 26				24,000	(22,500 × 0.16)+ (1,500 × 0.12)	3,780	12,500	0.12	1,500

Task 1.2

LABOUR VARIANCE SCHEDULE			
Department: Packing department		Month: May 1999	
Variance	*Actual cost*	*Standard cost*	*Variance*
	£	£	£
Labour efficiency			371.25 (F)
Labour wage rate			183.00 (A)
Total labour cost	£8,418.00	£8,606.25	188.25 (F)

Labour efficiency variance

102,000 cases packed should take	*1,275 hrs
but did take	1,220 hrs
Labour efficiency variance in hrs	55 hrs (F)
× Standard rate per hour	× £6.75
Labour efficiency variance in £	371.25 (F)

* Standard time to pack 1 case   = 45 seconds

    Number of seconds in 1 hour   = 60×60 minutes

                                         = 3,600 seconds

$\therefore$ Standard time to pack 1 case $= \dfrac{45\,\text{seconds}}{3,600\,\text{seconds}} = 0.0125$ hours

$\therefore$ Standard time to pack 102,000 cases $= 0.0125 \times 102,000 = 1,275$ hours

Labour wage rate variance

	£
1,220 hours of labour should have cost ($\times$ £6.75 per hour)	8,235
but did cost	8,418
Labour wage rate variance	183 (A)

Actual cost of labour

This is given in the assessment as £8,418.

Standard labour cost

Standard time to pack 102,000 cases (as calculated above) = 1,275 hours

$\therefore$ Standard labour cost to pack 102,000 cases = 1,275 hours $\times$ £6.75 = £8,606.25

Task 1.3

BUDGETED PRODUCTION SCHEDULE				
Product: Millennium Marmalade				Year: 2000
	PRODUCTION (JARS)			
	150,000	175,000	190,000	220,000
COST	£	£	£	£
Material (W1)	34,500	40,250	43,700	50,600
Labour (W2)	42,000	44,000	45,200	47,600
Overhead (W3)	60,000	65,000	68,000	74,000
Total cost	136,500	149,250	156,900	172,200
Cost per jar (£) (W4)	0.91	0.85	0.83	0.78

Workings

(1) **Variable cost of materials** $= \dfrac{£34,500}{150,000} = £0.23$ per jar

Material cost of 175,000 jars $= 175,000 \times £0.23 = £40,250$

Material cost of 190,000 jars $= 190,000 \times £0.23 = £43,700$

(2) **Labour costs**

We can use the high-low method to identify the fixed and variable elements of the labour costs.

	Volume	Total costs
	Jars	£
High	220,000	47,600
Low	150,000	42,000
	70,000	5,600

Variable labour cost $= \dfrac{£5,600}{70,000} = £0.08$ per jar

Fixed labour cost $=$ Total cost of 150,000 jars – variable cost of 150,000 jars

$= £42,000 - (150,000 \times £0.08)$

$= £30,000$

Labour cost of 175,000 jars $= £30,000 + (175,000 \times £0.08)$

$= £44,000$

Labour cost of 190,000 jars $= £30,000 + (190,000 \times £0.08)$

$= £45,200$

(3) **Overhead costs**

We can use the high-low method to identify the fixed and variable elements of the overhead costs.

	Volume	Total costs
	Jars	£
High	220,000	74,000
Low	150,000	60,000
	70,000	14,000

Variable overhead cost $= \dfrac{£14,000}{70,000} = £0.2$ per jar

Fixed overhead cost $=$ Total cost of 150,000 jars – variable cost of 150,000 jars

$= £60,000 - (150,000 \times £0.2)$

$= £30,000$

Overhead cost of 175 jars $= £30,000 + (175,000 \times £0.2)$

$= £65,000$

Overhead cost of 190,000 jars $= £30,000 + (190,000 \times £0.2)$

$= £68,000$

(4)   **Cost per jar**

$$150{,}000 \text{ jars} = \frac{£136{,}500}{150{,}000} = £0.91$$

$$175{,}000 \text{ jars} = \frac{£149{,}250}{£175{,}000} = £0.85$$

$$190{,}000 \text{ jars} = \frac{£156{,}900}{190{,}000} = £0.83$$

$$220{,}000 \text{ jars} = \frac{£172{,}200}{220{,}000} = £0.78$$

Task 1.4

(a)

BUDGETED PRODUCTION OVERHEAD SCHEDULE (EXTRACT) YEAR: 1999		
	Bottling department	**Packing department**
Allocated overheads (£)	85,000	96,000
Apportioned overheads (£)	246,000	194,000
Reapportioned stores overheads (£) (W1)	56,250	43,750
Reapportioned maintenance overheads (£) (W2)	34,240	34,240
Total production overheads (£)(W3)	421,490	367,990
Budgeted machine hours	17,381	11,807
Budgeted labour hours	14,605	16,919
Budgeted production overhead absorption rate (£) (W4)	24.25	21.75

Workings

(1)   **Reapportioned stores overheads**

	Bottling department £	Packing department £
Budgeted stores overheads = £125,000	56,250 (45%)	43,750 (35%)

(2)   **Reapportioned maintenance overheads**

	Bottling department £	Packing department £
Budgeted maintenance overheads = £85,600	34,240 (40%)	34,240 (40%)

(3) **Total production overheads**

Total production overheads are the sum of the following.

- Allocated overheads
- Apportioned overheads
- Reapportioned stores overheads
- Reapportioned maintenance overheads

(4) **Budgeted production overhead absorption rate**

$$\text{Bottling department} = \frac{£421,490}{17,381 \text{ machine hours}}$$

$$= £24.25 \text{ per machine hour}$$

$$\text{Packing department} = \frac{£367,990}{16,919 \text{ labour hours}}$$

$$= £21.75 \text{ per labour hour}$$

(b)

BOTTLNG DEPARTMENT OVERHEAD ABSORPTION SCHEDULE			
	March 1999	**April 1999**	**May 1999**
Actual production overheads (£)	31,650	32,398	32,880
Jars bottled	157,392	159,804	163,500
Standard machine hours produced (W1)	1,311.6	1,331.7	1,362.5
Budgeted production overhead absorption rate (£) (W2)	24.25	24.25	24.25
Overheads absorbed (£) (W3)	31,806	32,294	33,041
Over/(under) absorbed production overheads (£) (W4)	156	(104)	161

Workings

(1) **Standard machine hours produced**

Standard time to bottle one jar = 30 seconds

∴ In 1 minute, 2 jars will be bottled

∴ In 60 minutes, 2 × 60 jars = 120 jars will be bottled

$$\text{Standard machine hours produced} = \frac{\text{Jars bottled}}{\text{Standard number of jars bottled in 1 hour}}$$

		Standard machine hours produced

March 1999 $= \dfrac{157{,}392}{120}$ 1,311.6

April 1999 $= \dfrac{159{,}804}{120}$ 1,331.7

May 1999 $= \dfrac{163{,}500}{120}$ 1,362.5

(2) **Budgeted production overhead absorption rate**

This information is given in Task 1.4 (a)

(3) **Overheads absorbed**

March 1999 = 1,311.6 × £24.25 = £31,806

April 1999 = 1,331.7 × £24.25 = £32,294

May 1999 = 1,362.5 × £24.25 = £33,041

(4) **Over/(under) absorbed production overheads**

Actual overheads – absorbed overheads

	Actual overheads	*Absorbed overheads*	*(Under)/over absorption*
	£	£	£
March 1999	31,650	31,806	156 over
April 1999	32,398	32,294	(104) under
May 1999	32,880	33,041	161 over

SECTION 2

Task 2.1

(a) Higher.

(b) Under the First-In-First-Out method closing stock is valued at the prices of the most recent purchases whilst under the Last-In-First-Out method closing stock is valued at the cost of the oldest items in stock. Since the price of jars has increased between May 1st and May 20th 2000, closing stock valuations will be different under the two methods.

Task 2.2

The reorder level = maximum usage × maximum lead time (ie the maximum usage during the longest possible lead time). If there is any buffer stock this will need to be added also.

Task 2.3

(i) **Identification.** A unique reference is given to each item of stock which avoids any ambiguity and saves time.

(ii) **Production efficiency is improved.** If the correct material can be accurately identified from a code number, production hold-ups caused by the issue of incorrect material can be avoided.

Task 2.4

- Consideration of the previous years' labour wage rates
- The average labour wage rate in the industry in which Golden Plum Limited operates in.

Task 2.5

A standard labour hour produced is the quantity of work that could be produced by one worker in one hour if the worker was working in the standard way at the standard rate.

Task 2.6

(a) $\dfrac{\text{Number of employees leaving/being recruited during the period}}{\text{Average total number of employees during the period}}$

(b) Personnel department.

Task 2.7

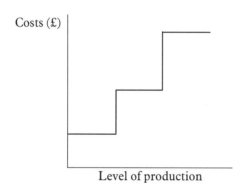

Example. **Rent** where accommodation requirements increase as output levels get higher.

Task 2.8

Labour. Supervisors' wages
Overheads. Rent

Task 2.9

Trend. There is a downwards trend on cost per jar from 91p per jar at a production level of 150,000 jars to 78p per jar at a production level of 220,000 jars.

Explanation. Fixed costs remain constant with changes in the level of production. Therefore, as production levels increase the cost per jar falls as the fixed costs are spread over a higher number of jars.

Task 2.10

A factory is divided into several production cost centres and also many service cost centres, but it is only the production cost centres that are directly involved in the production of jars of jam.

In order to be able to add production overheads to cost units (cost per jar of jam), it is necessary to have all the overheads charged to the production cost centres (bottling and packing departments).

The overheads of the service cost centres (stores and maintenance departments) are also apportioned to the production cost centres.

Task 2.11

(i)   Apportioned cost
(ii)   Allocated cost
(iii) Allocated cost
(iv) Apportioned cost

Task 2.12

PRODUCTION OVERHEAD CONTROL A/C

	£		£
Bank account	32,398	Work in progress (WIP)	32,294
		Profit and loss account	104
	32,398		32,398

SECTION 3

Task 3.1

<table>
<tr><td colspan="3" align="center">STANDARD COST REPORT</td></tr>
<tr><td>To: Accountant</td><td colspan="2" align="right">Period: Jan 1999 – May 1999</td></tr>
<tr><td>Description</td><td>Sub-variance</td><td>Total variance</td></tr>
<tr><td></td><td>£</td><td>£</td></tr>
<tr><td>MATERIAL</td><td></td><td></td></tr>
<tr><td>Material price</td><td>2,840 (A)</td><td></td></tr>
<tr><td>Material usage</td><td>390 (A)</td><td></td></tr>
<tr><td>Total material cost</td><td></td><td>3,230 (A)</td></tr>
<tr><td>LABOUR</td><td></td><td></td></tr>
<tr><td>Labour wage rate</td><td>890 (F)</td><td></td></tr>
<tr><td>Labour efficiency</td><td>2,875 (A)</td><td></td></tr>
<tr><td>Total labour cost</td><td></td><td>1,985 (A)</td></tr>
<tr><td>OVERHEADS</td><td></td><td></td></tr>
<tr><td>Overhead expenditure (W1)</td><td>13,980 (F)</td><td></td></tr>
<tr><td>Overhead capacity (W2)</td><td>10,428 (A)</td><td></td></tr>
<tr><td>Overhead efficiency (W3)</td><td>6,450 (A)</td><td></td></tr>
<tr><td>Overhead volume (W4)</td><td>16,878 (A)</td><td></td></tr>
<tr><td>Total overhead cost</td><td></td><td>2,898 (A)</td></tr>
</table>

COMMENTS

Sub-variances in excess of £2,500

- Materials price variance – £2,840 (A)
- Labour efficiency variance – £2,875 (A)
- Overhead expenditure variance – £13,980 (F)
- Overhead capacity variance – £10,428 (A)
- Overhead efficiency variance – £6,450 (A)
- Overhead volume variance – £16,878 (A)

Possible causes of material and labour variances

Material price variance

This adverse variance has probably arisen because of an unexpected increase in the price of glass. It is also possible that the price of glass might have been increased by the company's sole supplier (it might be a good idea for the company to obtain a number of other quotes for glass from other suppliers).

Material usage variance

There is an adverse material usage variance of £390 which might have arisen because the training of new operatives in the production departments has been reduced. The lack of training might mean that the new workers are wasting more materials than would normally be expected.

Labour rate variance

There is a favourable wage rate variance of £980. This may have been brought about by the fact that a proposed pay increase has not yet been implemented by the company.

Labour efficiency variance

There is an adverse labour efficiency variance of £2,875. This is a fairly significant adverse variance which might have been caused by the proposed pay increase not being implemented and also because of reduced training of new workers in the production departments.

Fixed overhead variances

(a) **Overhead expenditure variance.** This is the difference between the budgeted fixed overhead expenditure and the actual fixed overhead expenditure. The company has a favourable overhead expenditure variance which means that they spent less on fixed overheads than they budgeted for.

(b) **Overhead capacity variance**. This is the difference between the budgeted machine hours and the actual machine hours in the period. A large adverse variance indicates that far less machine hours were used in the period than budgeted.

(c) **Overhead efficiency variance.** This is the difference between the number of hours that actual production should have taken and the number of hours actually taken. The adverse variance suggests that the workforce took longer than expected to produce its actual production in January-May 1999.

(d) **Overhead volume variance.** This is the difference between the actual production at standard rate (standard machine hours produced) and budgeted production at standard rate. The standard hours produced were far less than budgeted which has resulted in a large adverse variance.

The most significant sub-variance is the adverse capacity variance of £10,428 and this should be brought to the attention of management and investigated in order to establish why it occurred.

Workings

(1) **Overhead expenditure variance**

	£
Budgeted overhead expenditure	178,359
Actual overhead expenditure	164,379
Overhead expenditure variance	13,980 (F)

(2) **Overhead capacity variance**

Budgeted hours of work	7,355 hrs
Actual hours of work	6,925 hrs
	430 hrs (A)
× Standard overhead absorption rate	£24.25
Overhead capacity variance	10,427.50 (A)

(3) **Overhead efficiency variance**

Standard machine hours	6,659 hrs
Actual machine hours	6,925 hrs
	266 hrs (A)
× Standard overhead absorption rate	£24.25
	6,450.50 (A)

(4) **Overhead volume variance**

The overhead volume variance is the sum of the capacity and efficiency variances ie £10,428 (A) + £6,450 (A) = £16,878 (A).

ANSWERS TO TRIAL RUN CENTRAL ASSESSMENT 3

SECTION 1

PART A

Task 1.1

STORES LEDGER CARD

Material: Cotswold Brick   Month: November 1999

Date	Receipts			Issues			Balance		
	Quantity	Cost per 1,000 £	Value £	Quantity	Cost per 1,000 £	Value £	Quantity	Cost per 1,000 £	Value £
Balance b/f November 1							19,500	1,100	21,450
November 6	10,500	1,150	12,075				30,000	(19.5 × 1,100) + (10.50 × 1,150)	33,525
November 8				14,000	(10.5 × 1,150) + (3.5 × 1,100)	15,925	16,000	16 × 1,100	17,600
November 13	16,000	1,175	18,800				32,000	(16 × 1,100) + (16 × 1,175)	36,400
November 15				19,000	(3 × 1,100) + (16 × 1,175)	22,100	13,000	1,100	14,300
November 22				10,000	1,100	11,000	3,000	1,100	3,300

Task 1.2

ELECTRICIAN BONUS AND EFFICIENCY SCHEDULE				
Description	**Northsite**	**Southsite**	**Westsite**	**Total**
Actual hours worked (W1)	140	140	140	420
Standard hours produced (W2)	162	132	159	453
Standard hours saved (W3)	22	-	19	41
Basic wages (£) (W4)	1,078	1,064	1,008	3,150
Bonus (£) (W5)	127	-	103	230
Total labour cost (£)	1,205	1,064	1,111	3,380
Labour efficiency (%) (W6)	116	94	114	108

Workings

(1)   **Actual hours worked**

All sites = 35 hours × 4 weeks = 140 hours

(2)   **Standard hours produced**

	2-bedroom house	*3-bedroom house*	*Total*
Northsite	72 (8 × 9)	90 (6 × 15)	162
Southsite	72 (8 × 9)	60 (4 × 15)	132
Westsite	54 (6 × 9)	105 (7 × 15)	159

(3)   **Standard hours saved**

Standard hours saved = standard hours produced – actual hours worked

Northsite = 162 – 140 = 22

Southsite = 132 – 140 = nil

Westsite   = 159 – 140 = 19

(4)   **Basic wages**

Northsite = 140 hrs × £7.70 = £1,078

Southsite = 140 hrs × £7.60 = £1,064

Westsite   = 140 hrs × £7.20 = £1,008

(5) **Bonus**

Bonus = 75% × standard hours saved at basic wage rate

Northsite = 75% × 22 hrs × £7.70 = £127 (to the nearest £)

Southsite = Nil standard hours saved ∴ Nil bonus

Westsite = 75% × 19 hrs × £7.20 = £103 (to the nearest £)

(6) **Labour efficiency**

$$\text{Labour efficiency} = \frac{\text{Standard hours produced}}{\text{Actual hours worked}} \times 100\%$$

Northsite $= \dfrac{162}{140} \times 100\% = 116\%$

Southsite $= \dfrac{132}{140} \times 100\% = 94\%$

Westsite $= \dfrac{159}{140} \times 100\% = 114\%$

Task 1.3

BUDGETED OVERHEAD SCHEDULE YEAR ENDING 31 DECEMBER 2000				
	Northsite	Southsite	Westsite	Total
	£	£	£	£
Allocated overheads	230,000	195,000	176,000	601,000
Apportioned overheads				
Head office and stores expenses (W1)	720,000	640,000	560,000	1,920,000
Depreciation (W2)	132,000	99,000	88,000	319,000
Total budgeted overheads	1,082,000	934,000	824,000	2,840,000
Total budgeted labour hours (W3)	15,750	14,000	12,250	
Budgeted overhead absorption rate per labour hour (W4)	68.70	66.71	67.27	

BPP PUBLISHING

Workings

(1) **Head office and stores expenses**

Total direct workers = 9 + 8 + 7 = 24

Northsite $= \dfrac{9}{24} \times £1,920,000 = £720,000$

Southsite $= \dfrac{8}{24} \times £1,920,000 = £640,000$

Westsite $= \dfrac{7}{24} \times £1,920,000 = £560,000$

(2) **Depreciation**

Total machine usage (hours) = 13,200 + 9,900 + 8,800
= 31,900

Northsite $= \dfrac{13,200}{31,900} \times £319,000 = £132,000$

Southsite $= \dfrac{9,900}{31,900} \times £319,000 = £99,000$

Westsite $= \dfrac{8,800}{31,900} \times £319,000 = £88,000$

(3) **Total budgeted labour hours**

Northsite = 9×35 hours $\times 50$ weeks = 15,750 hours

Southsite = 8×35 hours $\times 50$ weeks = 14,000 hours

Westsite = 7×35 hours $\times 50$ weeks = 12,250 hours

(4) **Budgeted overhead absorption rate per hour**

Northsite $= \dfrac{£1,082,000}{15,750} = £68.70$ per hour

Southsite $= \dfrac{£934,000}{14,000 \text{ hours}} = £66.71$ per hour

Westsite $= \dfrac{£824,000}{12,250 \text{ hours}} = £67.27$ per hour

Task 1.4

<table>
<tr><td colspan="3" align="center">BUDGETED JOB COST CARD
WESTSITE YEAR ENDING 31 DECEMBER 2000</td></tr>
<tr><td></td><td align="center">2-bedroom house
£</td><td align="center">3-bedroom house
£</td></tr>
<tr><td>MATERIALS: Bricks (W1)</td><td align="center">4,800</td><td align="center">6,000</td></tr>
<tr><td>Wood (W2)</td><td align="center">1,200</td><td align="center">1,500</td></tr>
<tr><td>Consumables (W3)</td><td align="center">600</td><td align="center">675</td></tr>
<tr><td>Furnishings (W4)</td><td align="center">7,200</td><td align="center">8,280</td></tr>
<tr><td>TOTAL MATERIALS</td><td align="center">13,800</td><td align="center">16,455</td></tr>
<tr><td></td><td></td><td></td></tr>
<tr><td>LABOUR: Bricklayer (W5)</td><td align="center">410</td><td align="center">492</td></tr>
<tr><td>Plumber (W6)</td><td align="center">56</td><td align="center">70</td></tr>
<tr><td>Electrician (W7)</td><td align="center">68</td><td align="center">113</td></tr>
<tr><td>Painter (W8)</td><td align="center">104</td><td align="center">130</td></tr>
<tr><td>TOTAL LABOUR</td><td align="center">638</td><td align="center">805</td></tr>
<tr><td></td><td></td><td></td></tr>
<tr><td>OVERHEADS (W9)</td><td align="center">5,583</td><td align="center">7,063</td></tr>
<tr><td></td><td></td><td></td></tr>
<tr><td>TOTAL COST</td><td align="center">20,021</td><td align="center">24,323</td></tr>
<tr><td>PROFIT (W10)</td><td align="center">10,011</td><td align="center">12,162</td></tr>
<tr><td>PRICE</td><td align="center">30,032</td><td align="center">36,485</td></tr>
</table>

Workings

(1) **Materials – 3-bedroom house**

Bricks = £4,800 × $\dfrac{200}{160}$ = £6,000

(2)   **Timber** $= £1,200 \times \dfrac{200}{160} = £1,500$

(3)   **Consumables**

Fixed cost $= £300$

$\therefore$ variable cost $= \dfrac{£600 - £300}{160 \, m^2}$

$= £1.875$ per m^2

$\therefore$ Consumables cost for 3-bedroom house $= £300 + (200m^2 \times £1.875)$

$= £300 + £375 = £675$

(4)   **Furnishings**

Fixed cost $= £2,880$

$\therefore$ variable cost $= \dfrac{£7,200 - £2,880}{160m^2}$

$= £27$ per m^2

$\therefore$ Furnishings cost for 3-bedroom house $= £2,880 + (200m^2 \times £27) = £2,880 + £5,400 = £8,280$

(5)   **Labour - bricklayer**

2-bedroom house $= 50$ hrs $\times £8.20 = £410$
3-bedroom house $= 60$ hrs $\times £8.20 = £492$

(6)   **Labour – plumber**

2-bedroom house $= 8$ hrs $\times £7.00 = £56.00$
3-bedroom house $= 10$ hrs $\times £7.00 = £70.00$

(7)   **Labour – electrician**

2-bedroom house $= 9$ hrs $\times £7.50 = £68$
3-bedroom house $= 15$ hrs $\times £7.50 = £113$

(8)   **Labour – painter**

2-bedroom house $= 16$ hrs $\times £6.50 = £104$
3-bedroom house $= 20$ hrs $\times £6.50 = £130$

(9)   **Overheads**

2-bedroom house $=$ Westsite overhead absorption rate $\times$ total labour hours
$= £67.27 \times (50 + 8 + 9 + 16)$ hours
$= £67.27 \times 83$ hours
$= £5,583$

3-bedroom house $= £67.27 \times (60 + 10 + 15 + 20)$ hours
$= £67.27 \times 105$ hours
$= £7,063$

(10) **Profit**

If profit = 1/3 of selling price
total cost = 2/3 × selling price
ie £20,021 = 2/3 × selling price

∴ Selling price (2-bedroom house) = $\dfrac{£20,021 \times 3}{2}$

= £30,032

∴ Profit = selling price – total cost
= £30,032 – £20,021
= £10,011

(Alternatively, if profit = 1/3 × selling price
and total cost = 3/2 × selling price
∴ profit = 1/2 × total cost
∴ profit (3-bedroom house) = 1/2 × £24,323
= £12,162

PART B

Task 1.5

(a) No. Last-In-First-Out is a method of costing stock so that any issues will be **valued** at the prices of the most recent purchases, but not necessarily used first (it is a costing method and not a method of stock control).

(b) The First-In-First-Out method issues stock items at the prices of the oldest items in stock at the time the issues were made. In contrast, the Last-In-First-Out method is the opposite and it values issues at the prices of the most recent purchases.

(c) The company would want to keep a buffer stock to cope with unexpected demand.

(d) (i) Each worker is paid according to the amount of good production.

(ii) Quality of work may be affected if workers become more concerned with the quantity of goods produced (rather than the quality).

(e) Direct labour.

(f) The standard time allowance could have been set by analysing the amount of work to be done on the 2-bedroom house and the speed and capability of the workforce involved. One method of doing this is a time and motion study.

(g) Annual depreciation charge = $\dfrac{\text{Cost} - \text{residual value}}{\text{Useful life}}$

= $\dfrac{£10,000 - £1,000}{5 \text{ years}}$

= $\dfrac{£9,000}{5}$

= £1,800 per annum

(h)   No. The most appropriate method would be the reducing balance method as it charges the largest amount of depreciation at the beginning of an asset's life and the machinery has most of its usage in the earlier years.

(i)

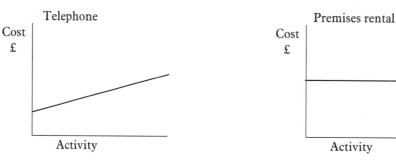

Type of cost: Semi-variable   Type of cost: Fixed

(j)   (i)   Machine hours.
       (ii)   This basis should be used where production is machine-intensive.

(k)   (i)   Site manager's wages.

       (ii)   Allocation is the process whereby whole cost items are charged direct to a cost unit or cost centre giving rise to allocated overheads.

              Apportionment in a procedure whereby common overheads are spread fairly between a number of cost centres giving rise to apportioned overheads.

(l)   Actual overheads – absorbed overheads
       = £2,240,000 – £2,170,000
       = £70,000 under recovery of overheads

SECTION 2

Task 2.1

STANDARD COST REPORT

Site: Southsite   Period: November 1999

Description	Sub-variance	Total variance
	£	£
MATERIAL		
Material price (W1)	6,140 (A)	
Material usage (W2)	8,840 (F)	
Total material cost		2,700 (F)
LABOUR		
Labour wage rate	1,890 (A)	
Labour efficiency	3,875 (F)	
Total labour cost		1,985 (F)
OVERHEADS		
Overhead expenditure	5,200 (A)	
Overhead capacity (W3)	15,000 (A)	
Overhead efficiency (W4)	7,800(F)	
Overhead volume	7,200 (A)	
Total overhead cost		12,400 (A)

Workings

(1)   **Material price variance**

	£
230,000 bricks should have cost (× £1.20)	276,000
but did cost	280,750
Material price variance	4,750 (A)

∴ Material price variance = £1,390 (A) + £4,750 (A)
                            = £6,140 (A)

(2)   **Material usage variance**

Standard usage	235,000 bricks
Actual usage	230,000 bricks
Material usage variance in bricks	5,000 bricks (F)
× Standard cost	× £1.20
Material usage variance in £	£6,000 (F)

∴ Material usage variance = £2,840 (F) + £6,000 (F)
                           = £8,840 (F)

415 **BPP**
PUBLISHING

(3)   **Overhead capacity variance**

Budgeted labour hours	1,600 hrs
Actual labour hours	1,350 hrs
Overhead capacity variance in hrs	250 hrs (A)
× Standard rate per hour	× £60★
Overhead capacity variance in £	15,000 (A)

$$\star \quad \frac{\text{Budgeted overheads}}{\text{Budgeted labour hours}} = \frac{£96,000}{1,600 \text{ hrs}}$$

$$= £60 \text{ per labour hour}$$

(4)   **Overhead efficiency variance**

Standard hours	1,480 hrs
Actual hours	1,350 hrs
Overhead efficiency variance in hrs	130 hrs (F)
× Standard rate per hour	× £60
Overhead efficiency variances in £	£7,800 (F)

COMMENTARY

Total variances

- Total material cost variance = £2,700 (F)
- Total labour cost variance = £1,985 (F)
- Total overhead cost variance = £12,400 (A)

Material variances

The favourable material cost variance of £2,700 is mainly due to the high favourable material usage variance of £8,840 which more than cancels out the adverse material price variance. The material usage variance is probably highly favourable because of the higher quality materials that are now being used. This will in turn account for the adverse materials price variance (since the company are now paying higher prices for their materials).

Labour variances

The favourable labour efficiency variance more than compensates for the adverse labour wage rate variance thus resulting in an overall favourable labour variance. The company has recently increased wage rates which will account for the adverse labour rate variance of £1,890 but may also have had an effect on the efficiency of the workforce and hence the favourable labour efficiency variance.

Overhead variances

The adverse overhead expenditure variance means that actual overheads were greater then budgeted overheads.

The adverse capacity variance means that the actual labour hours worked were less than budgeted.

The favourable efficiency variance means that the labour workforce worked more efficiently than expected.

The adverse volume variance means that the workforce produced less houses than they were budgeted to produce.

The total overhead variance was £12,400 (A) which means that the actual overhead incurred was greater than the overhead absorbed (ie there was an under recovery of overheads).

The most significant overhead variance which should be brought to the attention of the cost accountant is the adverse overhead capacity variance of £15,000.

ANSWERS TO SAMPLE CENTRAL ASSESSMENT

DO NOT TURN THIS PAGE UNTIL YOU HAVE
COMPLETED THE SAMPLE CENTRAL ASSESSMENT

ANSWERS TO THE SAMPLE CENTRAL ASSESSMENT

SECTION 1

Task 1

	1998 BUDGETED PRODUCTION COSTS		
Costs Units	750,000	1,000,000	1,250,00
Variable costs	£	£	£
Material	2,250,000	3,000,000	3,750,000
Labour	2,437,500	3,250,000	4,062,500
Overhead	2,062,500	2,750,000	3,437,500
Total	**6,750,000**	**9,000,000**	**11,250,000**
Fixed costs			
Labour	1,100,000	1,100,000	1,100,000
Overhead	1,750,000	1,750,000	1,750,000
Total	**2,850,000**	**2,850,000**	**2,850,000**
Total production cost	**9,600,000**	**11,850,000**	**14,100,000**
Cost per unit	**12.80**	**11.85**	**11.28**

Task 2

WAGE SCHEDULE				
Blowing dept: Team Alpha			Month: January 1998	
	Team	*Master Blower*	*Blower*	*Gen Assistant*
Wage rate (£)		8.60	6.40	4.20
Hrs worked	155	155	155	155
Total wage (£)		**1,333.00**	**992.00**	**651.00**
Standard hours produced	179			
Standard hours saved	24			
Bonus (£)		103.20	76.80	50.40
Total wage + bonus (£)		**1,436.20**	**1,068.80**	**701.40**

Task 3

	STORE CARD									

Material: Silica Sand   **MONTH: NOV 97**

Date	Receipts			Issues			Stock		
	Qty	*Cost per kg*	*Value*	*Qty*	*Cost per kg*	*Value*	*Qty*	*Cost per kg*	*Value*
Nov	'000 kg	£	£'000	'000 kg	£	£'000	'000 kg	£	£'000
Bal 1							1,470	2.00	2,940
5	860	2.15	1,849				1,470 860	2.00 2.15	4,789
9				1,060	860 @ 2.15 200 @ 2.00	2,249	1,270	2.00	2,540
14	1,100	2.25	2,475				1,270 1,100	2.00 2.25	5,015
18	1,050	2.20	2,310				1,270 1,100 1,050	2.00 2.25 2.20	7,325
21				2,300	1,050 @ 2.20 1,100 @ 2.25 150 @ 2.00	5,085	1,120	2.00	2,240
23	1,430	2.40	3,432				1,120 1,430	2.00 2.40	5,672
25				1,540	1,430 @ 2.40 110 @ 2.00	3,652	1,010	2.00	2,020
28				820	2.00	1,640	190	2.00	380

Task 4

(a)

Budgeted Production Overhead Schedule							

Year: 1998

Cost	Blow-ing	Cutting	Engrav-ing	Quality control	Stores	Maint-enance	Total
Cost centre	£'000	£'000	£'000	£'000	£'000	£'000	£'000
Allocated overhead	876	534	413	278	374	292	2,767
Apportioned overhead	1,138	793	541	311	416	324	3,523
Sub-total	**2,014**	**1,327**	**954**	**589**	**790**	**616**	**6,290**
Maintenance	280	145	95	48	48	(616)	
Stores	486	178	131	43	(838)		
Quality control	420	140	120	(680)			
Total budgeted overheads	**3,200**	**1,790**	**1,300**				**6,290**

(b)

	Blowing	Cutting	Engraving
Total budgeted overheads (£)	3,200,000	1,790,000	1,300,000
Budgeted labour hours	48,000	35,800	32,500
Budgeted overhead absorption rate £ per labour hour	66.67	50.00	40.00

(c)

Department	Time	Budgeted overhead absorption rate per labour hour	Overhead absorbed
	Minutes	£	£
Blowing	9	66.67	10.00
Cutting	7½	50.00	6.25
Engraving	12	40.00	8.00
Total			24.25

SECTION 2

Task 1

The cost per unit has moved downwards from £12.80 at 750,000 units to £11.28 at 1,250,000 units. The reason for this is that fixed overheads have remained the same with changes in the level of output. As a consequence, as more units are produced, fixed overheads will be spread over a greater number of units, which will reduce the unit cost. The variable overhead will remain the same at all levels of production.

Task 2

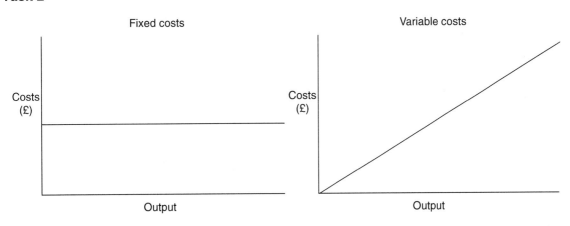

Task 3

Classification: Semi-variable cost
Example: Telephone costs

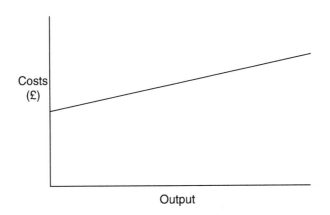

BPP
PUBLISHING

Task 4

(a) Benefits to workers

The wage payment that they receive can be increased within the normal working week if the conditions for the bonus are met. If a bonus is not earned, the basic wage based on time attendance will be received.

(b) Benefits to employers

Employers should have a motivated workforce with the introduction of a bonus system. The labour cost per unit will be reduced because only part of the cost is given to the employee as a bonus, and overheads per unit will be reduced as, ideally, more units will be produced.

Task 5

A time and motion study will have been undertaken to establish realistic times allowed for each operation that makes up the manufacture of the vases. These will then be aggregated to arrive at the standard times for the blowing team.

Task 6

(i)   Clock cards
(ii) Time sheets

Task 7

LIFO was chosen as the method to cost issues of silica sand in Task 3 of Section 1 as it is the method that costs issues to production at the most recent price, which is what the company wants.

Task 8

The weaknesses of LIFO as a method of costing issues and valuing stock include

(i)   Stock is valued at out-of-date costs.
(ii)   The method is not recognised by the Inland Revenue for tax purposes
(iii) The method is considered appropriate for external reporting purposes

Task 9

Holding cost   Ordering cost

(i)   Warehouse costs   (i)   Purchase department salaries

(ii) Financing costs   (ii) Purchase department overheads (telephone
      etc)

Task 10

(a) Economic order quantity.

(b) This method sets out to minimise the cost of ordering and holding stock by deriving an optimum order quantity and number of orders per year, given the level of demand by the company for that item of stock.

Task 11

Blowing department allocated overhead: Supervisor's salary
Blowing department apportioned overhead: Rent and rates

Task 12

Supervisors' salaries are allocated to a cost centre when they can be directly attributed to that cost centre. Overheads are apportioned to a cost centre when the cost centre has had the partial benefit of an overhead that has benefited a number of cost centres but cannot be directly attributable to any one particular cost centre. An example of this is rent and rates.

Section 3

Task 1

VARIANCE SCHEDULE			
Blowing dept			**January 1998**
		£	£
Material variance			
Material usage			4,236 (A)
Material price			1,125 (F)
Total			**3,111 (A)**
Labour variance			
Labour efficiency			1,750 (F)
Labour wage-rate			5,865 (A)
Total			**4,115 (A)**
Fixed overhead variance			
Expenditure			16,520 (A)
	Capacity	10,050 (A)	
	Efficiency	5,360 (F)	
Volume			4,690 (A)
Total			**21,210 (A)**

REPORT

The total material, labour and overhead variances are all adverse, as are all the sub-variances with the exception of the material price variance, fixed overhead efficiency variance and labour efficiency variance, which are favourable. In particular, the material usage variance, labour wage rate variance and all the fixed overhead sub-variances are significant as they are in excess of £4,000.

The material variances could have come about from the change in supplier. The supplies of material are cheaper but the quality might not be up to standard, hence the significant material usage variance of £4,236. The significant wage rate variance of £5,865 looks as if it was brought about by not budgeting for the full wage increase. However, the effect of this is lessened by the favourable labour efficiency variance.

The adverse total fixed overhead variance means that overheads were under-absorbed by £21,210. The most significant reason for this is the expenditure variance, which is £16,520 adverse. This is worrying as it means that actual overheads were greater than those budgeted. It would be expected that actual overheads would be greater than budget if actual activity was greater than budgeted. However, this was not the case as the budgeted level of production was not achieved, which is shown by the adverse fixed overhead capacity variance. This sub-variance shows that fixed overheads were underabsorbed by £10,050 because actual production was less than budget. The effect of this is ameliorated by the favourable fixed overhead efficiency variance of £5,360, giving a total volume variance of £4,690 adverse.

ORDER FORM

Any books from our AAT range can be ordered by telephoning 020-8740-2211. Alternatively, send this page to our address below, fax it to us on 020-8740-1184, or email us at **publishing@bpp.com.** Or look us up on our website: www.bpp.com

We aim to deliver to all UK addresses inside 5 working days; a signature will be required. Order to all EU addresses should be delivered within 6 working days. All other orders to overseas addresses should be delivered within 8 working days.

To: BPP Publishing Ltd, Aldine House, Aldine Place, London W12 8AW

Tel: 020-8740 2211   **Fax: 020-8740 1184**   **Email: publishing@bpp.com**

Mr / Ms (full name): _____

Daytime delivery address: _____

_____

Postcode: _____   Daytime Tel: _____

Please send me the following quantities of books.

	5/00 Interactive Text	8/00 DA Kit	8/00 CA Kit
FOUNDATION			
Unit 1 Recording Income and Receipts (7/00 Text)	☐	☐	
Unit 2 Making and Recording Payments (7/00 Text)	☐		☐
Unit 3 Ledger Balances and Initial Trial Balance (7/00 Text)	☐	☐	
Unit 4 Supplying information for Management Control (6/00 Text)	☐	☐	
Unit 20 Working with Information Technology (8/00 Text)	☐		
Unit 22/23 Achieving Personal Effectiveness (7/00) Text	☐		
INTERMEDIATE			
Unit 5 Financial Records and Accounts	☐		
Unit 6 Cost Information	☐	☐	
Unit 7 Reports and Returns	☐	☐	
Unit 21 Using Information Technology	☐		
Unit 22: see below			
TECHNICIAN			
Unit 8/9 Core Managing Costs and Allocating Resources	☐		☐
Unit 10 Core Managing Accounting Systems	☐	☐	
Unit 11 Option Financial Statements (Accounting Practice)	☐		☐
Unit 12 Option Financial Statements (Central Government)	☐		
Unit 15 Option Cash Management and Credit Control	☐	☐	
Unit 16 Option Evaluating Activities	☐	☐	
Unit 17 Option Implementing Auditing Procedures	☐	☐	
Unit 18 Option Business Tax FA00(8/00 Text)	☐	☐	
Unit 19 Option Personal Tax FA00(8/00 Text)	☐		
TECHNICIAN 1999			
Unit 17 Option Business Tax Computations FA99 (8/99 Text & Kit)	☐	☐	
Unit 18 Option Personal Tax Computations FA99 (8/99 Text & Kit)	☐	☐	
TOTAL BOOKS	☐	+ ☐ + ☐	= ☐

@ £9.95 each = £ ☐

Postage and packaging:
UK: £2.00 for each book to maximum of £10
Europe (inc ROI and Channel Islands): £4.00 for first book, £2.00 for each extra   P & P   £ ☐
Rest of the World: £20.00 for first book, £10 for each extra

▶ Unit 22 Maintaining a Healthy Workplace Interactive Text (postage free)   ☐ @ £3.95   £ ☐

GRAND TOTAL £ ☐

I enclose a cheque for £ _____ **(cheques to BPP Publishing Ltd) or charge to Mastercard/Visa/Switch**

Card number ☐☐☐☐ ☐☐☐☐ ☐☐☐☐ ☐☐☐☐ ☐☐☐☐

Start date _____   **Expiry date** _____   **Issue no. (Switch only)**___

Signature _____

REVIEW FORM & FREE PRIZE DRAW

All original review forms from the entire BPP range, completed with genuine comments, will be entered into one of two draws on 31 January 2001 and 31 July 2001. The names on the first four forms picked out on each occasion will be sent a cheque for £50.

Name: _____   Address: _____

_____

_____

How have you used this Devolved Assessment Kit?
(Tick one box only)

☐ Home study (book only)

☐ On a course: college _____

☐ With 'correspondence' package

☐ Other _____

Why did you decide to purchase this Devolved Assessment Kit? *(Tick one box only)*

☐ Have used BPP Texts in the past

☐ Recommendation by friend/colleague

☐ Recommendation by a lecturer at college

☐ Saw advertising

☐ Other _____

During the past six months do you recall seeing/receiving any of the following?
(Tick as many boxes as are relevant)

☐ Our advertisement in *Accounting Technician* magazine

☐ Our advertisement in *Pass*

☐ Our brochure with a letter through the post

Which (if any) aspects of our advertising do you find useful?
(Tick as many boxes as are relevant)

☐ Prices and publication dates of new editions

☐ Information on Interactive Text content

☐ Facility to order books off-the-page

☐ None of the above

Have you used the companion Assessment Kits for this subject?   ☐ Yes   ☐ No

Your ratings, comments and suggestions would be appreciated on the following areas

	Very useful	Useful	Not useful
Introductory section (How to use this Devolved Assessment Kit etc)	☐	☐	☐
Practice Activities	☐	☐	☐
Practice Devolved Assessments	☐	☐	☐
Trial Run Devolved Assessments	☐	☐	☐
AAT Sample Simulation	☐	☐	☐
Content of Answers	☐	☐	☐
Layout of pages	☐	☐	☐
Structure of book and ease of use	☐	☐	☐

	Excellent	Good	Adequate	Poor
Overall opinion of this Kit	☐	☐	☐	☐

Do you intend to continue using BPP Assessment Kits/Interactive Texts/? ☐ Yes   ☐ No

Please note any further comments and suggestions/errors on the reverse of this page.

Please return to: Nick Weller, BPP Publishing Ltd, FREEPOST, London, W12 8BR

REVIEW FORM & FREE PRIZE DRAW (continued)

Please note any further comments and suggestions/errors below

FREE PRIZE DRAW RULES

1   Closing date for 31 January 2001 draw is 31 December 2000. Closing date for 31 July 2001 draw is 30 June 2001.

2   Restricted to entries with UK and Eire addresses only. BPP employees, their families and business associates are excluded.

3   No purchase necessary. Entry forms are available upon request from BPP Publishing. No more than one entry per title, per person. Draw restricted to persons aged 16 and over.

4   Winners will be notified by post and receive their cheques not later than 6 weeks after the relevant draw date.

5   The decision of the promoter in all matters is final and binding. No correspondence will be entered into.